Advance Prais

Famous Faces Decoded

MEDIA PUNDITRY & PROGRAMMING

There's no one I would trust more to READ MY LIPS, not to mention my eyes, my eyebrows and everything else on my face than Dan Hill. He's the guy I go to when I need famous faces analyzed for one of my pieces, when I need someone to tell me which politician was lying during a debate. I'd be lying (and Dan would catch me) if I said Dan Hill isn't the best facial coder out there.

Jeanne Moos, CNN

I had the good fortune to interview Dan Hill a few years ago at the U.S. Open Tennis Championships in New York. Dan's an avid tennis fan, and I'm a lifelong player and lover of the game. So I was deeply interested in his study of facial coding and how it applies to tennis players. I have watched an extraordinary amount of matches over the years, and among the great gifts of my favorite sport is this: that for a couple of hours you can watch and study two supreme athletes to see not only the strategies, tactics, physical and mental capabilities they possess, but also see the primal power of their emotions.

Dan sees a lot more than most: sadness, anxiety, disgust, anger, fear, contempt. There are many different ways to be a tennis champion, and in the course of a match there are many facial cues to read and interpret—to understand better the process of champions, and sometimes their downfall. Dan Hill offers fascinating insights into the mind, heart, strengths and weaknesses of all manner of famous people: in politics, Hollywood, and for people like me, Center Court at Wimbledon. His work is illuminating, and you should know that as I write this, I'm smiling.

Mary Carillo, Tennis Channel, NBC Sports, HBO Sports

I love this book! Famous Faces Decoded *is a perfect reduction of Dan Hill's incredible facial coding abilities. In my competitive entertainment world, which is so personality driven, Hill's latest work is highly useful and relevant.*

**Benjamin Ringe, CEO and Executive Producer of
B.Bold Content Studios LLC**

General Business

Can you read the emotions on another person's face? Dan Hill sure can. Even better, he can teach you to do the same. In his terrific new book, Hill uses celebrity faces to help us improve our ability to identify and recognize other people's emotional states. FAMOUS FACES DECODED *is a valuable primer on understanding emotions, the rare book that manages to be both entertaining and enlightening—often on the same page.*

Daniel H. Pink, author of *WHEN* and *DRIVE*

In Famous Faces Decoded, *Hill shows the way to benefit from a spontaneous, real-life feedback loop as to what others in your life are feeling, thanks to what their faces reveal. Positive or negative emotions are incorrect labels, as Hill shows us. Instead the key is to understand how any emotion, from happiness to fear, can offer both reliable information about what motivates the other party and the likely behavior to expect. Armed with that knowledge, you can achieve better rapport and a better outcome for all involved.*

Jon Gordon, best-selling author of *The Power of Positive Leadership*

Leadership & Management

Recent research on leadership has found that the ability to recognize and understand emotions are among the best predictors of successful leaders. Rarely, however, are these emotional intelligence skills taught in business schools. Dan Hill presents a unique and highly entertaining roadmap to these skills. I highly recommend Famous Faces Decoded *as a way to improve your ability to read emotions in other people's faces. It's a great step towards increasing your own emotional intelligence.*

Steven Stein, Ph.D., CEO of MHS Assessments, author of *The EQ Leader* and coauthor of *The EQ Edge*

This is an extremely fascinating book on assessing the personality and emotional intelligence of people by observing their facial cues. The book uses famous faces to illustrate the technique, which is highly applicable to business in selecting people for jobs or promotions or in people's personal relationships. You will certainly enjoy this book. It makes a real contribution to our understanding of human behaviour and is a great read.

Professor Sir Cary Cooper, ALLIANCE Manchester Business School, University of Manchester, England

SALES PROSPECTS & CUSTOMERS

In Famous Faces Decoded, *you will learn to understand what other people are emoting, especially when their words don't match their facial expression, a critical tool for improving your emotional intelligence. More importantly, you will learn even more about yourself and the signals that you are giving others.*

Anthony Iannarino, bestselling author of *The Lost Art of Closing: Winning the 10 Commitments That Drive Sales*

With facial coding, Dan Hill again gives us another tool to help us read people and situations more clearly. Following his lead, you will add to your ability to interpret the words people say, but may or may not always mean.

Linda Richardson, founder of Richardson and author of *Changing the Sales Conversation*

This book is a must-read—and must-absorb!—for all those who embrace the Experience Economy. It will enable you to truly understand what your customers feel throughout your experience, enabling frontline workers as well as managers to more personally engage guests and enhance the emotional experience you design, create, and stage. Moreover, recognize that in the Experience Economy work is theatre, so experience staging itself is emotional labor. Famous Faces Decoded *will enable employees to not only act well, but act authentically.*

B. Joseph Pine II, coauthor of *The Experience Economy* and *Authenticity: What Consumers Really Want*

HIRING & PERSONNEL

Executive interviews are different from other interviews—they need to be, there's more at stake. Research shows that companies with great executive talent significantly outperform their competitors in revenue and EBITDA growth. The tactics and strategies in Famous Faces Decoded: A Guidebook for Reading Others, *will light your path to decoding facial expressions and separating fact from fiction. You'll set the world on fire where others get burned. Steeped in Hill's wry humor and unabashed candor, this book will quickly become your secret weapon!*

David Perry, Managing Partner of Perry-Martel Int'l, author of *Executive Recruiting for Dummies* and *Hiring Greatness: How to Hire Your Dream Team and Crush the Competition*

In running Philadelphia's most successful radio station for years, you get attuned to reading our on-air personalities carefully. They must be able to connect with the listeners. Dan has been a consultant with our radio station for years—so I'm familiar with his expertise in facial coding and his analytical abilities. Using those unique talents to analyze celebrities makes for a fascinating read!

Jerry Lee, Chairman of WBEB MORE-FM and President of the Jerry Lee Foundation

<u>LAWYERS & POLICE</u>

I don't think anyone could find a person who has greater insight in evaluating experts' sincerity and potential jurors than Dan Hill. To obtain objective insights into feelings is priceless. His ability to assist in jury selection in important cases cannot be measured. Dan has the ability to see the true reactions. More importantly, he is one of the kindest and nicest human beings anyone could ever meet.

Thomas V. Girardi, Trial Lawyer Hall of Fame inductee, former President of the International Academy of Trial Lawyers, and the lead attorney in winning a settlement in the famous *Erin Brockovich* case

For the next step in your "emotional intelligence" education, Famous Faces Decoded helps you recognize the emotions of the people you encounter. Dan deftly takes us through celebrity faces in order to guide us in reading the emotions of those we encounter in our own lives. He then takes us a step further, postulating on the WHY of each emotion to powerfully aid us in evaluating the true character of those we seek to understand.

Tanna Moore, MERITAS President & CEO

Police officers would be sorely remiss to overlook this book. It contains insights into decoding facial expression that, when used properly, relay so much more about people's emotions than what their words convey.

Dr. Renée J. Mitchell, Sacramento Police Department Sargent, President of the American Society of Evidence-Based Policing

CONSULTANTS

The intersection of soft and hard science is a messy place. Many social scientists get lost in reductionist, methodology-heavy approaches; others stay in the pop psychology lane. Both are unsatisfying to the bulk of people who just want to learn something valid and practical. Dan Hill delivers on both, and on a fascinating issue: how can you tell what other people are thinking and feeling? In Famous Faces Decoded, *he reveals hard research into this issue—yet writes it in real, colloquial English. What are the most common emotions? How can you spot them? Even more importantly, how do they relate to each other—and what do they mean? This is terrific! By using well-known celebrity examples, Hill brings solid scientific insight to the living room reading table. Read for fun, while learning insights for everyday use.*

Charles H. Green, founder and CEO of Trusted Advisor Associates and coauthor of *The Trusted Advisor*

SPORTS

Dan's a good guy with real insights. In figuring out how best to prepare and keep your players focused on shutting other teams down, every opportunity to know who you're going to war with is huge. This book does that. It gives you an understanding of people you can build on.

Tubby Smith, one of only five NCAA men's basketball head coaches to win 365 games in 15 seasons or less

Who would have thought that Dan Hill's facial profiling would assist in winning Olympic medals in the sport of diving, but that is just what happened at the 2016 Rio Olympic Games! Dan worked closely with me at the U.S. Olympic Trials for Diving in Indianapolis. His profiling of some of my elite athletes and coaches, followed by his great feedback in relation to their emotions under pressure, was insightful and put to good use. The result—four Olympic medalists! Thank you, Dan, and thank you for this fantastic new book that will assist me in taking coaches and athletes to another level in diving.

Steve Foley, High Performance Director USA Diving 2009–2017

In Famous Faces Decoded, *Dan Hill provides us with an essential tool to accurately read people's emotions and situations. Coaches and leaders in all walks of life will benefit greatly from his wisdom. We now have an effective way to immediately move people forward.*

TJ Kostecky, Men's Soccer Coach, LIU, Brooklyn

famous faces DECODED

A Guidebook for Reading Others

DAN HILL

Sensory Logic Books
www.SensoryLogic.com

1509 Marshall Street, N. E. Suite 400
Minneapolis, MN 55413, USA

Publisher's Cataloging-In-Publication Data
(Prepared by The Donohue Group, Inc.)

Names: Hill, Dan, 1959-
Title: Famous faces decoded : a guidebook for reading others / Dan Hill.
Description: Minneapolis, MN : Sensory Logic Books, [2018] | Includes
bibliographical references and index.
Identifiers: ISBN 9780999741641
Subjects: LCSH: Facial expression. | Emotions. | Personality. | Celebrities.
Classification: LCC BF592.F33 H55 2018 | DDC 153.69--dc23

Printed in the United States of America

LCCN 2018903981

Book cover by *the*BookDesigners
Book's interior design and illustrations by Karen Bernthal

*It is only shallow people who do not judge
by appearances. The true mystery of the world
is the visible, not the invisible.*

– OSCAR WILDE

By the age of 50, a man has the face he deserves.

– GEORGE ORWELL

*Fame simply means millions of people have
the wrong idea of who you are.*

– ERICA JONG

CONTENTS

Introduction

One of the Biggest Hiring Mistakes Ever

It's 1998 and the San Diego Chargers' brain trust has made what it considers to be a smart bet. Three miserable seasons removed from playing in Super Bowl XXIX, the Chargers have traded three draft picks and two current players to another team to secure the second overall pick in the upcoming NFL draft. Their trade leaves the Chargers sitting pretty, it seems, because almost every football expert agrees that in this year's draft, there are two prospects destined to be future star quarterbacks.

One of those quarterbacks will fulfill that destiny. Now retired, he awaits induction into pro football's Hall of Fame. The other will flame out and eventually go to prison. Which one will the Chargers get to choose, and even more importantly for the purpose of this story: which quarterback does the organization think it wants, and why?

In 1998 the team with the first pick of these two "sure winners" is the Indianapolis Colts. Half of the Colts' inner circle favors Ryan Leaf, believing Leaf has more upside and a stronger throwing arm. The other half favors Peyton Manning because he's "NFL-ready" and more mature.

Fortunately for the Chargers (or so they believe), Leaf prefers to play in San Diego given its great climate and more laid-back lifestyle. So Leaf blows off his pre-draft interview with the Colts, enraging their coach, and thereby tipping the Colts' choice to Manning.[1]

The Chargers are now free to select Leaf and relish their good luck. They don't see Leaf's maturity as a potential issue. Focused instead on Leaf's strong throwing arm, the Chargers also don't worry that the 20 pounds the guy has recently gained might indicate a suspect work ethic.

What happens next? Leaf is awarded a $31 million, four-year contract that includes the biggest signing bonus ever paid at that time to a rookie, and he rises to the occasion by *fumbling* the first snap of his regular-season career. Things go downhill from there. Leaf's third game features four fumbles, two interceptions, and only one out of 15 passes completed for a total of four yards. In short, Leaf's rookie season becomes, in the words of Chargers' safety Rodney Harrison, "A nightmare you can't even imagine."

After Leaf wins the final pre-season game in 2000, *Sports Illustrated* puts the quarterback on its cover with the headline "Back from the Brink." Hardly. In three years with San Diego, Leaf will post just four wins as a starter. That's over $7.75 million per victory. In the future, an episode of *NFL Top 10* will label Leaf the number one draft bust in the league's history. Even worse, NBC Sports analyst Michael Ventre will name Leaf "the biggest bust in the history of professional sports."

Ryan Leaf

Ryan Leaf had a career record of four wins, 17 losses, and a QB Rating of 50. (Here, he shows mostly anger and fear.) Compare that to Peyton Manning's record of 186 wins, 79 losses, and a QB Rating of 97—plus two Super Bowl victories and five NFL Most Valuable Player awards.

Now you could blame the Chargers' leadership for being dunderheads, but the truth is these kinds of mistakes occur all the time. For example, in 2014 the Cleveland Browns wasted a first-round draft choice on Johnny Manziel, a party boy soon out of the NFL. Beyond the gridiron, half of all new business hires, from CEOs on down through the ranks, fail within 18 months.[2] Romantic relationships likewise fail at an alarming rate, explaining why the most-read story in *The New York Times* in 2016 was "Why You Will Marry the Wrong Person."

The initial point of Leaf's story is to wonder, why would *any* team consider picking him? The overall point is to recognize that everyone misses helpful clues. While there's no foolproof method for successfully evaluating people and situations, the facial coding tool I'm sharing in *Famous Faces Decoded: A Guidebook for Reading Others* will certainly improve your odds.

> "*Jeff Foster, who runs the NFL's scouting combine, hired Hill in 2011 to evaluate top prospects. He said Hill had a 'master gift' for uncovering a football player's emotional DNA.*"
>
> — Excerpt from a front-page story in *The New York Times*[3] about my consulting work both in professional and NCAA Division 1 sports

Overcoming Limitations

Given the money involved and the rigor with which NFL teams approach the draft, you may rightly wonder: how do blunders like picking Leaf and Manziel persist? What's the underlying problem? My answer is that moving beyond the words people offer in job interviews or during other conversations means adhering to reality. Actions really do speak louder than words, and among the most frequently *overlooked* actions are facial muscle movements, subtle, but full of value.

Just as physical skills can be carefully gauged in settings like the NFL Combine—a week-long event where college players perform physical tests and sit down for interviews with general managers, coaches, and scouts—the same is true for emotional assessments. Gaining a sense of what in the NFL is referred to as "character" can be better handled than it is now through facial coding. What's this tool? Unlike *identity* recognition[4] based on scanning facial *features*, facial coding is *emotion* recognition based on facial *muscle activity*. That activity reveals people's current emotions and, over time, suggests their signature expressions and behavioral tendencies.

Emotions matter and the most tangible way to read them is in people's faces. How good are we at recognizing feelings? In *Emotional Intelligence 2.0*, the authors state that only 36% of us accurately identify our emotions as they happen.[5] That result is strikingly similar to my own research. When asked to indicate, from memory, the top two characteristic emotions that distinguish each of the celebrities I facially coded for *Famous Faces Decoded*, people chose correctly just 34.5% of the time. That score is based on comparing people's input (Voted) to the facial coding (Actual) results that came from a battery of photographs analyzed by expression.

Why weren't the voters I surveyed more on target? What hinders better emotional recognition that will, in turn, enable better decision-making? The answer is threefold in nature.

First, there's human nature and our tendency to believe lip-service affirmations, versus visual clues to the contrary. We want things to be rosy, so we don't always look closer. Second, our preconceptions get in the way of noticing what's literally happening before our eyes. Case in point: like the Chargers' leadership, the Colts' owner Jim Irsay swears by the idea that in the NFL "It's all about the freaking talent." Had Leaf not blown off his interview with their coach, it's altogether possible Leaf could have joined the Colts instead. Third, without a known method to follow, our visual instincts won't get sharpened.

How to Reliably Read People and Situations

Sherlock Holmes said it best when he remarked: "I have trained myself to notice what I see." Facial coding doesn't mean you have to go find information. It's already there; you just have to recognize it. This great tool originated with Charles Darwin, who was way ahead of his era as the first scientist to take emotions seriously.[6] From his studies, Darwin observed that there are three reasons why the face adroitly reflects and communicates our feelings:

- First is the *universality* of expressions. Yes, the intensity and duration of people's facial expressions may vary by culture, but the basic facial muscle activity by which emotions get conveyed doesn't change by gender, race, or ethnicity.[7]

- Second is the *spontaneity* of expressions. The face is the only place in the body where the muscles either attach just to facial tissue (such as the muscle surrounding the eyes or lips) or to a single bone and facial tissue. Other muscles in our bodies connect bone-to-bone.

- Third is the *abundance* of expressions. People have more facial muscles than any other species on earth, providing a rich signal system. Over 40 structurally and functionally autonomous muscles play a role in our facial expressions.

Almost a hundred years after Darwin published his book, *The Expression of the Emotions in Man and Animals* (1872), Paul Ekman and colleague Wally Freisen at the University of California, San Francisco, set to work on turning the tool into a methodology. The result was the Facial Coding Action System (FACS),[8] completed in 1978 and updated in 2002. In essence, FACS maps which specific facial muscle movements correspond to one or more of the seven core emotions FACS is capable of capturing. The overwhelming majority of academic experts on emotions support the tenets of Ekman's work,[9] and in 2009 *Time* magazine named him as one of the world's 100 Most Influential People.

Along the way, the tool has become part of popular culture. Facial coding was cited in depth in Malcolm Gladwell's best-seller, *Blink: The Power of Thinking Without Thinking* (2005).[10] It provided the basis for Fox's prime-time hit TV series *Lie to Me* (2009–2011), and guided Pixar's wildly successful movie *Inside Out* (2015).

Facial coding is also entering the mainstream of corporate America. A tech start-up called Emotient was at work on automating facial coding when sold to Apple in 2014. Facebook, Google, and Microsoft are all likewise pursuing the automation of facial coding.[11] The software isn't where it needs to be yet, but automated facial coding will continue to improve (and now that major companies are involved, probably quite rapidly). As of my writing this book, the leading software remains, most likely, in the range of only about 50–60% accurate.[12] So for now, at least, your best bet for quality remains knowledgeable, experienced manual facial coders (like myself), people who can attain accuracy levels of 90% or higher. Therefore, this book showcases results for celebrities manually coded in order to give you the most reliable examples and results possible.

Why You Should Care

Have you ever been in an ambiguous situation? Say a meeting with your boss where not all the cards are on the table. Or a first date where you find the other party seemingly inscrutable. Then, according to a UCLA professor's study that focused on three basic modes of communication, merely seven percent of the essential communication comes from words. The face and the voice deliver the rest, with the face delivering the lion's share: 55%.[13]

In short, don't focus so much on words—*watch* closely, instead. There's plenty to learn. Unlike IQ, all of us have the ability to improve our emotional intelligence (EQ) and that's good news. More emotionally intelligent people enjoy better interpersonal relations.[14] To do well in both your professional and personal life, you need a spontaneous, real-time feedback loop you can count on; and that's the information people's faces reveal. Moreover, perceiving emotions accurately is an essential skill

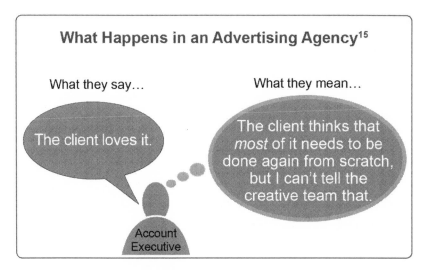

that opens the door to other, more complex skills, like using emotions to facilitate thought, understanding, and stronger rapport with others.

Do I use facial coding in my daily life? Absolutely. I would be crazy not to do so, considering that in tandem with EQ, it offers a great opportunity for improving interactions with others—and therefore outcomes.

The hotest new fields under the umbrella of emotional intelligence are social and personal intelligences, with the latter directly relevant to this book. Clearer, more productive communication arises from an enhanced ability to recognize the consequences of what we say and do as well as better anticipate the behavior of the people with whom we're interacting. A greater recognition of their emotions, motives, and personalities is crucial to reducing friction and gaining more acceptance from others.

In business, using a combination of facial coding and EQ, I've closed sales by reading prospects. When one person's lower lip stiffened in anger, signaling that I was trying too hard to get her to change her practice, I softened my approach. In another case, when the decision-maker's eyebrows were no longer knitted together, signaling focus, I returned to what had most intrigued him earlier in my presentation and regained momentum.

Off the job, I also use a combination of facial coding and EQ to assess the emotions, authenticity, and personality of people on the nightly news, in TV commercials, and in the countless movies I watch. However, I keep my wife trusting me by *never* telling friends what she might be feeling. Now, if only somebody was still willing to sit down and play poker with me.

What You'll Find Here

Famous Faces Decoded is structured around facial coding's seven core emotions and how they organize themselves, according to whether—for the person feeling them—they involve approach or avoidance behavior, and if they point to being dominant or submissive when interacting with others.[16] The size of each emotion's name in the accompanying chart indicates its frequency across my 173-person celebrity sample.[17] Some emotions, like happiness, occur much more often than does an emotion like disgust, and are correspondingly shown in larger type.

8

The three approach emotions of anger, happiness, and sadness get handled first. Then I tackle the spurning emotions of contempt and disgust, followed by the reactive emotions of surprise and fear. Each part ends with a short, simple quiz to test your newfound abilities.

Because happiness qualifies as the only clearly "positive" emotion of these seven, I explore it more elaborately. In my facial coding work, I distinguish between four, ever-weaker levels of happiness: joy, pleasure, satisfaction, and acceptance. But to simplify matters for the people who voted on the celebrities' distinguishing, characteristic emotions, I divided happiness into just two categories:

- Strong *happiness* is denoted by having *asterisks* around that term in the Voted results. In the facial coding, Actual results, asterisks adjoin the top two levels of happiness: *joy* and *pleasure*.

- Mild happiness appears without asterisks in the Voted results. In the Actual results, that outcome equates to the lower two levels of happiness: satisfaction and acceptance.

For a mock example of a celebrity's emotional profile, let's assume the voters believed Celebrity "X" favors big, intense smiles. So asterisks appear around *happiness* in the Voted results. Then because the facial coding confirmed the voters' collective judgment that strong happiness is commonly shown by this celebrity, the Actual results specificy the level of happiness, which in this case is *pleasure* with asterisks included. Meanwhile, Rare refers to the celebrity's facially coded, least common, least characteristic emotion, as compared to the other celebrities in my sample.[18]

Example of a Celebrity's Emotional Profile

──Voted──	──Actual──	──Rare──
happiness surprise	*pleasure* sadness	fear

Other special features in *Famous Faces Decoded* include two sets of Flash Portraits—emotional profiles that compare and contrast celebrities—plus an epilogue on ways to spot lying. The heart of this book, however, remains the seven, emotion-focused chapters. They're structured around each particular emotion's meaning, looks, and likely causes, along with four forms of each emotion, and finally the ways those forms may apply to your own life in a variety of circumstances.

In discussing these four forms, I touch on how people expressing themselves in those specific ways might react and how they could be described. In doing so, I'm certainly not looking to pass judgement on anyone. Nevertheless, to simplify matters and give you some practical guidelines for handling people and situations, I'm offering a way for you to take some of the guess-work out of what may happen next in your encounters with people, while preparing you for how you might best respond.

Becoming fluent in what emotions mean and their likely causes will boost your emotional literacy and serve as a first, easy level. Learning how each emotion shows on people's faces is the second level. Applying my forms of expression per emotion is the advanced, third level.

With this content, you can gain the inside track on understanding the reactions of others in your life, often beyond what they either don't consciously know or won't say. Every emotion has its own nuances and implications for future behavior. Discriminate between emotions and you can use that observed information wisely. To describe another person's feelings as simply "negative", for instance, is as inadequate as saying an army now marching in retreat has merely changed its direction. You can do better, and this book aims to help you get there.

part **1** one

approach

emotions

Anger

Pushing Ahead

What Anger Means

At the Plaza Hotel in midtown Manhattan, Cary Grant requests coffee and a pair of English muffins for breakfast. When the order arrives, there's the coffee but only three half slices. The other half slice of a muffin is missing. Determined to get a satisfactory explanation, Grant asks the waiter, calls the head of room service, and so on, up the chain of command. Then the movie star insists on having a call put through to the hotel's owner, Conrad Hilton, in Beverly Hills, despite it being the crack of dawn in California. When Hilton proves to be in Istanbul, Turkey, Grant still won't relent and has Mr. Hilton called there, instead, to complain.

Where's my half slice? Hilton knows. A hotel efficiency expert determined that most guests were leaving the fourth slice on their plates. So why bother to serve it?

Cary Grant

Welcome to anger, an emotion about wanting to be in control of your circumstances and make progress. In Grant's case, progress means the flurry of phone calls it takes to finally get an answer. Yes, the stakes are obviously small. But Grant's sense of having been taken advantage of, and determination to rectify matters, just as clearly looms large, no matter how zealously distorted his perspective might be.[1]

For this star of movies like *Bringing Up Baby* (1938) and *North by Northwest* (1959), what were the implications of wanting control? Start with being a well-known tightwad with money. Then add how Grant was so eager to dictate the behavior of the women in his life that his wife, Dyan Cannon, only half-jokingly called him "The Master."

As Cannon's rueful nickname for Grant implies, anger is often, at best, something of a mixed blessing. It's the most dominant, assertive emotion of the seven core emotions. Anger is also, like happiness and sadness, an approach emotion. In symbolic terms, rather than *to hug*, like happiness, or to be *longing for a hug*, like sadness, the essence of anger is *to hit*. Anger aids survival by enabling us to fight off threats or dismantle barriers that keep us from realizing our ambitions.

Although typically classified as a "negative" emotion, anger therefore joins the other so-called negative emotions in having an upside. Anger can help us eliminate a problem or pursue a superior solution. A person exhibiting this emotion is likely to be energetic and enterprising, focused and determined. Those qualities can be very attractive, at times.

Still, if someone's too hot-headed and grumpy, watch out. The reason most of us try to avoid physical fights is that we can never be sure if we will win and, even if we do win, whether we will come out of the fight seriously hurt. There can be more harm than gain, even as the supposed winner. Verbally expressed anger is cause for concern, too. Contrary to popular belief, anger is stoked instead of resolved by venting.[2] "Blowing off steam" can blow the whole place up, and with it the relationships we care about most.

Spotting Anger

Pick up early signs of this emotion in others and you may be able to defuse some situations before they get out of hand. That's the advantage of knowing an angry face *contracts* like a snake coiling to strike. People who get angry are aptly characterized as becoming red-faced and "boiling mad" because blood floods the face when they're incensed. More specifically, anger appears in nine ways on the face, including the following four ways when it's the only emotion being shown:

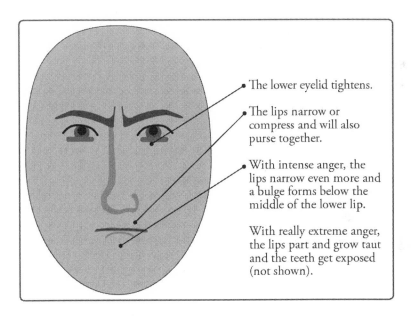

The lower eyelid tightens.

The lips narrow or compress and will also purse together.

With intense anger, the lips narrow even more and a bulge forms below the middle of the lower lip.

With really extreme anger, the lips part and grow taut and the teeth get exposed (not shown).

Next, there are five additional ways that anger gets expressed in tandem with other, specific emotions as listed here:

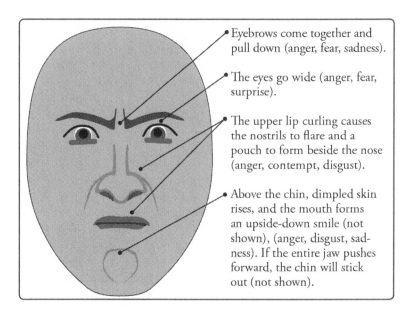

- Eyebrows come together and pull down (anger, fear, sadness).
- The eyes go wide (anger, fear, surprise).
- The upper lip curling causes the nostrils to flare and a pouch to form beside the nose (anger, contempt, disgust).
- Above the chin, dimpled skin rises, and the mouth forms an upside-down smile (not shown), (anger, disgust, sadness). If the entire jaw pushes forward, the chin will stick out (not shown).

Anger appears in more ways on the face than any other core emotion, but it's not just versatile—it's also pervasive. Among the celebrities analyzed for *Famous Faces Decoded*, on average a little over 30% of their emoting involves anger. Of the seven emotions this book covers, only happiness is more common. As to the emotions that might be classified as "negative" feelings, the next most common is fear, with merely one-third the frequency of anger.

Do men get angry more often than women? Studies find that's true, in part because men place more importance on status and power. War, with its opportunities for changes in fortune, is anger taken to extremes.[3]

TOP 10

Most Angry

Eminem
Douglas MacArthur
Joseph McCarthy
John Bonham
Leonardo DiCaprio
Kanye West
George Wallace
Khloe Kardashian
Angelina Jolie
Robert Redford

In *Famous Faces Decoded*, male celebrities show on average slightly more anger than their female counterparts and dominate the Top 10 list for Most Angry. Among them is somebody who's no stranger to war: General Douglas MacArthur.

In contrast, the Top 10 list for Least Angry is evenly split by gender and invites another way to look at anger. While excess anger can be detrimental, even fatal, a lack of anger can also have its shortcomings. Among other emotions that can also be motivating in their own way, anger helps you protect and promote yourself, seizing opportunities when they emerge. Appearing on the Least Angry list is Diane Keaton, who in a 1978 *New Yorker* profile admits that by junior high school she was always auditioning, "but I didn't seem to have much drive. I still don't really have it."[4]

TOP 10

Least Angry

Marilyn Monroe
Charles Schulz
Diane Keaton
Whitney Houston
Magic Johnson
Mary Lou Retton
Paul McCartney
Larry Page
John Lennon
Mariah Carey

How good are people at spotting anger? Maybe because it can be life-threatening not to detect anger, people are pretty good at recognizing this emotion. At almost 50%, anger comes in first for its level of detection accuracy (just ahead of mild happiness). These next three photographs illustrate ways in which anger appears, and the celebrities' emotional profiles indicate how well voters did in choosing the top two emotions that distinguish these famous people.

While the microphone Eminem is holding on stage at a concert obscures his mouth, from this photograph you can see the singer's severely lowered eyebrows. Also prominent are his tensed-up lower eyelids. Here is how Eminem has described his lyric-writing process: "If I'm mad at my girl,

I'm gonna sit down and write the most misogynistic fucking rhyme in the world. It's not how I feel in general, it's how I feel at that moment."[5] Not true. In actuality, Eminem is almost always angry. A staggering three-quarters of the singer's emoting involves anger.

Voted	Actual	Rare
anger contempt	anger fear	satisfaction

Eminem

Born Marshall Bruce Mathews III, the rapper Eminem was the best-selling musical artist of the 2000s in America. He's had 10 number-one albums on the *Billboard* 200 and sold over 172 million albums worldwide.

In Angelina Jolie's case, the photo shows one of the two signature ways in which she most frequently emotes. While the slight smile Jolie often relies on is absent here, note the combination of tense lower eyelids and the lips lightly pressed together. That look is the prevalent mode in which this actress expresses anger. Unlike Eminem's more explosive version of anger, with Jolie anger smolders like a fire where you don't see the flames, but can smell the smoke beyond the next ridge of trees.

Voted	Actual	Rare
anger sadness	acceptance anger	*pleasure*

Angelina Jolie

Angelina Jolie won an Academy Award for Best Supporting Actress in *Girl, Interrupted* (1999) and directed *Unbroken* (2014). Her humanitarian efforts have included being a Special Envoy for the United Nations High Commissioner for Refugees.

This is classic George Wallace: a show of defiance. The lower eyelids are tight, and the lips are pressed together tightly enough to create a bulge beneath the middle of the lower lip. In addition, there's a hint of a curled upper lip. Wallace tried but failed to prevent black students from enrolling at the University of Alabama while the state's governor. Later insisting he wasn't a racist, Wallace remains most famous for having proclaimed in 1963: "Segregation now, segregation tomorrow, segregation forever."

Voted	Actual	Rare
disgust anger	anger disgust	satisfaction

George Wallace

The longest-serving governor of Alabama, George Wallace sought the Democratic party's presidential nomination in 1964, 1972, and 1976. Running as an independent in 1968, he became the last third-party candidate to win any electoral college votes.

What May Cause Anger

Check out Ranker's online list of people's favorite songs about anger and aggression emerges as the de facto theme. In first place is "Killing in the Name" by Rage Against the Machine, and it goes on from there. Anger can occur for many reasons, as this set of seven likely causes makes clear.

1. We seek to control our circumstances, including resources.

Eminem's upbringing is bereft of financial resources or security. The future singer's drug-addled mom takes most of his teenage wages but still kicks him out of the house for not helping to support her. Eminem's dad is out of the picture so early Eminem never meets him. The artistic output that follows is "horror-core" humor, without limits, from a singer who commonly expresses anger through tightened lower eyelids and firmly pressed lips. An example of this grim humor: on *The Slim Shady LP* (1999), Eminem's alter-ego dumps his murdered girlfriend in a lake, aided by their baby daughter. "We'll roll her off the dock," Eminem sings, adding, "No more fighting with Dad, no more restraining order." In an alternative world of *judges-be-damned*, it's as if Eminem's alter-ego Slim Shady is sanctioning murder as the ultimate form of control.

2. Kept from making progress toward a goal, we tend to become angrier the more we feel a barrier to progress is unfair.

In 1984 a nearly flawless John McEnroe is in the middle of a year in which his winning percentage will exceed 95%. The tennis star will conquer almost every event, including the Swedish Open. In Stockholm, however, McEnroe unleashes a monumental temper tantrum[6] triggered by a serve called "out". McEnroe's diatribe follows: "That ball was right on the line, *right* on the line. You've made no mistakes in this match yet, *right?*" This is McEnroe taunting the chair umpire, redirecting his competitive attention away from the opponent across the net (who remains the real barrier to victory in the match). Not waiting for an answer, McEnroe reiterates: "No mistakes *whatsoever.*" When the umpire remains silent, McEnroe's eyes go wide, his lips part, his teeth get bared, and his lower lip turns out. Displaying the kind of a look you see when a dog is growling over a lost bone, the tennis star verbally unloads: *"Answer the question! The question, jerk!"*

Jeers and boos rain down from the Swedes filling the arena. The judge issues a code violation. In response, McEnroe smacks a ball into the bleachers at a loud-mouthed fan objecting to his outburst. Distracted or perhaps more like *unhinged*, McEnroe loses the next point and with it that game.

At the changeover, the verbal violence turns physical. Gripping his tennis racket as if it's a golf club, McEnroe whacks his tennis bag. Then he hits a teeshot that connects with his water bottle, sending it into the air, across the front row of spectators. Water splatters the King of Sweden as it goes by. The judge screams *"Code violation!"* repeatedly as McEnroe starts swatting anything in reach. With a forehand swing, the left-hander destroys a courtside flower arrangement. Then finally spent from rage, McEnroe hides beneath a blue towel he drapes over his head in embarrassment as he sits down to regain some composure. Two years later, the burnt-out star takes a half-year sabbatical from tennis, signaling the end of his reign.

3. In reaction to feeling lost or confused, we focus on solving the problem.

After Angelina Jolie's parents divorce, a rocky relationship with her famous father, Jon Voight, doesn't help matters. The future actress's first career ambition as a teenager is to become a funeral director. From insomnia to depression so severe that Jolie tries to hire a hit man to end her life, upheaval consumes her. But starting with *Lara Croft: Tomb Raider* (2001), her breakthrough movie, Jolie finds professional success and settles into her tell-tale expression of anger: eyes narrowed in a piercing gaze. In adulthood, anger once turned inward begins to help power an outwardly-focused career.

Not easy to typecast, Jolie has become a humanitarian advocate for conservation, education, women's rights, and refugees, all without entirely shedding her past. At the same time as promoting those warm-hearted causes, Jolie remains in her own words, "just a punk kid with tattoos," one of which declares: "What nourishes me destroys me." Go figure, or go search for clues in Jolie's past. Reverse the tattoo's motto by putting "destroys" ahead of "nourishes" and you've got another part of Jolie's teenage years. The actress admits to having once upon a time cut herself repeatedly because pain felt "somehow therapeutic to me."

4. To survive a challenge or threat, we go on the attack, possibly relieving stress.

For four long years in a row, Michael Jordan's challenge is to get his Chicago Bulls past the Detroit Pistons in the NBA's Eastern Conference play-offs. The "Bad Boys" Pistons relish roughing up Jordan and always win the head-to-head matchup, until finally in 1991 Jordan pushes himself and his teammates hard enough to prevail.

As dominant in practice as in actual games, Jordan punches two teammates in the face during scrimmages and taunts many others.[7] Among those under siege is "Medical Bill" Cartwright, as Jordan likes to call him. Believing Cartwright has "bad hands," Jordan throws him a series of impossible-to-catch passes until finally the center pulls Jordan aside and tells him to stop or else "you will never play basketball again because I will break both of your legs." A notoriously vindictive Hall of Fame speech in 2009, in which Jordan derides many former coaches, teammates, and even his own children, shows his Airness has not yet learned to ease up. It's a verdict supported by the many ways Jordan shows anger off-court, including: lowered eyebrows, tightened eyelids, and a flaring upper lip.

5. We resist the status quo or a change in circumstances, often because our expectations have been violated.

The put-down is that, over the years, critics' descriptions of Robert Redford suggest he's a somewhat bland, bankable "golden boy."[8] While no one particular form of anger most characterizes Redford, a look of lips firmly pressed together in annoyance comes the closest. In response to being typecast, Redford wants more than merely to be seen as a safe-sex presence on-screen. He expects something more of himself. So even as Barbara Streisand, Redford's co-star in *The Way We Were* (1973), reportedly drools over filming scenes like their fireside courtship in Malibu, Redford is already aiming for something higher. For him the movie is really about "The questionable nature of true free speech," more so than being a steamy romance.

Not happy with Hollywood conventions, Redford has now long ago become an eco-activist and the creator of the alternative Sundance Film Festival in Utah. In doing so, he's supporting artistic endeavors that mirror his independent, *I-won't-buckle-under* mindset. Stubbornly resolved not to play the game the usual way, Redford has made all the money he might need and has moved on to striving for merit instead.

6. Feeling demeaned and resentful, we seek to preserve and enhance our own identity or that of a group to which we belong.

The son of a former Black Panther party member and an English literature professor, Kanye West advocates for what he calls examples of Black Excellence that will enhance his race's identity. West is also famously, even *notoriously* outspoken. That trait suits a guy whose signature expression of anger is the intense version in which firmly pressed lips cause a bulge to form below the lower lip. After Hurricane Katrina strikes New Orleans, West punctuates a live 2005 telethon for its victims by ad-libbing a comment that strikes many people as plausible given the sorry state of America's race relations, namely, "George Bush doesn't care about black people."

A second, surprising off-script moment occurs during the 2009 MTV Video Music Awards. The musician Taylor Swift has taken the stage to accept the award for Best Female Video for "You Belong with Me." Believing that Beyonce deserves the award for "Single Ladies (Put a Ring on It)," West responds by seizing the stage, grabbing the microphone from Swift, and proclaiming Beyonce's video "one of the best videos of all time." Again, the point is to challenge a status quo that favors whites. This injustice, however, doesn't match the scale of Katrina's aftermath. West's anger has gotten the better of him. In response, the musical artist gets banished for the remainder of that year's MTV show and called a "jackass" by President Barack Obama.

7. We fight against injustice, seeking to rectify situations that are contrary to our values.

It's fair to say that both men caught up in a nationally televised exchange during the Army-McCarthy Hearings of 1954 feel a sense of injustice. Prolonged, intense anger verging on rage belongs to only one man, though. That's Senator Joseph McCarthy, whose displays of anger overwhelmingly favor narrowed eyes. For McCarthy, the injustice is that he believes Communist traitors lurk inside the U.S. government. For his counterpart, the U.S. Army's chief legal counsel Joseph Welch, the injustice lies elsewhere. Welch believes McCarthy's hearings have become a witch hunt harming the lives of decent, patriotic Americans.

Their conflicting views come to a head when Welch says: "You've done enough. Have you no sense of decency, sir, at long last? Have you left no sense of decency?" Ducking the question, McCarthy patronizingly resumes by saying "I know this [line of questioning] hurts you, Mr. Welch." Quick with a retort, Welch replies, "I'll say it hurts," which he offers with a sad, wistful smile and just a touch of anger.

Four Forms of Anger

A dog is a dog is a dog. Well, not really. As everyone knows, not all dogs in the park are as likely to growl at another dog as some are. Likewise, anger isn't a monolithic, one-size-fits-all emotion. While a testy Thunderstorm look might be vaguely comparable to a pit bull, the happiness-infused expression I'm calling the Golden Blend comes closer to being like a gentle Golden Retriever. The other two forms of anger fall somewhere in between that first pair in terms of their positive versus negative orientation.

As the chart shows,[9] Thunderstorm is more intense as well as more negative than the other most assertive version of anger: Battle Ready. Both forms are nevertheless problematic. They most closely adhere to anger's *hit* instinct and are assertive, even hostile. Concentration and Golden

Blend are the remaining forms of anger, which involve more subdued, constructive reactions. Of them, Golden Blend qualifies as a slightly positive feeling because it mixes anger with mild happiness.

Thunderstorm

Sometimes, angry people's lips tighten so severely that a bulge forms below the center of their lower lip. Much less common is when their lips form a hyper-tense, teeth-bared growl. Either way, stay alert. Danger lurks. With the tell-tale bulge, also look for suddenly thin lips that may almost disappear from view. These visual clues serve as a warning that you may be physically or verbally struck.

- Thunderstorm: The lips are pressed tight, creating a bulge below the middle of the lower lip.

- Other signs of anger: The raised chin adds a slight jaw thrust. The lower eyelids are likewise somewhat tense.

In this photo, Hillary Clinton reveals one of her signature looks: grim determination. It's entirely possible to imagine such a look on her face during a famous scene in Joe Klein's *Primary Colors,*[10] a thinly disguised novel about Bill and Hillary Clinton. I'm referring to the moment when the character almost certainly modeled on Hillary says to her husband: "You could have been such a

Hillary Clinton

great president if you weren't such an undisciplined shit." Note that both members of this power couple appear in the Top 10 list for Thunderstorm.

TOP 10
Thunderstorm

Jimmy Page
Kanye West
Joe Frazier
Bill Clinton
Donald Trump
Rush Limbaugh
Peyton Manning
Jeb Bush
Hillary Clinton
Barack Obama

Who are the other celebrities who fill out the list? Those most prone to this lashing, forceful version of anger range from heavy-metal, Led Zeppelin guitarist Jimmy Page; to a former heavy-weight boxing champion, Smokin' Joe Frazier; and enough politicians to remind us that politics is often called a *blood sport.* Fully half the list is taken up by politicians, among them three candidates from 2016: Donald Trump, Hillary Clinton, and an often straining, deeply frustrated Jeb Bush.

Battle Ready

When people's upper eyelids rise, their eyes widen as if their eyeballs are protruding. At other times, the eyes may narrow while the lower eyelids grow tense. The most intimidating version of this look combines the two movements. Then you're being stared down in a manner similar to how cats arch their backs to look larger and more intimidating in a hostile encounter.

Joseph McCarthy

- Battle Ready: The lower eyelids are tight, and the eyes about as wide as the lowered eyebrows permit.

- Other signs of anger: The inner eyebrows are lowered, and the lips are slightly pressed together.

Anger constitutes over 60% of Joseph McCarthy's entire emoting, double the average for the celebrities in *Famous Faces Decoded*. "McCarthyism is Americanism with its sleeves rolled up" is how the Senator once described his style of going after alleged Communists during the 1950s Red Scare that he avidly promoted. Implicit in *sleeves rolled up* was McCarthy's eagerness for a fight. The hearings he held were almost like televised boxing matches, with witnesses either fighting off or succumbing to McCarthy's verbal punches.

Battle Ready

Eminem
Joseph McCarthy
James Dean
Angelina Jolie
Charles Manson
Michael Milken
Kurt Cobain
Taylor Swift
Roger Clemens
Jack Welch

This Top 10 list is full of compelling figures. For example, besides two convicts—mass murderer Charles Manson, and former junk bond king Michael Milken—there's General Electric's former CEO, Jack Welch.

How did Welch earn the intimidating nickname "Neutron Jack"? In downsizing the company's ranks, Welch would fire any employee caught in the bottom 10% of GE's annual performance reviews.

Concentration

A less adversarial version of anger is when the eyebrows lower and knit together, creating a vertical wrinkle between them. The deeper the wrinkle and the more firmly someone's lips may simultaneously press together, short of forming a Thunderstorm bulge, the more that person is focused on the matter at hand. Note that this expression often reveals some confusion, as the puzzled person strives for clarity and a restored sense of control.

Tom Hanks

- Concentration: The eyebrows knit together, creating vertical wrinkles between them. Firmly pressed lips complete the look.

- Other emoting: The lower eyelids are slightly tense, a sign of anger. Skin that's drawn toward the eyes suggests sadness.

Tom Hanks has admitted that "Everybody has something that chews them up and, for me, that thing was always loneliness." Many a time, though, he won't say much, especially to the media. Seen by voters surveyed for *Famous Faces Decoded* as happy and happier, a nice, trustworthy guy, Hanks's version of anger involves maintaining control and self-control alike. For instance, Hanks tells a *Guardian* journalist[11] he's happy to talk "about absolutely anything." Queries lead to answers that stymie the journalist, and Hanks even pretends not to hear some questions—so resistant is he to sharing anything that would make good copy.

Concentration

Douglas MacArthur
Jay-Z
John Bonham
Eminem
George H. W. Bush
Ronald Reagan
George Harrison
Johnny Cash
Leonardo DiCaprio
Tom Hanks

The epitome of someone being either well focused or at times too narrowly focused, Concentration features a Top 10 list that consists entirely of male celebrities. Well focused? That might be Leonardo DiCaprio, who has admitted to being "unhappy doing things that I'm not passionate about." As a candidate for too narrowly focused, consider Douglas MacArthur. The general's insistence on pushing his U.S. troops ever farther north during the Korean War brought China into the conflict.

Golden Blend

A good strategy for coming across as powerful, yet not dangerous, is to blend anger and happiness. That emotional tandem combines backbone with warmth. Socially acceptable anger is anger that appears restrained and nicely balanced by happiness. Put yet another way, to combine a smile with signs of assertiveness demonstrates calm resolve.

- Golden Blend: There's both a pert smile and lips pressed hard together.

- Other signs of anger: Tight lower eyelids are joined by an upper lip that slightly rises and could curl if the lips weren't so firmly clinched.

Taylor Swift

Golden Blend

Estee Lauder
Khloe Kardashian
Douglas MacArthur
Angelina Jolie
Amy Schumer
Kim Kardashian
Leonardo DiCaprio
John Bonham
J. K. Rowling
Edward Snowden

Taylor Swift has become a one-woman musical empire, whose statement "Careers take hard work" fits her frequent, steely, eyes-narrowed look. An album and a concert tour titled *Fearless* (2008) surely overstate Swift's degree of equanimity. Nevertheless, she's intrepid in carving out a path for herself. More angry than happy, Swift mostly shows slight smiles in keeping with her recent remark: "In terms of being happy, I've never been closer to that."[12]

The Top 10 list for Golden Blend is loaded with female talent. Besides Amy Schumer and her zinging humor, add Estee Lauder and, two generations later, the likewise enterprising Kardashian sisters: Khloe and Kim. Finally, there's J. K. Rowling, the very rare case of an author rewarded for her talent by becoming a billionaire.

Applications in Your Life

In your own life, when might you see these four forms of anger? How might you best react to them, given what causes people to feel anger?

Thunderstorm: If you're advising a client, this look surely means trouble. Your counsel is already being rejected, big-time. If you're an attorney addressing a jury, this look could mean your opening arguments have left the jurors utterly clueless and feeling dumb about the points you're

Thunderstorm

Nasty
Irritable
Bad-tempered
Ardent
Decisive

trying to make. If you're a company manager and see this look around the meeting table, odds are staff isn't on-board with the new initiative and timetable you've just laid out. To them it's a bridge too far. In your home life, a partner showing the Thunderstorm look is about to escalate your disagreement. Ditto regarding the chat you're trying to have with your teenage son about his emerging lifestyle habits.

People showing the Thunderstorm look are caught up in the most intense, assertive version of anger. Feeling ardent, even nasty—they have a pre-ferred outcome and they want that outcome *now*. They will almost surely be opposed to any alternative approaches you may suggest.

Among the various causes of this form of anger, the likeliest triggers involve people perceiving a direct challenge to their well-being. That might mean an offensive remark was made, or there's been a threat to their deeply held values. In response, lower the temperature with a dialogue conducted in private that emphasizes what's feasible going forward. Stay in the moment. Don't let these people grab the extra ammunition that comes from rehashing why their being challenged is unfair. They might feel like they've been treated disrespectfully. Humiliation hurts. Repair that wound by honoring their input on how the two of you can most wisely join forces to minimize the risk of future harm.

Battle Ready: You could well be dealing with someone who antici-pates trouble and welcomes it. As a sports coach, you're not likely to impose your will on a headstrong player showing this look without encountering, at a minimum, sullen insubordination. As an angel inves-tor trying to give helpful advice to a much younger entrepreneur, you

Battle Ready

Forceful
Bossy
Tough
Determined
Brave

might soon find yourself being rebuffed. In a clash of opinions with somebody at a party, don't expect that person to softly agree-to-disagree.

With a Thunderstorm look, the die is already cast; expect an attack. By comparison, with a Battle Ready look *defiance* could entail either an offensive or defensive stance, depending on how you respond to receiving a stare-down. These people don't like to be bossed around, but ironically they might be just fine with becoming rather bossy themselves.

The likely causes of this look range from people resenting unfair barriers to progress, to their resisting the status quo because expectations are now being violated. How best to respond to people feeling stymied? Play to their need to compete and win, and don't be shy about appealing to their pride in themselves, their family, or organization. If barriers are involved, emphasize how the approach you're suggesting increases efficiency and enables break-through progress. If instead these people are hostile to change, emphasize how whatever you're proposing will restore their autonomy and grant them respect. Reinforce your proposal with precedents that demonstrate the likelihood of their landing on the winning side, provided they now get on-board.

Concentration: People who exhibit this look may be either mildly perplexed by what they're hearing or super attentive to details. If you're a corporate trainer, you should hope for the latter but confirm it isn't the former. Otherwise, the people listening to you may soon drift away. This look from a boss suggests the door is still open to redefining a project based on your input, so gently pursue the matter. In your personal life, you might be making headway with a partner not sold on how you like to handle money or other contentious matters.

Concentration

Persistent
Dependable
Diligent
Serious
Tidy

Concentration is mild in tone, and you can easily work with people showing this form of anger. It suggests qualities like being diligent and dependable. Catch your breath and relax. Take this look as a sign of commitment by the other party in terms of getting things done smoothly.

The likeliest triggers concern people seeking to control their circumstances, or else feeling that they're lost and confused. If it's a matter of control, avoid giving direct orders or simply "going around" these people. Either move will reinforce their sense of lacking power. As to possible disorientation as a cause, remember that anger makes people get tunnel vision. Therefore, respond by gently getting them to broaden their perspective. Maybe there's a key detail they've overlooked? Revisit essential details in a step-by-step manner that won't be overwhelming. Because the underlying problem could be that they're not feeling able to absorb new information, restore confidence by accentuating what they *are* good at doing.

Golden Blend: How fortunate you are. Whomever you're interacting with is likely to exhibit both fortitude and flexibility. If you're a customer service representative trying to resolve a shopper's complaint, that person won't "go off" on you so long as you listen well. If you're a headhunter, you're witnessing the kind of leader you want to consider putting in a delicate, "turn-around artist" position at a client company. As a woman on a date, you would much rather see this look from the guy than a Battle Ready expression.

Golden Blend

Dynamic
Adventurous
Boisterous
Courageous
Pro-active

The qualities of people who frequently experience the Golden Blend of anger and mild happiness are fortuitous. Expect them to be adventurous and lively. After all, this pair of approach emotions, taken together, reinforces a pro-active orientation.

As to likely causes for this look, people who have just resolved a challenge and are, therefore, experiencing relief from stress is one reason why happiness might be in the mix. Another cause could be people regaining a sense of equilibrium. They no longer feel "lost" because clarity has arrived regarding a previously perplexing issue. Fortunately, these aren't people prone to venting. They won't let anger counter-productively feed on itself, making them just that much angrier. Instead, you can work with them to resolve conflicts or confusion. Without rushing, paraphrase any problem that arises to ensure you two see it similarly. Then jointly explore what the optimal outcome might look like, emotionally speaking, before moving on to possible solutions.

Summary

Anger and ambition often fit like a glove. When we want to get things done, remove barriers to progress, and exert control over our destiny, anger can come in handy. It serves as the rocket fuel that keeps us focused. It's also the epitome of getting our hands—and fists—around a problem to solve our dilemma. That's all good, but implicit in my reference to *fists* is why anger can be so problematic. This emotion is functionally suited to help us hit out at people, objects, and viewpoints we consider to be blocking our progress and preferences.

By helping us fight off threats, and thereby survive and thrive, anger is central to life and a frequent emotion that the male celebrities in this book show much more often than their female counterparts. In anger, the face's muscles contract and tense up. We're preparing for conflict and not open to others, whom often get viewed as opponents to conquer. With anger, people skills suffer. So while this emotion can energize us in fighting against injustices, with anger, securing a desired outcome can take precedence over showing concern for the individuals involved.

Happiness

The Luxury Emotion

What Happiness Means

It's known as *Ellen's* "Puppy Episode." Ratings are down and desperate to achieve its version of happiness (commercial success), the network proposes introducing a puppy as a love interest for the show's star. In contrast, Ellen DeGeneres is seeking personal happiness and prefers an authentic love interest. Ready to "out" herself, she pushes for a script full of halting and apprehensive dialogue, leading to self-confession.[1] Here, DeGeneres's character Ellen Morgan is talking to Susan, who has only recently revealed she's a lesbian and admitted she thought Ellen was one, too.

Ellen DeGeneres

Ellen: You know how you said in the room, you know, that you thought, maybe I was … I was thinking about it, and …

Susan: Are you saying what I think you're trying to say?

Ellen: What do you think I'm trying to say?

Susan: Oh, I'm not going to say it again and be wrong.

Ellen: No, you're not wrong. You're right. This is so hard …
I'm so afraid to tell people. I mean … I'm just … Susan
…

Then just as Ellen is turning back toward Susan, she puts one hand on a service counter and accidentally presses the airport's PA system, making a private moment *very* public.

Ellen: I'm gay.

With that admission, a huge, beaming smile flashes across Ellen's face. Welcome to happiness! This emotion is basically a "me"-"we" proposition. People feel their happiest when they're being true to their own values (me) and are simultaneously supported, externally, by others (we) who endorse them for being who they genuinely are. In this case, DeGeneres has affirmed her sexual orientation. By doing so, she's cleared the path to realizing a greater degree of fulfillment, which is what happiness is about. In affirming oneself and, in effect, hugging oneself, a person can become more emotionally available to others, too.

Because the essence of happiness is to *hug* oneself as well as other people, it could almost go without saying that happiness is an approach emotion. Happiness brings people together. It's a matter of affection and affiliation. Happiness helps individuals approach situations, social or otherwise, as opportunities to be embraced, rather than as risks to be avoided.

Like anger, happiness qualifies as a dominant, approach emotion. The difference between the two feelings is vast, however, in regards to tonality and intent. While anger is aggressively dominant, imposing itself on others, happiness is *affirmatively* dominant. With happiness, people are invited to bask in its warm glow. The only facial display capable of being seen at distances of as great as 300 feet,[2] robust smiles foster cooperation, serving as the emotional equivalent of a "Welcome, Open for Business" sign.

Put so simply, happiness may seem like an easily realized emotion. But as Woody Allen has joked, "Happiness makes up in height what it lacks in length." Of the seven core emotions, happiness emerges as the one clearly upbeat emotional sensation. Why does it stand alone? The answer is that from a survival point of view, *life is hard and then you die.* In other words, happiness could be considered a luxury emotion—not as vital as the other, "negative" emotions that assist us in handling challenges.

Nevertheless, happiness isn't a trivial emotion. Thomas Jefferson enshrined "Life, Liberty and the pursuit of Happiness" in America's Declaration of Independence, and none of us wants to go without happiness if we have anything to say in the matter.

Happy people aren't just happy. Studies indicate that happy people tend to live longer and be more creative—brainstorming superior solutions more quickly than those who are less content.[3] Like all emotions, happiness is contagious. So an opportunity to be around cheerful, optimistic people can feel good, making happy people a magnet for attention. Who doesn't want the glow of happiness? And who doesn't harbor the hope of future happiness, however fleeting?

Spotting Happiness

A happy face *lifts up* as if a flower welcoming the sun. More specifically, happiness appears in only two ways on the face:

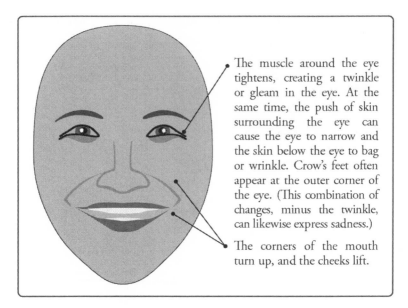

The muscle around the eye tightens, creating a twinkle or gleam in the eye. At the same time, the push of skin surrounding the eye can cause the eye to narrow and the skin below the eye to bag or wrinkle. Crow's feet often appear at the outer corner of the eye. (This combination of changes, minus the twinkle, can likewise express sadness.)

The corners of the mouth turn up, and the cheeks lift.

To detect these few signals sounds easy enough, now doesn't it? In order for you to fully grasp how happiness works, though, I want to share a secret I've learned from my two decades of facial coding: happiness is actually *four slightly different but equally essential feelings rolled up into one emotion.* To tease out the various manifestations of happiness, let's delve deeper into this emotion's *four levels*: joy and pleasure (again, as noted in my introduction, both qualify as strong *happiness* with asterisks if appearing in a celebrity's emotional profile), and satisfaction and acceptance (both qualify as merely mild happiness, appearing without asterisks, in any of the Actual, Voted or Rare results).

How does each level of happiness get revealed?

- The highest level of happiness is joy, which can't be faked. When you're truly, exuberantly happy, the muscle around the eye constricts, causing a twinkle in the eye and the skin around the eye to push in and change its shape. This look is accompanied by a smile and usually a pronounced lifting of the cheeks.

- The second highest level of happiness is pleasure. In this case, there's no gleam in the eye but there's still a big (often toothy) grin that lifts the cheeks until they touch or almost touch the eye sockets.

- The third level of happiness is satisfaction. These are either more subdued, genuine smiles or instead *social smiles:* instances where you may not really feel that happy, but you manage a smile when told to say "Cheese." With these smiles, the cheeks will rise slightly; however, the smile doesn't carry high into the cheeks. Mostly, the action consists of how the corners of the mouth lift just enough to clearly signal a smile.

- The lowest level of happiness is acceptance. While the cheeks barely move, if at all, one or both corners of the mouth rise ever so slightly. An acceptance level smile still signals happiness, but of the grimmest sort. A Thomas Hardy poem describes this look: "The smile on your mouth was the deadest thing / Alive enough to have strength to die."[4]

While only contempt shows up in as few places on the face as happiness, it's no contest between those two feelings when it comes to frequency. Among the celebrities facially coded for *Famous Faces Decoded*, almost 35% of their emoting involves happiness. It's the single most common emotion among the seven core emotions, edging out anger, which comes in second for frequency. Together, happiness and anger constitute two-thirds of all the emotions coded for this book.

Within my 173-person sample, which gender shows more happiness? The answer is women by a wide margin, with joy and acceptance being the levels at which the female celebrities notably outdistance their male counterparts. No single explanation covers the reasons why. To this day,

TOP 10

Most Happy

Ellen DeGeneres
Charles Schulz
John Lennon
Mariah Carey
Mary Lou Retton
Martha Stewart
Diane Keaton
Magic Johnson
David Letterman
Jim Henson

though, it's probably fair to suggest that women may get routinely judged more favorably based in part on their emotional warmth, whereas for men it's more likely to be their degree of self-assertion. Put another way, at least trying to appear happy is probably more important for the typical woman.

The greater prevalence for happiness among women is revealed in the Top 10 list for Most Happy. Female celebrities represent about a third of the celebrities facially coded for this book, but they hold down half of these top ten slots. In contrast, the list of the Least Happy celebrities contains only one woman, Hillary Clinton, who comes in 9th in a list headlined by her 2016 election foe: Donald Trump. Overall, in *Famous Faces Decoded* the emotions of anger and happiness, *to hit* or *to hug*, split by gender. In terms of which feeling the celebrities display most often, the men favor anger and the women various levels of happiness.

Least Happy

Donald Trump
Aaron Rodgers
Barack Obama
Eminem
George H. W. Bush
Cam Newton
Johnny Cash
Douglas MacArthur
Hillary Clinton
Charles Manson

Given that robust smiles are the only facial display readily evident at a distance, it shouldn't come as a shock that people are good at recognizing happiness. At almost 47% accuracy, mild happiness came in second best (after anger) in terms of strength of detection, with strong *happiness* close behind. The following four photographs illustrate differences between the various levels of happiness, and the celebrities' emotional profiles indicate how well voters did in choosing the top two emotions that distinguish these famous people.

Despite it being a forced smile that contains an element of fear, Mary Lou Retton is nevertheless also expressing *joy*. There's a gleam if not quite a twinkle in her eyes, and a broad, equally gleaming, white-toothed grin. Retton's natural exuberance made her a crowd favorite at the 1984 Summer Olympics, and afterwards she became the first female athlete ever to grace the front of a Wheaties box.

Voted	Actual	Rare
happiness surprise	*joy* *pleasure*	anger

Mary Lou Retton

At the 1984 Olympics, Mary Lou Retton won a gold medal in the individual all-around gymnastics competition, plus two silver and two bronze medals. In a 1993 sports study, Retton tied for first as America's most popular athlete.

Also in the strong *happiness* category is Mariah Carey. The earpiece malfunction that doomed her New Year's Eve 2017 concert in Times Square and led Carey to walk off the stage in a huff isn't as representative of her emoting as is the broad, *pleasure* smile on display here.

Voted	Actual	Rare
happiness sadness	*pleasure* *joy*	anger

Mariah Carey

Mariah Carey's 1995 hit single "One Sweet Day" continues to be America's longest-running, number-one song ever. She was the world's best-selling recording artist during the 1990s.

Moving on to mild happiness, Diane Keaton's *satisfaction* smile includes a hint of assertive anger around the eyes. This look is in keeping with a 2013 interview in which Keaton told a journalist: "I'm going to say what I think. I'm more outspoken, less afraid. It used to be that every movie bore such weight. Now I think, 'Who cares?'"[5]

Voted	Actual	Rare
happiness *happiness*	*joy* satisfaction	anger

Diane Keaton

Born Diane Hall, Diane Keaton has starred in *The Godfather* (1972), *Annie Hall* (1977), and *The First Wives Club* (1996), among other movies. Her films have grossed over $1.1 billion in North America alone.

David Letterman's craggy, *acceptance* smile indicates a comedian who has seen it all. "I'm just trying to make a smudge on the collective unconscious," Letterman has ironically said of his ambitions in life.

Voted	Actual	Rare
happiness surprise	*joy* contempt	surprise

David Letterman

David Letterman hosted, in total, 6,028 episodes, of first *Late Night with David Letterman* on NBC and then the *Late Show with David Letterman* on CBS. In 2013, he surpassed Johnny Carson as America's longest-running, late night talk show host.

What May Cause Happiness

Let's briefly revisit *Ellen's* "Puppy Episode." Imagine you're the show's director and lately your star hasn't been the same. Not only are the ratings down, but Ellen DeGeneres is unhappy that the U.S. Congress passed the Defense of Marriage Act a year ago. Her suggestion to "out" herself inspires the biggest true smile you've seen from DeGeneres in quite some time. Are you going to turn down her idea or take it to the network's executives?

In weighing your choice, you're wise to the various reasons why happiness occurs.

1. We're suddenly more fulfilled, having experienced some kind of success or improvement in our circumstances. (Pride is a likely, related feeling in this case.)

No, no, I'm really him, Charles Schulz finds himself insisting at his Central High School class reunion in St. Paul, Minnesota. Nobody believes him. So finally Schulz proves he really is the *Peanuts* cartoonist by drawing Charlie Brown for the former classmates gathered around him. It isn't the first time Schulz has been doubted. When he proposed to the woman on whom his comic strip character Lucy is likely modeled, her mom intervened. Told that Schulz wouldn't amount to much, the woman married a fireman instead.[6] Twenty years later, *Happiness Is a Warm Puppy* (1962) has hit the best-seller list. The previously hardscrabble, often gloomy Schulz is now a rich, radiantly smiling man. He's got both a twinkle in his eyes and a bank account that's growing by over $30 million a year.

2. We harbor reasonable hope for the future, having made progress toward a goal we have. Optimism seems warranted. (Relief is a likely, related feeling in this case.)

At a Christie's auction of Hollywood memorabilia in 1999, Mariah Carey picks up for $662,500 a chipped, white baby grand piano that had belonged to Marilyn Monroe's mother "and was a piece of" the actress's childhood. Why the purchase? For starters, Monroe is the namesake of Carey's daughter and Carey's biggest inspiration. So while Carey won't ever play the purchased piano, or even tune it, she's bought it to preserve "what she [Marilyn] cared about."[7]

More deeply, however, the piano calls to mind for Carey her own childhood instability. Her parents' divorce when Carey was three years old led to a childhood in which Carey, her mom, and siblings moved together through a string of 13 marginal homes across Long Island. Nowadays, Monroe's piano serves as a touchstone for Carey, a way to stay grounded. The singer is happy and grateful for her success, often flashing large smiles, while mindful of how sad life can sometimes be.

3. We've achieved security and are no longer surrendering to circumstances beyond our control. Certainty brings comfort.

Convicted of insider stock trading in 2004 and sentenced to a five-month term in a federal correctional facility, Martha Stewart faces for the first time ever doubters about the on-going viability of her one-woman business empire. How wrong those doubters prove to be. Soon, Stewart is active again in her magazine, *Martha Stewart Living*, which might as well be renamed *Martha Stewart Working* given her copious output. Besides a wealth of other products, Stewart even begins to sell a line of homes modeled on her private estates. To focus on the merchandise alone misses the underlying point, however. As Stewart notes, her version of domestic order means gladly offering "not a fantasy, but a reality that looks like a fantasy." In supporting her brand, Stewart reveals in photographs a penchant for big pleasure smiles, the second highest level of happiness. In contrast, eye-twinkling joy eludes Stewart as much as her taking a rest from her many endeavors.

4. Our identity gets affirmed, individually or as part of a group. We experience a sense of belonging, whether based on family, friends, or romantic bonds. We've begun to feel cared about.

While Brian Epstein at first manages The Beatles, and George Martin becomes their producer, the band's leader is unquestionably John Lennon. Lennon formed the band's various lineups beginning in 1957 and urged The Beatles on with the promise they were headed "for the top." Now they're stars, and as my chart Beatles' Emotions Through the Years shows,

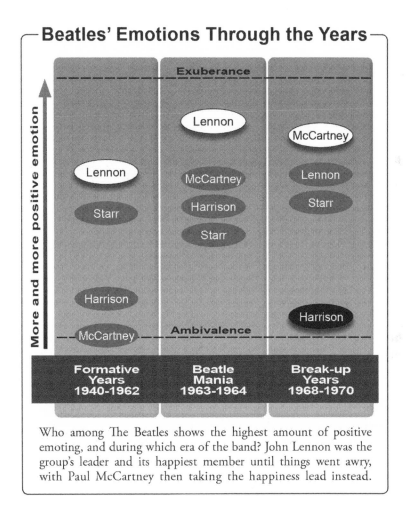

Beatles' Emotions Through the Years

Who among The Beatles shows the highest amount of positive emoting, and during which era of the band? John Lennon was the group's leader and its happiest member until things went awry, with Paul McCartney then taking the happiness lead instead.

Lennon is enjoying their early success the most. Granted, he rarely hits the high note of true, joyful smiles. But for a guy whose seaman father wandered off and mom died early, hit by a car, Lennon must find solace in being, as Paul McCartney later acknowledges, the one "we all looked up to" within a tight, cohesive group.[8]

Then the dynamic changes. First, George Harrison in 1968, followed by Lennon in 1969, each momentarily leaves the band before being coaxed back. When The Beatles officially break up in 1970, McCartney will explain (and complain): "I didn't leave the Beatles. The Beatles have left."

In the band's final stage, McCartney emerges as the happiest Beatle, usurping Lennon's role as the group's cheerleader. Cajoling the others to rediscover their group spirit has become the veiled message in McCartney songs like "Get Back." Trying to direct Lennon, however, is doomed to fail. In the end, Lennon objects to McCartney's departure notice, saying: "I started the band. I disbanded it. It's as simple as that." Well, actually it isn't quite that simple. During the break-up years, Harrison leaves The Beatles first in terms of feeling much less positive than his bandmates.

5. We indulge in sensory delight, and in whatever is amusing or introduces variety. We relish both the moment and any pleasing distractions.

When Julia Child is cooking in Paris, her husband Paul notices that his six feet, two inches tall wife is often stirring a pot she stoops to reach. So when they move to America, Paul designs a more suitable kitchen that becomes the setting for Child's in-home TV shows, starting with *The French Chef* in 1963.

It isn't just the food she cooks that Child finds delicious.[9] In describing her house in Cambridge, Massachusetts, on camera, Child says in her breathy, warbly voice: "If we could just have the kitchen and the bedroom, that would be all we'd need." Another time, she writes her husband: "I want to see you, touch you, kiss you, talk with you, eat with you, ... eat you, maybe." To a city near where the Puritans had landed, Child brings a joyful, eye-twinkling determination not to "cater to the flimsies": those who only go halfway, in whatever room of the house.

6. Finding a purpose larger than ourselves gives life meaning.

It's 1963 and Gloria Steinem, who by her nature favors modest, satisfaction level smiles, isn't currently very happy. Then again, Steinem's not experiencing her undercover, freelance journalism assignment as a Playboy Bunny for the fun of it. The future cofounder of *Ms.* magazine has something more in mind. In publishing a two-part expose in *Show* magazine, she's offering a reality check on Hugh Hefner's monthly essays dubbed "the Emancipation Proclamation of the sexual revolution." Steinem's happiness comes, in this case, from knowing the gig's grin-and-bear-it hassles are ultimately worthwhile.

What's involved?[10] After getting tested for venereal diseases, Steinem receives her Bunny outfit. The shoes with their three-inch heels are so agonizing that after two weeks on the job, Steinem's feet will forever remain half a size larger. Meanwhile, the corset is easily at least two inches too small, except the bust, which gets issued with only D-cups. All in all, the outfit is so tight that even to sneeze might break the corset's zipper. As for filling the D-cups, like almost all of her new colleagues, Steinem resorts to stuffing them. The options are many: sanitary napkins, gym socks, and the solution the New York City Playboy Club's wardrobe mistress imposes on Steinem. A pair of plastic, dry-cleaning bags get stuffed inside her costume.

"Sir, you are not allowed to touch the Bunnies" is the refrain taught in the orientation lecture for the latest hires. In reality, however, saying "no" doesn't do any good because the men continually try anyway and, when rebuffed, they will tweak Steinem's tail as she walks by. Once, when she rejects a customer's advance, he angrily responds, "What do you think I come here for, the roast beef?" On Steinem's final evening of duty, she overhears a fellow Bunny say of a customer, "He's a real gentleman. He treats you just the same whether you've slept with him or not." Thereby confirmed is Steinem's conclusion that a male-defined sexual revolution leaves plenty to be desired.

The aftermath of the exposé's publication is that, at first, Steinem is miserable. Hefner will claim that Playboy Bunny recruiting perversely improves, despite the bad publicity; and Steinem gets endless requests to repeat the feat, only this time as a prostitute. Offered an advance for a book deal to transform her recent undercover experience into a lush romantic fantasy, Steinem sends the money back. On the other hand, Steinem can ultimately say she's glad she wrote her famous scoop because "My exposé of working in a Playboy Club has outlived all the Playboy Clubs, both here and abroad."

7. We believe opportunity exists as part of a society where people largely play by the rules and there's a sufficient degree of justice.

That opportunity exists, Beyonce has never had cause to doubt. "I grew up upper-class. Private school. My dad had a Jaguar. We're African-American, and we work together as a family,"[11] Beyonce has said of her upbringing. Her childhood home was something of a showpiece. Picture a four-bedroom, brick-and-stucco mansion made possible by both her father's work as a salesman, first for Xerox and later for Johnson & Johnson, and her mother owning a highly successful hair salon. A work ethic that leads to success has been the hallmark of Beyonce's life. "Repetition, repetition," her father, Matthew, would preach after he left his job to manage Beyonce's first (childhood) band, Destiny's Child. To this day Beyonce repeatedly works and reworks her act. I'm never satisfied," she says, adding: "I've never met anyone that works harder than me in my industry."

At the same time, though, does Beyonce believe that opportunity broadly exists within a society where if people play by the rules, they can count on justice? Not exactly. Increasingly, Beyonce may flash joyful smiles while singing her songs but she hovers more in the range of acceptance level smiles when she raises issues on stage like, "Do you want your daughter to have 75 cents when she deserves $1?" Politeness and success aren't a natural pairing, a sad truth Beyonce credits her dad for helping her first realize regarding the cutthroat world of entertainment.

Four Forms of Happiness

Go down the cereal aisle in your local grocery store, and every box with a cartoon character—from Tony the Tiger to Capt'n Crunch—will be the happiest person ever to appear at a breakfast table. To interject some realism, let's be honest: many people aren't exactly thrilled to pull themselves out of bed in the morning. If they do smile at dawn, those smiles won't be ear-to-ear grins but, rather, instances of mild happiness.

Earlier, I introduced four levels of happiness: joy, pleasure, satisfaction, and acceptance level smiles. Now I'm taking those four levels of happiness and taking one level of smiling and putting it front and center per form. In simplest terms, Camouflage equates to satisfaction smiles; Plugging

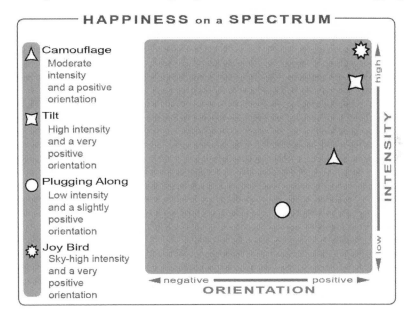

along to acceptance smiles; and Joy Bird to—what else—joyful smiles. More specifically, think in terms of this formula: happiness level X is always *minus* the other three happiness levels. In the case of Camouflage, for instance, the amount of satisfaction level smiles *minus* the amount of joy, pleasure, and acceptance level smiles, shown per celebrity *over time* defines which celebrities are prone to displaying the Camouflage form of happiness. The exception is Tilt, which occurs when joy and pleasure—both strong levels of happiness—aren't equally shown over time. (If you're somewhat confused, don't worry. This should all become clearer in the pages to follow.)

Put another way, the first two forms of happiness, Camouflage and Tilt, reveal that this emotion can be less straightforward than you might have expected. Be alert whenever you encounter people emoting in these ways; what you see may *not* be what you get. Happiness isn't always pure sunshine. In contrast, the other two forms of happiness, Plugging Along and Joy Bird, are straightforward ones you can rely on.

Camouflage

These instances involve people who show lots of satisfaction, while also being low on all of the other levels of happiness. Satisfaction level smiles can be due to polite reserve or else people trying to ingratiate themselves with others. Either way, when satisfaction level smiles serve as social smiles, they become a matter of Camouflage, a technique commonly used by people and animals alike to protect themselves from "predators". (The obvious comparison here is celebrities trying to ward off the paparazzi.)

With Camouflage comes complexity. Yes, happiness might seem like the easiest gig in town among the seven core emotions. How can you get a smile wrong? Then again, with smiles frequently deployed to bond with others and *deflect* trouble, watch out. Social smiles definitely pose the risk of not being detected for what they may actually be: less a matter of happiness than Camouflage, hiding other, more negative feelings.

Kim Kardashian

- Camouflage: A modest smile is being offered, accompanied by a slight lift of the cheeks. (To know that Camouflage is truly the form involved, over time the other levels of happiness should rarely appear.)

- Other emoting: Note the tense lower eyelids, and how the inner eyebrows are slightly lowered, indicative of anger most of all.

Camouflage smiles suggest being able to navigate socially in a calculating manner. Kim Kardashian has proven to be the most adroit of the Kardashian sisters—boosting her status through not only the TV series *Keeping Up with the Kardashians*, but also a home-sex video, and a book of selfies entitled *Selfish*.[12] Now Kim Kardashian-West after her marriage to Kanye West, she's the star whose fans sometimes include girls wearing t-shirts that say, "All Hail KKW."[13] Of evenings that were once spent partying with current frenemy Paris Hilton, Kardashian-West recalls: "We knew exactly where to go, where to be seen, how to have something written about you."

Who are the other celebrities appearing on the Top 10 list for Camouflage? Bandmates John

TOP 10

Camouflage

John Lennon
Larry Ellison
Jeb Bush
Peyton Manning
Chuck Berry
Ray Croc
Lindsey Vonn
Kim Kardashian
Ringo Starr
Cam Newton

Lennon and Ringo Starr appear, an outcome that might in part reflect their learning to mug for the cameras during the media blitz they faced as The Beatles. Also here is somebody who knows TV camera crews as well as Kardashian-West does: former NFL star quarterback Peyton Manning, now one of America's preeminent pitchmen.

Tilt

Okay, hang in there with me on this explanation. To understand if people exhibit Tilt, you need an emotional baseline. What's their happiness emoting pattern over time? Do they exhibit lots of joy, but not much pleasure; or is it the reverse? Do they show lots of pleasure, but not much joy? When you recognize a disparity involving the two levels of strong happiness, you've found a case of Tilt. Something is out of balance whenever the two highest levels of happiness being expressed by people, over time, vary a lot in terms of frequency. That one level is largely, curiously absent hints at instability. Look out for an unresolved tension in people exhibiting this form of happiness, a tension that begs the question: why the huge disparity?

pleasure smile   acceptance smile

Whitney Houston

- Tilt: Here I've dramatized the form's emotional asymmetry by juxtaposing a pleasure smile next to a mere acceptance smile. Note how vast the difference is between these two photos taken the same day.

Highly pertinent in this case is that no examples of a joyful smile exists among the photos available from that day's concert.

- Other emoting: In the right photo, the chin is pushing up in a sign of anger, disgust, and sadness.

In simplest terms, Whitney Houston's immense talent was greater than her emotional stability. Pleasure, yes, but rarely did joy characterize her feelings in even her happiest moments. Gifted with an incredible voice, beauty, a mother who sang behind Aretha Franklin and Elvis Presley, Dionne Warwick for a cousin, and Darlene Love as her godmother, Houston had it all. But against her parents' wishes, she married a "street guy" named Bobby Brown. Then Whitney's childhood nickname, Nippy, alluding to a comic strip character prone to problems, quickly became prophetic.

TOP 10

Tilt

Ellen DeGeneres
Mark Zuckerberg
David Letterman
Bill Wyman
Whitney Houston
Jack Welch
Bill Cosby
John Lennon
Jennifer Aniston
Joe Montana

Among the biggest Tilt celebrities are two linked to substance abuse: Houston, with her serious drug habit; and David Letterman, a recovering alcoholic. Then there's Bill Cosby, now serving jail time for sexual misconduct. Still another example is John Lennon, whose first solo album after The Beatles broke up featured therapeutic primal screaming as a way to cope with his mother's early death.

Plugging Along

In this case, people show plenty of acceptance smiles but the other three levels of happiness rarely occur. An acceptance smile is a mere toehold of receptivity, akin to *that's the worst joke I ever heard, but at least you tried to humor me.* Habitually expressed, such a smile might also bring to mind Garrison Keillor's radio show quip about a reserved Norwegian-American man who "loved his wife so much he almost told her." While acceptance smiles represent the lowest, most begrudging level of happiness, there is nevertheless an upside to them. People who barely smile often plug along in a quiet, steady manner. They don't go too high or too low emotionally, and are unlikely to oversell themselves.

Amy Schumer

- Plugging Along: Observe the slight, acceptance level smile. (Over time, by comparison the other levels of happiness rarely appear.)

- Other emoting: The lowered eyes and eyebrows, and especially the deep furrow in the right cheek, all indicate sadness.

Opposed to idle chitchat given an "insatiable" work ethic,14 Amy Schumer instead favors what caused her breakthrough on Last Comic Standing: "I kept it honest on the show and it served me well." In that vein, these are Schumer's takes on a variety of topics. On Hollywood schmoozing: "I don't pretend to be nice." On childhood: "It was a 24-hour comedy boot camp in our house ... but for really sad reasons." And on hooking up: "I always thought sex was funny." After being photographed nude by Annie Liebowitz, Schumer tweeted her photo, writing: "Beautiful, gross, strong, thin, fat, pretty, ugly, sexy,

TOP 10

Plugging Along

Amy Schumer
Angelina Jolie
Bernie Madoff
Douglas MacArthur
John Bonham
Steven Spielberg
Andy Warhol
Dustin Hoffman
Elton John
Jimmy Page

disgusting, flawless, woman. Thank you." Can you see why you might expect slight, wry smiles from this comedian?

Also on the Top 10 list for Plugging Along is Steven Spielberg. As is true of Schumer, with Spielberg exuberance gives way to getting the work done. In hindsight, Spielberg dismisses most of his creative efforts as "sugar substitutes."[15] Typically what you get with this director is a whisper of a smile and low, long tracking shots that simulate a world in which challenges loom large, but not insurmountable.

Joy Bird

To qualify, people will be unusually given to broad, joyful smiles, complete with twinkling eyes, and do so in greater proportion than they show other levels of happiness. They're signaling rapture. It's hard to dislike Joy Birds, unless you're indulging in envy. These proverbial happy campers tend to be elastic in their thinking and may also exhibit a great ability to schmooze. But even this strongest form of happiness has a potential downside: happiness can leave us unfocused.

That caveat aside, what is it about joy that makes it special? Joy is a social magnet. The old cliché, "Smile, and the world smiles with you; cry, and you cry alone," didn't come about by chance.

Joyful smiles help people make their way through uncomfortable situations. Such smiles say *winner,* echoing why a female peacock chooses the male with the most dazzling plumage. Beautiful feathers showcase a male who will be a strong, healthy partner. With people, in turn, joyful smiles can offer the prospect of sharing in the victor's good fortune.

Mark Zuckerberg

- Joy Bird: The push of skin surrounding the eyes and a big smile say it all.

Sure, being one of the richest people on earth doesn't hurt. But joy would still define Mark Zuckerberg's manner, for better and for worse, even without the money, I believe. Joy gives Zuckerberg the flair, the energy to climb the next mountain. Joy can also simultaneously cause him to be surprisingly blasé about key details. For instance, in *Chaos Monkeys*[16] a former Facebook staffer describes how hard it was to get Zuckerberg to focus on something that was hardly a minor matter: monetizing the company's user base prior to its IPO. Although *follow the money* is the lifeline of business, apparently Zuckerberg isn't always willing or able to adhere to that dictum.

TOP 10

Joy Bird

Ellen DeGeneres
Mark Zuckerberg
Jack Welch
Little Richard
Barack Obama
Mary Lou Retton
Bill Wyman
Michael Phelps
LeBron James
Tiger Woods

Others on this Top 10 list radiate "sweet dreams." They've achieved greater success than they could have ever imagined, and now they can bask and relax in its glow. That's especially true of Ellen DeGeneres, whose way forward in life wasn't obvious back when she held a variety of jobs ranging from being a waitress at T.G.I. Friday's to a vacuum cleaner saleswoman. It's likewise true of much-beloved Mary Lou Retton, whose big break came when an opening was created for her on the U.S. gymnastics squad because a teammate got injured prior to the 1984 Summer Olympics.

Applications in Your Life

In your own life, when might you see these four forms of happiness? How might you best react to them, given what causes people to feel happy?

Camouflage: Social smiles are, by definition, displayed more for others than as an expression of happiness deeply felt. The effort to maintain a satisfaction level smile not necessarily genuine can prove to be exhausting. If seen on employees working the checkout counter, maybe this isn't the most natural role for them in

the store. If you're either an advertising agency's creative director or a management consultant, Camouflage might be a sign that your client has reservations about your approach. If you're a guy reflecting on a first date, during which you saw this pattern a lot, you may want to reconsider whether your comments at dinner were truly amusing.

People who exhibit the Camouflage form will tend to be circumspect, adaptable, and friendly, but not overly so. In terms of happiness, they're keeping their cards pretty close to their chests, whatever the reason.

A plausible explanation for this form of happiness arises from people feeling like they've achieved security, but only just barely or temporarily. Occasional sensory pleasure doesn't resolve their underlying sense of discomfort. These are people whose happiness is of modest proportions or else a mask. How best to respond? Help them reduce the risk of their happiness fading away, and they'll be grateful. What are the threats? Have they taken unwise risks? Double-check their decision-making process with them, but realize that most likely they will be most receptive to listening to your advice only if they seriously falter. Therefore, patience is necessary.

Tilt: Don't rashly assume that the intense happiness you're seeing is rock solid. That warning applies to the job prospect you might want to meet a second or even a third time before hiring. Or it could apply to a family member struggling with substance abuse, an eating disorder, or recovery from an injury or lay-off, and not doing as well as you believed. Giving them *more* emotional support than would otherwise appear to be required could be in order.

In a case of Tilt, those exhibiting this pattern may be unreliable and restless precisely because, over time, they can't land squarely on both of the top two rungs of happiness. Either joy or pleasure eludes them. They may get really high emotionally, but then they don't come down gently from joy into pleasure; instead, they crash. Taken the other way around, they might feel plenty of pleasure but can't quite attain joy.

Why is Tilt occurring? Sudden success may not feel sustainable, or sensory attractions are really distractions from serious problems that haven't gone away. Those are among the possible causes. You may best develop rapport with these people by helping them to repeat their success, especially if that success entails what they care about most. By identifying possible improvements that will help them build on previous success, you can prove your value and earn their trust. At the same time, these people are likely to be edgy, early adopters who pursue trends. Appeal to their natural curiosity and work with them to generate new possibilities for delight.

Plugging Along: If you're a job candidate, sales person, or marketing manager repeatedly receiving only a faint smile from somebody you must win over, try harder. You haven't yet carried the day. A female shopper showing this pattern may still be searching for the item with enough emotional benefits to get her past a high price point. See the signs of Plugging Along in an employee you think is loyal, and don't be surprised on receiving two-weeks' notice or less. Children taking piano lessons but barely smiling aren't nearly as excited about the lessons as parents paying for them in the belief that the training is worthwhile.

In general, people prone to the slight smiles of the Plugging Along version of happiness will be fastidious, understated, or exhibit both traits. They don't lose sight of what they want, and don't give much away.

Delayed gratification is a probable, underlying cause for this form of happiness being expressed. These are people who may either have reasonable hopes for future progress or believe, in general, that they're operating in an environment in which a tenuous but fair opportunity for advancement exists. How best to respond? First, don't impede; they probably know where they're headed. Second, seek to understand if what motivates them is more a matter of achieving task-related goals or of securing social affiliation. If the former, seek to cooperate by ensuring the goals get reached quickly and well. If the latter applies, however, then how the outcome gets viewed and validated by others is the key. In that case, you'll build a tighter bond with them by emphasizing how others will appreciatively react to whatever angle you're proposing.

Joy Bird: This emotional tendency reflects the type of flight attendants Southwest Airlines likes to hire: people who are cheerful and adept at building rapport with passengers. In fact, anybody in the hospitality industry should ideally be near this mark. Charismatic leaders, who might excel at both the people skills of motivating employees as well as

Joy Bird

Charismatic
Upbeat
Impulsive
Convivial
Elfin

conceiving big-picture business plans, also belong here. Finally, should you want a partner who's a good conversationalist, start here.

When it comes to the Joy Bird form, expect conviviality as well as some impulsivity. These people are riding a wave of enjoyment. The hunt for the next source of rewards will appeal to them most.

The likely causes of this, the highest level of happiness, predominating will be profound. Either these people have had their identity affirmed—namely, a feeling of being cared for and belonging—or they've found a purpose that gives their life meaning. What might be your role in all of this? Know that these people often prefer dreaming over paying attention to crucial details. Help them be on guard. If a situation involves far more risk than potential reward, let them know. Just don't overplay your hand or expect too much in the way of behavioral change. Joy Birds are often people with an expansive sense of themselves, so don't crowd their parade.

Summary

The rule of thumb is that once our basic needs are met, then the pursuit of happiness can rightly assume ever greater importance in our lives. But studies show that happiness benefits our physical, psychological, and social well-being at *all* times. Smiles make things happen, helping us, in part, through making a positive impression on others. Everyone likes to feel welcomed, and smiles do a nice job of it. Providing an emotional high that's often contagious, happiness enables us to bond with others.

In mind/body terms, smiling literally cools the head and creates a sense of comfort. People who are happy won't struggle to maintain their vigor due to lost hope. They will instead believe effort matters. The single most frequent of the seven core emotions celebrities show in *Famous Faces Decoded*, happiness gets displayed by the women far more than by their male, play-it-cool counterparts.

Sadness

A Rear View Mirror

What Sadness Means

His eyes are glistening with tears, and sweat is as visible above his upper lip as it was the evening of his first presidential debate with John F. Kennedy in 1960. Richard Nixon stands before members of his administration and White House staff the morning after his resignation on national TV, ready to give his last speech as a politician.[1] The evening before, Nixon's address had been scripted and brief. This one will be extemporaneous and in its ramblings nearly 18 minutes long.

Besides gallows humor, the speech will feature less than genuine self-depreciation, scarred pride, and self-righteous anger. But what will emotionally stand out the most from Nixon's farewell on August 9, 1974 is sadness, with self-pity and anguish joined at the hip. "We'll see you again," Nixon says and winces, before closing his eyes

Richard Nixon

momentarily. Regrets follow. "I should have been by your offices and shaken hands," Nixon says, choking up. Far greater depths of sadness are ahead. "My mother was a saint," Nixon finds himself saying, voice quavering, a tear now taking over his left eye as he recalls her tending to "two boys," two brothers of Nixon's, both "dying of tuberculosis."

Next, an aide brings Nixon the book he requested so everyone can, by implication, hear of another president's fellow misery. That would be Theodore Roosevelt's grief upon losing his wife: "And when my heart's dearest died, the light went from my life forever." This president's own wife, Pat, isn't dead; she's standing nearby. She's not mentioned even once by Nixon, though, as he starts to sniffle, fighting back sobs. By then White House counsel Leonard Garment is, as he later recounts, thinking to himself as he sits in the audience: *Oh, my God, he's beginning to break down. A binge of free association. Money, father, mother, brothers, death. The man is unraveling right before us. He will be the first person to go over the edge on live television.*

Luckily, things never quite reach that point. Sadness can involve a sense of irrevocable loss and is an approach emotion: we long to be hugged and consoled. In August of 1974, however, Nixon is having none of that because sadness is also a submissive emotion, an admission of having been wounded. The essence of sadness is a cry for help, not something Nixon can permit himself. To admit to needing emotional support would go against the line he loves in *Patton* (1970): George C. Scott declaring that "Americans love winners" and "will not tolerate a loser."

A saddened Nixon can't consciously allow himself to feel sad because to do so would mean he's become a loser. So he likewise can't bring himself to directly address losing the presidency. Instead, Nixon pulls himself back from the abyss, tightens his lips in anger and, near the end of his rambling remarks, proclaims: "Always give your best, never get discouraged, never be petty." Further advice that might best apply to Nixon himself follows: "Always remember, others may hate you but those who hate you don't win unless you hate them" (a small smile), "and then you destroy yourself."

Incapable of lightness on that day (everything is going wrong, why *even his watch has stopped working*), Nixon is nevertheless on to something that many people can relate to by denying himself sadness. In America, where we're serenaded with "Don't Worry, Be Happy," sadness can seem embarrassing. In line with *Patton*, it's as if sadness is an emotion we're not supposed to feel. Terms like "sad sack" or being a "downer" put a derogatory spin on an emotion that serves a legitimate purpose in life.

In Pixar's *Inside Out*, a happy, hockey-playing girl from Minnesota is forced to relocate with her family to San Francisco. In the movie, the personified character of Sadness becomes something of a hero given the emotion's redemptive ability to slow us down and help us reflect on, and rectify, what's painful. That's the process Nixon is short-circuiting. Ashamed of feeling weak and vulnerable, he's pretending as if nothing bad has happened as he boards a helicopter after the speech. Standing outside its door, Nixon waves to the people on the South Lawn as if he's just won another campaign.

Spotting Sadness

A sad face *wrinkles* as if its owner is a crumpled piece of paper. Sad people display some of the most obvious emotional clues, including: tears, sobs, and hang-dog looks. Those overt signals aside, sadness can nevertheless also be as subtle as any of the emotions in terms of how it gets displayed. More specifically, sadness appears in seven ways on the face—two of those when it's the only emotion being shown:

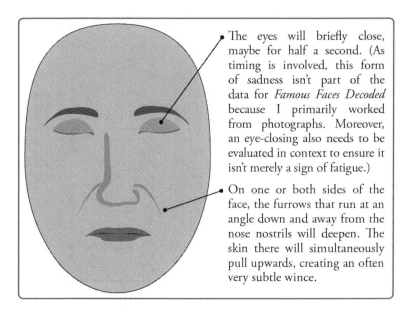

The eyes will briefly close, maybe for half a second. (As timing is involved, this form of sadness isn't part of the data for *Famous Faces Decoded* because I primarily worked from photographs. Moreover, an eye-closing also needs to be evaluated in context to ensure it isn't merely a sign of fatigue.)

On one or both sides of the face, the furrows that run at an angle down and away from the nose nostrils will deepen. The skin there will simultaneously pull upwards, creating an often very subtle wince.

There are another five ways that sadness gets expressed. In each of these cases, one or more of the other core emotions will likewise be shown:

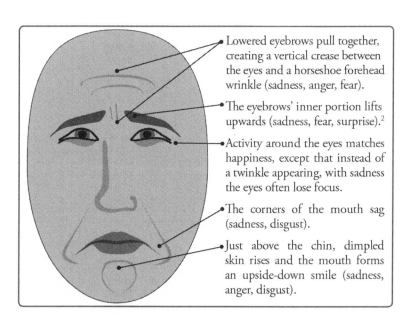

Lowered eyebrows pull together, creating a vertical crease between the eyes and a horseshoe forehead wrinkle (sadness, anger, fear).

The eyebrows' inner portion lifts upwards (sadness, fear, surprise).[2]

Activity around the eyes matches happiness, except that instead of a twinkle appearing, with sadness the eyes often lose focus.

The corners of the mouth sag (sadness, disgust).

Just above the chin, dimpled skin rises and the mouth forms an upside-down smile (sadness, anger, disgust).

Compared to the dominant, approach emotions of anger and happiness, the *submissive*, approach emotion of sadness is relatively rare (at least in public, the source of the photographs I had access to for facial coding purposes). While those two other approach emotions each account for over 30% of the celebrity emoting captured in *Famous Faces Decoded*, the average amount of sadness is a little above 8%. Male celebrities contributing to that average show nearly a third more sadness than their female

TOP 10

Most Sad

Donald Trump
Richard Nixon
Hillary Clinton
Marlon Brando
Tiger Woods
Johnny Cash
Janis Joplin
Jay-Z
John McEnroe
Cam Newton

counterparts. Accordingly, the Top 10 list for Most Sad consists largely of men enduring various degrees of anguish. Hillary Clinton and Janis Joplin are the only two women to appear, both of whom I might note have been derided by their critics as insufficiently feminine.

Greater male sadness will be surprising to anyone who assumes men so favor anger as a coping mechanism that they're not vulnerable to sadness. The Top 10 list for Least Sad may, likewise, surprise people because it mostly involves females.

TOP 10

Least Sad

Martha Stewart
Estee Lauder
Sandra Bullock
Joe Montana
Diana Ross
Kate Winslet
Jackie Onassis
Howard Stern
Ellen DeGeneres
Jimmy Page*
Gloria Steinem*
* Two-way tie

Donald Trump has said: "Women are much tougher and more calculating than men"; maybe he's right.

How good are people at spotting sadness? With a detection accuracy rate of 23%, the result for sadness ties for second worst. (Only the rate for contempt is lower.) In the Top 10 list for Most Sad, the celebrities not recognized by this book's voters as prone to sadness consist of Donald Trump, Hillary Clinton, and John McEnroe. The following three photographs illustrate ways in which sadness appears, and the celebrities' emotional profiles indicate how well voters did in choosing the top two emotions that distinguish these famous people.

Don't let Janis Joplin's good-sized smile distract you from what else is evident here. The right inner eyebrow is slightly raised and the eye below it is unfocused and surrounded by pushed up skin. Sadly happy, Joplin isn't even close to feeling elated.

Voted	Actual	Rare
sadness anger	sadness *joy*	anger

Janis Joplin

Janis Joplin was a major female rock star when she died from a heroin overdose at age 27 in 1970. Her cover of "Me and Bobby McGee" hit number one after her death, and she was posthumously inducted into the Rock and Roll Hall of Fame in 1995.

Sadness is evident here from the downcast eyes that belie Jay-Z's smile. There's also a fairly pronounced crease in the upper right cheek, as it is pulled obliquely upwards near the base of the nose. "I'm hungry for knowledge," Jay-Z says. "The whole thing is to learn every day, to get brighter and brighter." This contemplative look is the signature expression of a guy whose albums include *The Blueprint* (2001), released back when Jay-Z was laying the foundation for not only his musical career but his entire business empire.

┌─Voted─┐	┌─Actual─┐	┌─Rare─┐
happiness contempt	sadness fear	satisfaction

Jay-Z

Born Shawn Corey Carter, Jay-Z has sold over 100 million albums and won 21 Grammys. Besides holding the U.S. *Billboard* record with 14 number one albums by a solo artist, he's a certified sports agent in pro basketball and baseball.

Back at the White House for Hubert Humphrey's funeral, post Watergate fiasco, a sad Richard Nixon has baggy skin around his eyes. Notice, too, the slightly downturned lip corners that accompany the downcast gaze and the subtle wrinkle between the eyebrows. Furthermore, Nixon's cheeks are raised and puffed, despite the absence of an uplifting smile. As Nixon's 1968 election opponent, Humphrey campaigned as "The Happy Warrior." In contrast, a childhood neighbor lady once said of Nixon: "He wasn't the kind of boy you would pick up and hug."

┌─Voted─┐	┌─Actual─┐	┌─Rare─┐
anger contempt	sadness anger	surprise

Richard Nixon

After serving as Dwight Eisenhower's V. P., Nixon was the only U.S. President ever to resign (1974). He opened diplomatic relations with China, engaged in détente with the Soviet Union, and established the Environmental Protection Agency.

What May Cause Sadness

Taken to extremes, sadness becomes depression.[3] In those cases, the depressed person will often feel trapped in an adverse past they can't get out of their heads. But even with ordinary sadness, there's a tendency to see the world through a rear-view-mirror perspective, whereby past disappointments can color and limit faith that future situations will turn out well. The following set of seven causes explores the overly strong internal focus that is such a part of feeling this emotion.

1. We're dealing with rejection, often involving a sense of having been abandoned as part of suffering from isolation.

Back for her 10th high school class reunion, Janis Joplin is asked by a clueless TV interviewer: "Did you entertain in Port Arthur?" (meaning, did she ever sing there in her home town along the Texas coast). "Only when I walked down the aisles," the rock star cackles in response. The reality, however, is much more painful than Joplin is letting on.[4] How can she forget incidents like being named "Ugliest Man on Campus" after escaping Port Arthur for a stop at the University of Texas in Austin?

In the way she bellows, cries, and stamps her feet, Joplin-the-performer can find pleasure, or at least release, from what Joplin-the-person is suffering through. Cheerful, yet melancholy. A white woman singing—maybe the correct verb is *overwhelming*—the blues. Those are among Joplin's many contradictions, all of them hard to sort out. "I can't talk about my singing," she tells an interviewer. "I'm inside it. How can you describe something you're inside of?"

To witness Joplin immersed in performing, watch the video of her squeezing everything she can out of "Piece of My Heart" (1969). In it, she goes from the sad, anxious lifting of her inner eyebrows when the song begins to a fist-pumping, joyful look by the end. Along the way, she's invited members of the audience up on stage. By song's close, Joplin is singing encircled by adoring fans at close range. All the same, she's still only holding a microphone in her arms. That's in keeping with Joplin's signature remark: "Onstage I make love to 25,000 people, then I go home alone."

2. We're dealing with a loss of self-esteem (or even just the prospect of losing it).

Psychologists are all over Donald Trump, trying to explain his personality. The overwhelming verdict is that Trump is the ultimate narcissist.[5] That's a personality disorder the Mayo Clinic calls the mark of fragile self-esteem, noting that those who suffer from narcissism "may be generally unhappy." If it's true that Trump is a prime example of narcissism, what stumps the psychologists is that they can't point to the usual culprit: parents who aren't affirmative, causing the child to long for praise from others. By all accounts, Trump had a good relationship with both his parents, and especially his dad, at whose funeral in 1999 Donald spoke, saying Fred Trump's greatest achievement was his "fantastic son."

If buildings make the man, witness TRUMP stenciled in 20-foot high letters on the tower Trump has branded alongside the river in downtown Chicago. Or hear how Trump bragged after 9/11 that, with the Twin Towers gone, his building at 40 Wall Street was now the tallest in downtown Manhattan.[6] Notably lacking the contentment signaled by happiness, Trump admits that "It's the hunt that I believe I love" and so "I aim very high, and then I just keep pushing." In business, that approach might be justifiable. But in the context of groping women (as Trump grotesquely boasted about doing on the *Access Hollywood* tape that emerged during the 2016 campaign), it's as if Trump's being so often in the grip of sadness has somehow crippled his sense of decency and fair play.

3. We're dealing with a loss of praise and social support.

At age 12, Johnny Cash goes off fishing one Saturday while his older brother Jack stays behind, cutting wood to help make money for the family.[7] Using a giant framesaw, Jack loses his balance and gets fatally injured. "I had to take out too many of his insides," the doctor admits to Cash's parents after doing what he could for the boy. For years after Jack's death, Cash's father, Ray, will say: "John, you should be more like your brother. You're lazy, no account [sic], shiftless."

Cash will subsequently wish he died that day. Feeling guilty and sad, he often tells himself: "I want to be more like" my brother Jack "to get my father to finally accept me." In times of trouble, Cash will wonder "What would Jack (an aspiring preacher) do?" and the country music legend's first commercial hit will be the song, "Cry, Cry, Cry" (1957).

4. We're dealing with disappointment, often related to high, unrealistic expectations.

In April of 1994, the internet's stunning growth causes Jeff Bezos to quit his job at a New York City hedge fund. "Regret-minimization framework" is how he describes deciding to take the risk.[8] In running Amazon, Bezos is philosophical about setbacks he can't entirely let go of: "I've made billions of dollars of failures at Amazon.com. Literally billions of dollars of failures," he says in an interview, comparing those experiences to "getting a root canal with no anesthesia."

How to explain the man the *Harvard Business Review* has called "The Best-Performing CEO in the World"? How can Bezos both dwell on and yet overcome a litany of costly failures and disappointments? The answer is he plunges onward into many new ventures, some of which pan out big-time. While his biological father used to be in circuses, Bezos is his own dream machine. Bezos is still the same guy who, as a high school valedictorian, told *The Miami Herald* his goal in life was "to build space hotels, amusement parks, yachts and colonies" for millions of people orbiting the earth. It's a dream Bezos retains, even at the risk of setting himself up for yet another, possible disappointment by literally aiming so high and far away.

5. We're dealing with physical pain, possibly involving a general loss of health and functionality.

With a track record of locking teachers in rooms, as well as setting fires, Marlon Brando fails high school and is no more accepting of authority figures upon reaching Hollywood. What's behind the pattern?[9] Try a father who beat him and an alcoholic mother whom a young Brando searched the local bars for many a night, in hopes of bringing her home. Those influences will all come together in *The Godfather* (1972), when Brando plays a macho, thuggish man turning gentle and sensitive in old age. For Brando, any scenes that require anger inspire memories of "my father hitting me." In contrast, for scenes requiring compassion he calls on memories of the boy whose mother "chose a bottle over caring for me." By mid-life, one of Brando's favorite quotes has become the Jesuit motto: "Give me a child until he is seven and I will give you the man."

6. We're dealing with the loss of a treasured object.

As Tiger Woods gives his press conference apology in early 2010 before a hand-picked audience, he barely shows any emotion. It's as if the script has been ghost-*written* before being ghost-*read* by Woods. When the golfer says he has "bitterly disappointed all of you" seated before him, nobody's home, emotionally speaking. Woods shows no visible sadness, no regret, regarding his affairs with other women. Left unacknowledged, the scandal's moment of greatest drama: Woods crashing his Escalade into a fire hydrant around 2:30 a.m., with his wife Elin allegedly in pursuit.

When does Woods emote during the press conference? Rarely while talking about his wife and kids. Passion kicks in far more when the topic turns to tournament trophies. At the press conference and in subsequent media interviews, Woods winces often—and convincingly—whenever the question concerns getting back on tour to post more golf victories.

7. We're dealing with a sense of hopelessness and helplessness. (But should despair reach the point of feeling worthless, depression has set in.)

According to Nirvana grunge rock star Kurt Cobain, the band's name is from the Buddhist concept of "freedom from pain, suffering and the external world." But what if the pain is mostly internal? In Cobain's suicide note, he doesn't shy away from admitting to sadness or pointing to its likely, original source: his parents' divorce. "There's good in all of us and I think I simply love people too much, so much that it makes me feel too fucking sad. The sad little sensitive, unappreciated, Pisces, Jesus man," he writes, taking a gibe at himself. Loathing and self-loathing intermingle. "Since the age of seven, I've become hateful towards all humans in general," Cobain confesses before adding, "Only because it seems so easy for people to get along and have empathy."

Age seven was two years before Cobain's parents divorced, but storm clouds were probably already gathering in their relationship. The suicide note's divorce reference builds on a 1993 interview[10] in which Cobain recalls turning defiant and withdrawn after his parents' divorce because "I desperately wanted to have the classic, you know, typical family. Mother, father. I wanted that security, so I resented my parents for quite a few years." With no band as of yet, one of Cobain's favorite boyhood activities was repeatedly drawing the character "Creature from the Black Lagoon" to express—and distance—himself from his own misery.

Four Forms of Sadness

Besides the ordinary version of rain, there's freezing drizzle as well as "snain": a rain/snow mix. Why, there are even sun showers. So it follows that there can't be only one form of sadness, and there isn't. The first two forms, Deflated and Shaken, signal feeling needy and thrown off-balance in ways that challenge one's sense of being a worthwhile person. In addition to sadness, Deflated can also involve fear more so than surprise. It's very much about low-grade suffering and anxiety. Despondent people feeling this way are probably more likely to slow down but may, instead, cope by engaging in a flurry of activity to "paper over" their discomfort. Then with Shaken, surprise gets favored over fear in being yoked to sadness. With this form, it's more about a set-back leaving a forlorn and rattled person yearning for relief.

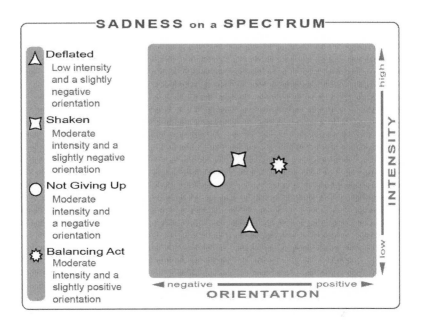

In contrast, the other two forms of sadness, Not Giving Up and Balancing Act, draw on either disgust and anger, or happiness—and thereby demonstrate resiliency. With the third form, Not Giving Up, a feeling of loss gets challenged by the intervening influence of anger and disgust. Finally, with Balancing Act the inherent call for help that sadness involves has now been answered by a reason for happiness to enter the picture.

Deflated

The single most clear-cut way people exhibit sadness is when the cheeks rise, sometimes just slightly, producing wrinkles from the edge of the nostrils down to the top, outer corners of the lips. This wincing movement also pushes up the skin below the eyes so that they narrow at the corners. When this look is combined with the inner eyebrows rising, you're typically moving from what might be sadness merely hinted at, to a more funda-mental desire to escape suffering.

Donald Trump

- Deflated: The inner eyebrows are raised, and wincing wrinkles appear in both cheeks.

- Other signs of sadness: The eye-brows are knitted together, and the skin near the eyes is baggy.

TOP 10
Deflated

Humphrey Bogart
Donald Trump
Janis Joplin
Hillary Clinton
Peyton Manning
Larry Page
Cam Newton
Larry Ellison
Woody Allen
Jeff Bezos

Donald Trump's supporters believe that his empathy for the challenges many of them face means he will truly "drain the swamp" in the na-tion's capitol. Detractors insist that "Make America Great Again" says more about his ego than anything else, and that any sadness Trump feels involves self-pity rather than concern for others. What both sides would agree on is that with its apoc-alyptic language about an "American carnage," Trump's inagural address was a strikingly grim departure from most new presidents' more uplifting remarks.

Besides Trump, others on the Top 10 list for Deflated who may override sadness with a flurry of activity include the entrepreneurial, high-tech trio of Larry Page, Larry Ellison, and Jeff Bezos. Then there's Woody Allen, who has said of his more than 50 movies: "I would erase all but a few."[11] High self-expectations, if not always met, can be one source of sadness. Another source explains Humphrey Bogart and Janis Joplin also appear here, for in their own way both of them struggled for affirmation. In Bogart's case, the actor unsuccessfully sought affection from his taciturn parents while growing up. In Joplin's case, outside of her family she never did find much acceptance in her home town or even Texas at large.

Shaken

A cheek-raising wince, combined with a mouth falling open with surprise, reveals people caught off-guard. They're freshly vulnerable to discouragement. Given their shock on feeling sadness, these people look like the equivalent of someone who's just tripped during a walk, landing on the pavement in pain.

- Shaken: The crease in the cheek fits this look, even though the mouth hanging open in grief is replaced here by lips pressed tight.

- Other signs of sadness: The eyes are downcast and the eyebrows are lowered in reflection suitable for prayer.

Johnny Cash

Besides the premature loss of his brother Jack, the other most devastating loss in Johnny Cash's life was

75

Shaken

Donald Trump
John McEnroe
Hillary Clinton
Serena Williams
Mary Lou Retton
Elton John
Johnny Cash
Adele
Janis Joplin
Bill Clinton

when his wife died.[12] Day after day, Cash would sit in his wheelchair by June Carter Cash's bed as she lay gravely ill, begging her not to leave him. Then after her death, there was additional rear-view-mirror behavior. Not only did Cash pay an artist to paint June's face on the elevator doors of his office, he would also frequently resort to picking up the phone to talk to June as if nothing had changed.

Headlining the Top 10 list for Shaken, you'll find Donald Trump and John McEnroe. Both men are notoriously thin-skinned, befitting the theory that a cause of sadness can be the absence of enough praise (or success) to bolster one's self-esteem. In contrast, three celebrities on this list have experienced another cause of sadness: the irrevocable loss of somebody important to them. Removed through death or separation early in their lives was Jack in Cash's case, and the fathers of, respectively, both Adele and Bill Clinton.

Not Giving Up

A rodeo clown's painted face showcases a frown. But with a real frown, not only will the lip corners sag. You'll also find that the skin below them simultaneously pouches. Add in an upward chin thrust that puckers the chin and lifts the lower lip, and you've got an upside-down smile. These sad smiles mix in anger and disgust, creating a resolute flavor. Think in terms of sadness, but not resignation; of disappointment that can and will be recovered from. You can likewise think of this look as showing a determination to "get my life back" to where it was previously.

- Not Giving Up: The chin area lifts, and the mouth corners sag.

- Other emoting: A tight-lipped smile and the tension in the lower eyelids can't be ignored, adding happiness to anger, and indicating pride that in some instances may border on arrogance.

Elon Musk

"Sooner or later" Elon Musk has proclaimed, "we must expand life beyond this green and blue ball—or go extinct." His goal is to establish a Mars colony within the next generation[13] and ensure the people living there can use electric transportation. (After all, the atmosphere on Mars lacks the oxygen ordinary cars require.) Given his company's electric cars, how nicely that plan suits the agenda of the CEO of both Tesla Motors and SpaceX. Or so a cynic might say. But you have to hand it to Musk for his never-say-die spirit. Spat on by a disbelieving Russian space designer when he first began to conceptualize a "Mars Oasis," about the only serious things Musk has ever quit on were his first two marriages.

At #11, Musk just barely misses the Top 10 list for Not Giving Up. Those on this list are all world-class athletes or politicians with a single exception: Andy Warhol. As a boy, that artist suffered from a nervous system disease known as St. Vitus' Dance and became a frequently bedridden hypochondriac who, like Musk, was an outcast at school.

TOP 10

Not Giving Up

Barack Obama
Aaron Rodgers
Andy Warhol
Jeb Bush
Bill Clinton
Peyton Manning
Tom Brady
Ted Williams
Roger Clemens
Venus Williams

Balancing Act

Happiness and sadness are opposites that often blend together. We benefit from sadness when the emotion helps enrich our understanding of a loss, including how we might best recover. At other times, sadness helps us anticipate a disappointment and prepare for the hurt. Sadness combined with offsetting amounts of happiness, however, can be even better, ensuring we extract the benefits of sadness without giving in to that feeling.

Mariah Carey

- Balancing Act: This modest smile almost surely would not lift the cheeks so much if wincing wasn't also involved.

- Other emoting: A slightly distended lower lip hints at disgust.

Music and her own bruised self-esteem went together for Mariah Carey from the start. Why, even her first name derives from the plaintive song "They Call the Wind Maria," from the 1951 Broadway musical *Paint Your Wagon*. After her parents' divorce, a youthful Carey would find solace in singing along to music on the radio at night. From such salvation, her career was born.

Other celebrities in the Top 10 list for Balancing Act include: Ringo Starr, whose first drum was a gift the

TOP 10

Balancing Act

Mary Lou Retton
Charles Schulz
John F. Kennedy
Diane Keaton
Ringo Starr
Janis Joplin
Venus Williams
Whitney Houston
Mariah Carey
Jim Henson

often hospitalized boy latched onto; and the Muppets creator Jim Henson, surely the Walt Disney of his era. In helping to establish *Sesame Street* in 1969, Henson was affectionately described by a colleague as having a "whim of steel." Henson's most famous character is alter-ego Kermit the Frog. A good, stable blend of happiness and sadness himself, Kermit sometimes expresses melancholy but is most famous for an open, red mouth that resembles a Valentine whenever he smiles big-time.

Applications for Your Life

In your own life, when might you see these four forms of sadness? How might you best react to them, given what causes people to feel sadness?

Deflated: This look can be synonymous with a cry for help. Somebody crying for help will—in a best-case scenario—also be somebody who empathetically hears other people's cries for help in turn. Somebody who's feeling Deflated may, therefore, prove to be a good listener, able to acknowledge the other party's point of view without merely giving in to it. In negotiations, an adept leader will have sonar-bat instincts for the other party's pain points. The business stakes might be smaller, but the same goes for somebody good at creating customer loyalty by resolving complaints. They'll address a disappointed customer's underlying emotional need and not just the surface request. Acquaintances can turn into good friends with the sensitive disposition this look frequently suggests.

All of the above examples assume a best-case scenario. At other times, people feeling this way may compensate by "revving their engines."

Overriding the sadness they're suffering from, they're not likely to show much patience as they storm ahead.

Among the probable causes of someone feeling Deflated is an on-going, pervasive sense of having been rejected, resulting in isolation. Add to that a feeling of being both helpless and hopeless. How best to respond and assist that person? The clearest antidote is to promote a counter-sense of belonging. What interactions can you suggest that will bolster a deep feeling of connectedness? To offset the notion of being incapable, suggest tasks where the person's likelihood of success is greatest.

Shaken: Here the profile may tip from someone empathetically sensitive to floundering. Sales may not be a good career for people for whom each new failure feels like a shock— no matter how many pep talks they receive. On the other hand, a doctor feeling this way and genuinely dismayed by the rapid deterioration of a patient's condition will move quickly to pursue remedies. This is just the look you expect from a close friend or family member concerned about a relapse in your own health.

People expressing this look are combining sadness with an element of surprise, even alarm. Their situation may have just turned dismal. They're going to feel insecure and off-balance, and in need of plenty of support.

Yes, a sudden change in people's health can explain this look on their faces. But so could an unexpected loss of self-esteem or a disappointment caused by having had higher expectations than proved realistic. How might you respond to people feeling Shaken? Honor the pain, especially if physical in nature. Don't rush to change the topic as that will constitute yet another, unwelcome surprise. As to set-backs of a more social or psychological nature, if true, affirm that the change of fortune didn't result from their own shortcomings. Point out the larger forces involved, and also why the status quo was untenable. Then suggest plausible goals that, when realized, might restore hope and assurance.

Not Giving Up: Being determined, despite setbacks, is an essential quality for any innovator to succeed. If you're a marketing director, you should remember that if the people in your TV spots don't realistically show pain, then you're not high-lighting the value of your client's happiness-inducing, brand solution. Peaks need valleys to reveal their contrasting height. As an employee,

a Not Giving Up look is a badge of honor when given a near-impossible deadline for a project. If a weekend warrior athlete, you don't want to see this look on the face of an opponent you're currently beating on a racquetball court or during a softball game.

People with a Not Giving Up look are buttressing sadness with feelings of anger and disgust. They're wounded but likely to persevere—even forcefully so. Express condescending sympathy at your own risk.

A loss of praise and accompanying social support may have been the trigger. Otherwise, this look may be due to newfound health concerns that introduce limitations these people aren't quick to accept. How best to respond? Show that they're still counted on to contribute. Don't give up on them. In whatever you're doing together, give them the latitude to operate freely and pro-actively. Share stories of adversity conquered, as these are people who will readily identify with examples of resolve.

Balancing Act: It's a delicate dance, not giving in to sadness while also not blindly smothering it with fake happiness. Nurses are called on to manage the Balancing Act every work shift. People in human resources must find a similar balance. In posting job descriptions, they would best serve applicants by acknowledging both the upsides and the challenges inherent in the roles

people will be taking on. In a marriage, don't imagine the other person will utterly change to your liking. To permit some disappointment will paradoxically give the relationship the emotional space required for it to realistically prosper.

People who show the Balancing Act look are managing, to one degree or another, to skillfully leaven sadness with happiness. They're able to suffer through a loss with a degree of levity and enduring acceptance. Considerate, they're also more likely to be amiable than the average person during trying circumstances.

Two of the causes that might be most applicable are, first, when high expectations prove to be a little too high; and second, when a treasured object long enjoyed has now been lost. Chances are that people capable of happiness despite a setback are on their way to healing, but how might you contribute? Together, you can explore what the let-down meant to them in ways they might not have been aware of. You might also help keep them from lunging too impulsively after a suspect solution in an attempt to fill an aching void. Whatever the underlying needs involved, see if those needs can be addressed in a new, more constructive manner.

Summary

Some people may think that rich-and-famous celebrities are too wealthy to ever feel worthless and sad, but of course that's not true. Charlie Chaplin could still convincingly play his character The Tramp, with the Tramp's wincing smiles, long after the actor had achieved fame and fortune. While nobody supposedly knows you when you're down and out, everybody knows what it's like to feel beaten down at times. We also all instinctively know the sadness look: the frowning, "long" face that comes from feeling blue.

Grief can overwhelm us, and misery can make us literally groan in agony. Even less intense versions of sadness can make us want to hide. Ashamed of feeling weak and vulnerable, we often pretend as if nothing bad has happened. With sadness, every facial muscle movement, subtle or otherwise, serves a greater purpose. It signals our need for help as we seek the support required to persevere and prosper. How else does sadness help us? For one thing, it releases hormones that help foster empathy and compassion. For another, it aids in reflection by slowing us down so that we don't rashly jump into another disaster. Accordingly, sadness can lead to being very good at attending to the small details that might make a big difference at times. Finally, when "down", remember: so close and *yet so far* is the distance between sadness and happiness, as the same lips turned down in a frown will, in rising, offer a smile.

Approach Emotions Quiz
(in answering, focus on each emotion's four forms and not the personalities involved)

1. Which of these three celebrities best embodies the elated **Joy Bird** form of happiness?

| Joe Montana | Jack Welch | Katharine Hepburn |

2. Which one of these celebrities shows the **Concentration** form of anger in the purest, most simple way, without other emotions?

| George Harrison | Leonardo DiCaprio | Barry Bonds |

3. Which of the following celebrities best fulfills the requirements of the **Balancing Act** form of sadness?

| LeBron James | Princess Diana | Patsy Cline |

ANSWERS

1. Happiness

Camouflage
Tilt
Plugging Along
Joy Bird

The **Joy Bird** form is calculated by joy minus the other three levels of happiness. In that sense, no conclusion can be drawn from a single photograph, though Hepburn is the best answer here. She's just "letting it fly," showing only over-the-top happiness. Welch's broad smile touches on joy, but he is also exhibiting purposeful anger given his piercing stare. Montana's smile is likewise broad, but simply doesn't go far enough in animating his full face, which the Joy Bird form requires. In Montana's case, there's also sadness as revealed by the right downturned corner of the mouth and the wince in the cheek above it.

2. Anger

Thunderstorm
Battle Ready
Concentration
Golden Blend

The **Concentration** form starts with lowered eyebrows that also pinch together, creating a vertical wrinkle between the eyebrows. Then the form adds lips pressed together. All three photographs show the correct activity involving the eyebrows. Only Harrison, however, shows a mouth with lips pressed together in anger, and no other emotion entering the picture. Bonds is the runner-up because, while his mouth reveals anger, his upraised chin introduces disgust. Less fitting is DiCaprio, whose tight mouth conveys a contradictory acceptance level smile, a part of happiness.

3. Sadness

Deflated
Shaken
Not Giving Up
Balancing Act

The **Balancing Act** form is best enacted by an equal blend of happiness and sadness, so count out James. Yes, he displays two signs of sadness: the corner of his lower left lip sags a bit and there's an upper chin thrust. But he's not showing any happiness. Between Princess Diana and Patsy Cline, it's a close call for the best choice. Both have a fairly broad smile. Both also show sadness because their lower eyelids have deepened furrows from pushed up skin. Ultimately, though, the nod goes to Cline. Why? While the country singer shows some extraneous disgust (a flared upper lip), Princess Diana introduces not one but *two* other emotions besides happiness and sadness. Notice how Princess Diana not only shows anger (a taut lower right eyelid), but also fear (a stretched, tight smile).

flash

Personality insights revealed by
facial coding comparisons

family

&

romance

John F. Kennedy — Robert F. Kennedy

John F. Kennedy	Robert F. Kennedy
Voted	**Voted**
happiness	happiness
surprise	*happiness*
Actual	**Actual**
satisfaction	sadness
sadness	acceptance
Rare	**Rare**
surprise	contempt

Voters saw the two brothers as upbeat, especially Robert Kennedy, though in reality sadness also filled them both. What separates them emotionally is what they didn't feel very often. A rarely surprised John Kennedy contrasts with a rarely contemptuous Bobby, who of the two was younger, smaller, and quite possibly more empathetic. Bobby grew "not by reading books, as brother Jack had." Instead, "experience transformed him," Larry Tye writes,[1] in praising Bobby's 1968 campaign for its spontaneity. For example, the candidate won over a crowd in Nebraska by ad-libbing, "There goes my farm program" when the wind blew away the pages of his prepared speech, leading to a rousing, improvisational, from-the-heart address.

Serena Williams — Venus Williams

Serena Williams	Venus Williams
Voted	**Voted**
happiness	happiness
anger	surprise
Actual	**Actual**
disgust	*joy*
contempt	sadness
Rare	**Rare**
joy	contempt

Voters saw both tennis stars as mildly happy. In fact, Serena Williams's perceived anger is often actually disgust and Venus Williams's mild happiness deserves to be upgraded to joy. Those two corrections aside, the big difference between the two sisters is Venus's tender sadness versus Serena's contempt—a sign of superiority you could say Serena has earned. Back in 1992, when the sisters were both still tennis juniors, their father, Richard, said[2] that Venus would be a champion, but Serena is "like a pit-bull dog. Once she gets ahold of you she won't let go." Then he rightly predicted that "Serena will probably be a better player than Venus," despite excellence from both.

Janet Jackson — Michael Jackson

Janet Jackson:
- Voted: surprise, happiness
- Actual: fear, *joy*
- Rare: anger

Michael Jackson:
- Voted: sadness, fear
- Actual: surprise, fear
- Rare: anger

Voters saw emotional darkness for Michael Jackson, versus a sunnier picture for his sister. Granted, Janet Jackson is more capable of happiness than Michael was. But what the siblings have in common is fear, which makes sense given how their dad behaved. In Michael's autobiography, *Moonwalk*, he remembers how Joe, his father, would critique the family rehearsals in Gary, Indiana: "If you messed up, you got hit, sometimes with a belt, sometimes with a switch."[3] And yet well into adulthood the "King of Pop" (who could move backwards while seemingly walking forward) still lived with his parents, believing, "Oh, no. I think I'd die on my own. I'd be so lonely."

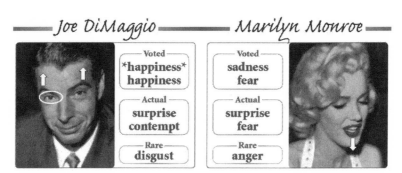

Joe DiMaggio — Marilyn Monroe

Joe DiMaggio:
- Voted: *happiness*, happiness
- Actual: surprise, contempt
- Rare: disgust

Marilyn Monroe:
- Voted: sadness, fear
- Actual: surprise, fear
- Rare: anger

Newly retired from the New York Yankees, Joe DiMaggio saw some publicity shots of Marilyn Monroe and asked her for a date. Their brief marriage ended abruptly. After Monroe filmed the skirt-flying subway grate scene in Manhattan for *The Seven Year Itch* (1955), DiMaggio beat her and she left him. Were they hopelessly mismatched? Shared surprise aside, the signs weren't good. The voters were off-base to see DiMaggio as happy. A smirk isn't a smile. The slugger's contempt and Monroe's fear couldn't have been a very good dynamic. Most likely the more she was anxious, the more he would have disrespected her for feeling ill at ease.

Kardashian Sisters

Khloe Kardashian

Voted
sadness
happiness

Actual
anger
acceptance

Rare
fear

Kim Kardashian-West

Voted
happiness
surprise

Actual
satisfaction
contempt

Rare
fear

Kourtney Kardashian

Voted
happiness
sadness

Actual
acceptance
anger

Rare
fear

Voters perceived differences between the three sisters, with Kim Kardashian-West the most upbeat, Kourtney Kardashian somewhere in between, and Khloe Kardashian the least cheerful. Yes, Kim and Kourtney show mild happiness. Anger rather than sadness best defines Khloe, however. By comparison, Kim stands out for showing contempt. What none of the three feel is much fear, which figures. The title of *Keeping Up with the Kardhasians* updates the cliché, "keeping up with the Joneses," the first family in Newport, Rhode Island to build a Guilded Era mansion. Nowadays, put cameras in a California mansion and, voilá, the secure, privileged lifestyle the Jones' dinner guests saw has become what the Kardashian viewers see on TV.

Pitt, Aniston & Jolie

Brad Pitt

Voted
sadness
happiness

Actual
satisfaction
anger

Rare
fear

Jennifer Aniston

Voted
happiness
happiness

Actual
satisfaction
joy

Rare
fear

Angelina Jolie

Voted
anger
sadness

Actual
acceptance
anger

Rare
pleasure

Having left one woman (Jennifer Aniston) and having been left by the other woman here (Angelina Jolie), the interesting question becomes: was Brad Pitt emotionally well matched with either one? Voters saw Aniston and Pitt as more compatible based on their sharing mild happiness. But someone close to Pitt has said of Jolie: Pitt saw "a very adventurous person who was grabbing onto life,"[4] which he preferred. Indeed, Jolie and Pitt share an affinity for the aggressive emotion of anger, versus Aniston's sunnier disposition. The intriguing result is that despite her reputation for being somewhat neurotic, the one argument in favor of Aniston being better suited for Pitt is that they both rarely show fear.

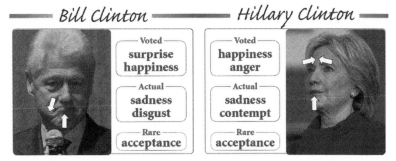

At the 2016 Democratic Convention, Bill Clinton certainly did his best to shape the Clintons' relationship as a romantic fairy tale that began with boy-meets-girl on a college campus. In truth it's been a tumultuous marriage, with both the couple's closeness as well as their venting evident for their staffs to witness. While voters saw this couple as sympatico in sharing mild happiness, closer to reality is mutual sadness. Then add disgust for Bill and contempt for Hillary Clinton, and harsher feelings enter the picture. Who can be tougher to handle? Former White House Chief of Staff Leon Panetta[5] recalls this difference between the couple: while Bill "could be a screamer, too," Hillary's temper when feeling sadly let down by aides "had much more sustained velocity, for a longer period of time."

Voters saw no difference between father and son, despite there being some emotional daylight between them. Sadness helps to define George H. W. Bush, who was a worrier. Critics would say that George W. Bush should have been more concerned in office himself, rather than declare "Mission Accomplished" in Iraq. At the 2004 Republican convention, George W. said, "Some folks look at me and see a certain swagger—which in Texas is called walking." George W. also taunted Iraqi insurgents by telling them to "Bring it on." Self-confident contempt defines George W. to a degree that wasn't true of his polite, more modest dad.

More emotionally buttoned-up than her dad (which isn't hard to do, given his style), Ivanka Trump stands out for emotional displays centered around the spurning emotions of disgust and contempt. Disgust is a feeling Donald Trump and his daughter share. But to see an occasion of them not on the same page, watch the 2013 *Wendy Williams Show* episode[6] in which they're asked what they have in common. "Either real estate or golf," Ivanka says. Then she reveals intense disgust and fear, followed by a sort of baffled, masking smile. That's because Donald, pointing at her, has instead answered with a grin, "Well, I was going to say sex, but I can't relate that to her."

Music's royal couple makes it work,[7] despite vastly different upbringings and emotional displays. Aided by attending first an elementary school and then a high school devoted to the fine arts, Beyonce was already on her way to selling 60 million records as a member of the group Destiny's Child by the time she was 16 years of age. Voters see Beyonce as happy, and she is. Try as he might, Jay-Z can't escape emotional scars. Raised in the projects in Brooklyn, he began selling crack on the streets at age twelve. Sure, he smiles some—but not much. Satisfaction is rarely felt. Jay-Z shows sadness and fear instead of the self-confident contempt that voters saw in him. He's down, she's up, and together recent troubles in their marriage have resulted in some of their best solo work ever.

part **2** two

emotions

Contempt

Cool or Cruel?

What Contempt Means

The year 2005 will forever loom large in Tom Cruise's life. In April, he begins dating the actress Katie Holmes in a romance the media quickly dubs "TomKat". The following month, Cruise madly jumps around atop a couch on *The Oprah Winfrey Show* while declaring his newfound love for Holmes. Then in November, Cruise marries Holmes in a Church of Scientology ceremony held in Italy. Besides wedding vows, the actor is thereby affirming his faith that a galactic emperor named Xenu sent frozen souls to earth to inhabit human bodies.[1]

Scientology also happens to blame psychiatry for condoning the use of drugs prescribed for treatment. So three days after the couch jump, Cruise publicly criticizes Brooke Shields for using Paxil to cope with her postpartum depression, causing Shields, in turn, to tell Cruise to "stick to saving the world from aliens."

Tom Cruise

Happy to milk the controversy, Matt Lauer of NBC's *The Today Show* now invites Cruise to give an interview.[2] During it, Cruise promptly criticizes Shields again for her use of medication rather than something like vitamins to cure her depression. Yes, Cruise tries to walk the criticism back a little by saying, "I really care about Brooke Shields." But then he states, "I know that psychiatry is ... is a pseudo science."

Lauer's various attempts to get Cruise to tolerate the kind of treatment plan that worked for Shields finally leads Cruise to sputter aloud, "Matt, Matt, Matt, you don't even—*you're glib*. You don't even know what Ritalin is." To stress his point, Cruise jabs his finger at Lauer at the same time as his upper lip repeatedly curls in contempt.

A full three years later, Cruise will semi-apologize: "I came across as arrogant. That's not who I am." Well, maybe; but there's no denying what viewers saw that day. Cruise was clearly dismissing Lauer's attempts to find some middle ground, and in doing so feeling contempt: an emotion about relishing one's superiority to others.

From the introduction to *Famous Faces Decoded*—namely, the Nature and Frequency of Emotions chart—you already know the score. Contempt is a dominant as opposed to submissive emotion. But here's the flavor of this emotion: you're basically *annointing* yourself as someone worthy of exaltation. The essence of contempt is almighty spurning. If you're feeling smug, you feel like you're riding high. You've found other people and circumstances unworthy, meaning you can freely disregard them as beneath you. Given a desire to simultaneously keep away from what's been tainted by mediocrity, contempt also qualifies as an avoidance rather than an approach emotion. While happiness means you're a "hugger", with contempt you believe you're better than others. So you're excluding people, rather than embracing them.

The standard definition of contempt is that this emotion consists of a cross between anger and disgust. But left out, and sorely needed in order to fully grasp contempt, is a degree of happiness.[3] Think of the old cartoon character Snidely Whiplash and his evil smile as contempt personified.

The upside of contempt is that it serves as an expression of self-assurance. You're happy going negative. In judging others, you condescendingly conclude that you know best. The downside is that unwarranted contempt can rob you of the benefit of collaborating with others. Feeling contempt makes it hard to get along well with anyone tagged as deficient. The all-too-human urge to see ourselves as superior is a by-product, if not the linchpin, of hierarchies ranging from England's and India's respective class and caste systems, to a company's organizational chart.

Spotting Contempt

A contemptuous face *smirks* as if that person is giving you a mocking salute. These smirks are mostly unilateral, occurring on just one side of a person's face. More specifically, there's only a pair of ways in which contempt gets shown:

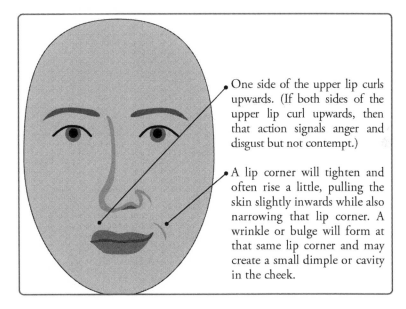

One side of the upper lip curls upwards. (If both sides of the upper lip curl upwards, then that action signals anger and disgust but not contempt.)

A lip corner will tighten and often rise a little, pulling the skin slightly inwards while also narrowing that lip corner. A wrinkle or bulge will form at that same lip corner and may create a small dimple or cavity in the cheek.

Most Contempt

Bill Gates
Aaron Rodgers
Neil Armstrong
J. K. Rowling
David Letterman
Tom Brady
Barack Obama
Cam Newton
Hillary Clinton
Hank Aaron

Contempt is a comparatively rare emotion but often toxic when it does appear. In *Blink: The Power of Thinking Without Thinking*, Malcolm Gladwell visits the Love Lab at the University of Washington. The lab utilizes facial coding for marriage counseling and has found that nothing is more accurate in predicting a couple's eventual divorce than strong feelings of contempt for one another. With merely 15 minutes of coded videotape per couple, the accuracy rate linking emotions like contempt to divorce reaches 90% range.[4]

Among the celebrities analyzed for *Famous Faces Decoded*, on average only a little over 3% of their emoting involves contempt. Think of contempt as the opposite of a diamond ring. Both come in small packages. But the ring represents a big gift, whereas contempt is frequently a big problem.

Of further note is that, except for the weakest level of happiness, namely acceptance, no other emotional state exhibits a larger gender split than contempt does. Male celebrities in this book are, as a group, almost twice as likely to reveal contempt as their female counterparts, with the Top 10 list for Most Contempt nearly half full of cocky male athletes.

Least Contempt

James Dean
Martha Stewart
Princess Diana
Robert Redford
George Harrison
Leonardo DiCaprio
Diana Ross
Jim Henson
Mickey Mantle
Tom Hanks*
Charles Schulz*
*two-way tie

Turning to the Top 10 list for Least Contempt, what do we find? Mickey Mantle aside, athletes are absent. Instead, two visual artists appear: the Muppets creator Jim Henson, and the *Peanuts* cartoonist Charles Schulz. Also gracing the list is the "People's Princess": Diana, Princess of Wales. The opposite of aloof, she physically touched and emotionally comforted those suffering from leprosy and AIDS. When her cause then became clearing land mines, Princess Diana traveled to Angola. There she obligingly walked through a field of mines—twice—ensuring more publicity, because some of the paparazzi hadn't caught her first effort on camera.[5]

How good are people at spotting contempt? Abysmal, for at 21% contempt is the emotion voters were least able to detect accurately. The following two photographs illustrate how contempt reveals itself, and the celebrities' emotional profiles indicate how well voters did in choosing the top two emotions that distinguish these famous people.

A post on Yahoo Answers parallels voters' misidentification of Bill Gates as a happy camper. The person wonders aloud: "I once read a book, and it briefly said Bill Gate [sic] was an arrogant person. Is he really an arrogant person in real life? He doesn't look like it (at least from his physical appearance)." My advice is to look at the photo shown below more closely. The expression that accompanies many of Gates's smiles is a smirk. An upwardly-angled, dimpling of the lip corner is contempt's tell-tale mark.

⎯Voted⎯	⎯Actual⎯	⎯Rare⎯
happiness *happiness*	contempt satisfaction	fear

Bill Gates

Born William Henry Gates III, Bill Gates cofounded Microsoft and led it until 2006 when he began splitting his time between the company and the Bill & Melinda Gates Foundation. He's often been ranked the richest person in the world.

A version of the lip-corner smirk is when the mouth pulls wider but wrinkles instead of lifts, creating a tense, horizontal slit. You can see that version in this photo of J. K. Rowling, along with a slight acceptance level smile and just a hint of a raised upper lip. Maybe you wouldn't notice such subtlety, but I bet Rowling's husband Neil Murray does. He admits that when Rowling is "very stressed, she'll detach herself and only trust one person, and that's herself."[6]

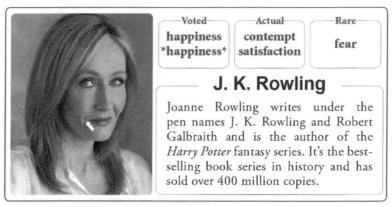

Voted	Actual	Rare
happiness *happiness*	contempt satisfaction	fear

J. K. Rowling

Joanne Rowling writes under the pen names J. K. Rowling and Robert Galbraith and is the author of the *Harry Potter* fantasy series. It's the best-selling book series in history and has sold over 400 million copies.

What May Cause Contempt

In deciding whether contempt is a cool or cruel emotion, consider the positive meanings of "cool": qualities such as staying calm or being socially hip. But when the definition of cool proceeds to *not* showing much interest in, nor affection for others, a cool, slightly cold emotion can become downright mean. So in the end, the answer is that contempt is both cool and cruel. The emotion's range of nuances will become clearer from this set of six likely causes of contempt.

1. Our faith in behaving properly ensures that when violations occur, our instinct is to pull back from anyone perceived as breaking the rules.

Why does Neil Armstrong get chosen to be the first person to walk on the moon in 1969? Part of the answer is his sense of decorum, anchored by not having a big ego.[7] NASA officials don't have to worry that fame will go to his head. Proof that NASA chose well is a story about a woman coming up to Armstrong on a putting green years later and asking him, "Are you somebody that I should know?" Armstrong's reply: "Probably not." In the astronaut's case, humility counter-intuitively leads to good-natured scorn for behavior he doesn't condone.

Another story brings that point home. In this case, Armstrong is on a golf course in 2002 with Clint Eastwood so that the two men can discuss a possible movie about NASA and Armstrong's experiences. A strong sense of honor means that sooner than later, however, Armstrong takes his bag of clubs off Clint Eastwood's cart and walks away. The two men have irreconcilable viewpoints about the new movie idea. Eastwood's prior release, *Space Cowboys* (2000), had involved lots of free-wheeling behavior by U.S. Air Force pilots. Armstrong believes *Eastwood has got it all wrong*. The prospective movie won't be any more honest—and therefore not worth making—because it would again fail to emphasize careful, engineering-based procedures over wild, colorful personalities.

2. We regard another person or group of people as inferior, meaning any act of exclusion or correction is for everyone's good.

The code of conduct for the regrettably few, big-time female politicians in America is fraught with assumptions about how a woman "should" behave. Add in how any candidate handles an election defeat, and the standard for female leaders becomes even more difficult.

In a Portsmouth, New Hampshire coffee house in January of 2008, Hillary Clinton gets asked by one of the 15 women gathered there how she does it, how she finds the fortitude to get up and hit the campaign trail day after day. "It's not easy, it's not easy," Clinton initially says, shaking her head. Her eyes are watery long before she finishes her answer. Clinton has just come in third, behind Barack Obama and John Edwards in Iowa's caucus voting among Democrats. It was a crushing defeat that now leads to a softening of her robotic (and surely often sexist) "Ice Queen" image.

At a campaign event later the same day as the Portsmouth coffee house scene, Clinton lingers on stage, takes every question, and for once doesn't show any contempt. It's this more emotionally open version of Clinton who comes back to win the New Hampshire primary the following Tuesday, after having been far down in the polls.

Fast forward to 2017, and how has Clinton handled losing to Donald Trump? Many people would say not so well,[8] after Clinton re-emerges 100 days into Trump's presidency to begin a flurry of appearances. At a Women for Women International luncheon, she talks of potential supporters who "got scared off" by late-breaking events during the campaign and smirks with contempt. Is it James Comey, Julian Assange, or voters lacking backbone who trigger these expressions? Or all of the above, and more? (When asked as part of a *New Yorker* profile if she stands by her remark that a larger number of Trump's backers were "irredeemable" and a "basket of deplorables," Clinton bypasses the opportunity to be generous and instead declares: "I don't take back the description.")

Clinton likewise often smirks on stage at a 2017 Code Conference. There, she discusses everything from the digital voter files she received from the Democratic National Committee ("poor, nonexistent, wrong"), to lucrative speeches for Goldman Sachs defended anew ("they paid me"). Quickly, a consensus has emerged regarding those events and Clinton's memoir, *What Happened*. That consensus paints the former candidate as more derisive and defensive, rather than reflective, about accepting her role in losing the election.

3. We consider the actions of others to be amoral transgressions, and so we become filled with distrust.

After having been promised artistic freedom when he signs up (as a teenager) with Warner Brothers in 1977, Prince has by 1993 had enough. Now he appears in public with the word "slave" across one cheek and a sneer at the corner of his mouth, ready to change his name to an unpronounceable "Love Symbol." The impetus for these anti-corporate moves is Prince's sense of having been commercially exploited. He isn't alone. Other musicians also often feel that way about their record labels, but typically don't have the means to fight back. Prince's motivation for rebelling also arises from African-Americans' history of enslavement. As the rock star observes: "I don't own Prince's music. If you don't own your masters, your master owns you."[9]

4. Our confidence in being superior leads us to assert power and status.

It's often said that a company's culture starts at the top. So when a reporter covering Microsoft's anti-trust case in 1999 hears a senior aide to Bill Gates rant about "sub-50-IQ people" wrongly daring to question the company's business practices,[10] you've got to question, in turn, Gates's influence. By then, Gates is already well known for an imperial management style exemplified by his interrupting managers' presentations with comments like, "That's the stupidest thing I've ever heard!" and "Why don't you just give up your options and join the Peace Corps?" Certainly, the judge presiding over the anti-trust case isn't enamored of Gates (and may be rather smug himself). Afterwards, this judge says of Microsoft's CEO: "I think he has a Napoleonic concept of himself and his company, an arrogance that derives from power and unalloyed success."[11] (Over the years following the anti-trust suit, the beneficent efforts of the Bill & Melinda Gates Foundation will improve Bill's image, but his smirking doesn't go away.)

5. We've been deeply hurt or insulted by somebody and, as tolerance shrivels, we either take revenge or disengage from others.

J. K. Rowling is 14 years old when she discovers her life-long heroine. That would be the author Jessica Mitford, who headed to Spain during that country's Civil War to fight against fascism. Later in life,[12] Rowling will describe Mitford as someone who "liked nothing better than a good fight, preferably against a pompous and hypocritical target." Cast in similar terms will be Rowling's famous young wizard. How fitting that Harry Potter's destiny is to fight Lord Voldemort, a character whom Rowling has described as a "raging psychopath," without remorse, who believes he's superior to everyone else.

Rowling's childhood unfolds in a home with an ill mom and a dad who frightens her. Not "particularly happy" growing up, Rowling has compared living with her parents to the Stockholm syndrome: you're a hostage who must "make friends with the warders."

Nowadays, Rowling's oppressors are members of the media. Their incessant questions often get greeted by the defensive barrier of a raised upper lip and a jeering twist of the author's mouth. Some 50 times Rowling has taken legal action against the press to protect her privacy. That her publisher has developed the practice of "denial marketing," whereby the "more people want, the less you give," suits Rowling's outlook perfectly well. Rowling's husband, Neil Murray, certainly knows the score. Murray admits that when his wife is "very stressed, she'll detach herself and only trust one person, and that's herself."

6. We reject others, finding them unworthy of our attention (thereby, eliminating the need for us to engage with them).

When Barack Obama bursts upon America's political stage, his message of hope and kindly, joyful smiles predominate. But with the 2008 Pennsylvania primary looming, Obama has become the front-runner and now Hillary Clinton and the press are targeting him. In a Philadelphia debate, a gotcha question makes Obama tilt his head back, scoff, and literally look down his nose at the media panelists, revealing a desire to avoid the stench-in-the-trench of politics. Given his simultaneous desire—to run the country—could being aloof limit Obama's effectiveness as a leader?

In office, Obama won't stroke the egos of members of Congress to ensure legislation gets passed. Selling is a task he delegates to Joe Biden and company.[13] Instead, Obama stays true to his 2008 inaugural speech, with its call to resist "pettiness and immaturity" (even as some opponents rely on less dignified tactics). As a result, the President gets characterized by his White House advisors as preferring to play "chess in a town full of checkers players" because he's a decent guy who would "rather be right than win."[14]

Four Forms of Contempt

Why might contempt be such a hard emotion for a marriage to survive? In essence, how the face displays this emotion matches up well with an instinct to move up and away from the object of derision. Contempt differs from the other emotions in *Famous Faces Decoded* because those who feel it aren't always as much in "the throes" of an emotion (like for instance, raging anger, trembling fear, or blissed-out happiness). Instead, they're people for whom an attitude toward someone or something have

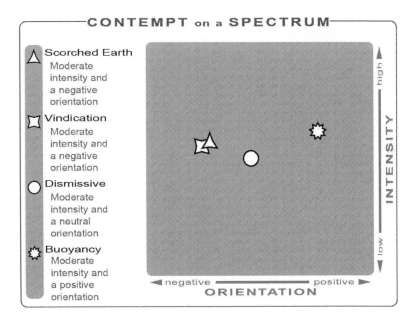

crystallized and be re-activated in response to the latest input. So regardless of which form pertains, the intensity levels are always moderate.

Of these four forms of contempt, the first two, Scorched Earth and Vindication, are decidedly negative, combining corrosive contempt with either vengeful anger or disappointed sadness. By adding different levels of happiness, the other two forms, Dismissive and Buoyancy, range from conveying modest, self-contained assurance to the outright enjoyment that comes from believing you've achieved supremacy. What unites all four of these forms is that with contempt the themes of distrust and disrespect are forever in play.

Scorched Earth

With contempt usually defined as a mixture of disgust and anger, Scorched Earth qualifies as contempt on steroids. With this form, throw in an extra dollop of anger because of the expression's eyes-narrowed glare or lips pressed firmly together. The result is a hard, high-pressured look. Frequently, the contemptuous person's anger arises from feeling betrayed. People haven't been meritorious, despite their promises. So anger reflects a desire to take control of the situation by using scorn to punish those people for not being true to their word.

Given its air of self-righteous indignation, Scorched Earth equates to *you let me down, how dare you!* The subsequent behavior doesn't have to be spiteful, however. By analogy, a constructive use of this feeling is akin to the way forest fires can enable new growth. Burned vegetation from forest fires puts nutrients back into the soil. New plants also

Prince

become possible, thanks to more sunlight reaching the forest floor.

- Scorched Earth: There's just a hint of the left lip corner pulling back and upwards as a sign of contempt. However the pressed lips and tense lower eyelids show anger for sure.

- Other emoting: The cocked left eyebrow reveals wariness (surprise and fear).

Scorched Earth

Douglas MacArthur
Eminem
Joseph McCarthy
Khloe Kardashian
John Bonham
Kanye West
Bill Gates
Leonardo DiCaprio
Prince
Jimi Hendrix

In general, an abrasive manner and a Scorched Earth expression are likely to go together. Here's a vivid example. In San Francisco to audition for his record contract with Warner Brothers, an 18-year-old Prince finds time to go see Carlos Santana. This is how Prince's first manager remembers the meeting:[15] "We open the door. It's an all-white house with all-white carpeting. Carlos says, 'Come in, please. Please take off your shoes.' I say, 'Prince, you gotta remove your boots.' But Prince replies, 'I don't remove my boots for anyone.'" What's the outcome? The two musicians chat while the manager cleans up a trail of mud.

Prince aside, how about the other celebrities in the Top 10 list for Scorched Earth? Are any of them mild mannered? The answer is certainly *no* in regards to Led Zepplin's John Bonham, who died in his sleep at age 32 after consuming 40 shots of vodka. Such behavior wasn't unusual for a drummer whose highly energetic solos during the group's instrumental song "Moby Dick" often lasted for half an hour on stage. At times, Bonham would deliberately break his drumsticks part way through his solo and resort to banging on his drum kit with bloodied, bare hands.

Vindication

A second form of contempt involves people expressing sadness. They might be disappointed that so-and-so can't, in their estimation, be trusted enough to bother with. Or they might feel isolated and lonely, suspecting that somebody close to them isn't a capable ally. A feeling of Vindication means the disdainful person's doubts have proven to be justified. In that sense, Vindication is a consolation prize. While it would have been better not to have found a defect or outright failing in the other party, at least you can regard yourself as being perfectly fine.

With sad contempt, a frown or wince accompanies the usual signs of contempt. Since sadness is part of the mix, the spirit of Vindication becomes a matter of *you let me down, leaving me feeling disappointed and wishing you could do better.* Scornful chagrin rules the day. The upside is that this form of contempt can be powered by a strong desire to ensure justice gets served.

- Vindication: Although this photo shows a wax replica at Madame Tussauds, the look is spot on. The wrinkle that rises near the right corner of the mouth hints at contempt, while the eyes are downcast in sadness.

- Other emoting: A tight-lipped smile is accompanied by an upward chin thrust.

Hugh Hefner

Back when *Playboy* magazine launched in 1953, *no* out-weighed *yes*: anti-homosexual and anti-interracial marriage laws still ruled the land, and The Pill was not yet available. Even using the word "pregnant" on TV was not allowed. At the same time, the phrase "objectifying women" was on few people's radar screens, Hugh Hefner's perhaps least of all. And yet Hefner's crusade for *male* sexual freedom—separating sex from

Vindication

Hank Aaron
Hillary Clinton
Bill Gates
Donald Trump
Cam Newton
Roger Clemens
Andy Warhol
Ringo Starr
Elvis Presley
Barack Obama

sin—became for him a matter of righteous indignation.[16] Fast forward a few decades, and Hefner's smug stance remained intact right up until his death, by which time the guy was simply, sadly, out of date. His Los Angeles Playboy mansion had been sold to the billionaire owner of Twinkies, with the proviso that Hefner got to live out his days on the premises, playing some tennis and watching old movies.

Among the celebrities in the Top 10 list for Vindication, it could be said that Andy Warhol and Elvis Presley most clearly echoed Hefner's libertine lifestyle and decline. Another trio that also catches my attention on this list consists of Hank Aaron, Cam Newton, and Barack Obama. These African-Americans soon found in their careers a need to transcend prejudice related to the color of their skin. As an "ambassador" for his race, for example, Obama likes to quote Martin Luther King, Jr.'s statement that "The arc of the moral universe is long, but it bends toward justice." Needless to say, such a viewpoint requires great patience amid countless disappointments involving likely or suspected racism.

Dismissive

Welcome to partly-sunny contempt as mild happiness enters the picture. Rather than *sneering*, think in terms of *snickering*. This more upbeat feeling may come from the disdainful person concluding that others can be safely disregarded. Then again, the happiness may involve feeling relieved—even liberated from—the need to interact with someone never quite welcome in the first place. In both those cases, the usual signs of contempt go well with satisfaction or acceptance level happiness. The spirit of being Dismissive reflects self-contained, disciplined happiness, as in *I'm better than what's around me and I'll see my way through.*

Lindsey Vonn

- Dismissive: The smile of forbearance for getting photographed in public is a perfect fit for this look. Likewise, the look is well illustrated by the smirk evident in the raised right lip corner.

- Other emoting: The slightly tense lower left eyelid and the raised chin add a note of anger.

With the ultra-competitive Lindsey Vonn, it's all about grit and being "the captain of the ship."[17] On her way to becoming the most successful American ski racer ever, the number of injuries Vonn sustained during practices and competitions was astonishing. For instance, Vonn won races while skiing with her arm in a brace. Regarding her life off the slopes, "I did my own thing for a while" is the way Vonn laconically describes a six-year lapse in talking to her dad after having been coached by him until the age of 16. Men remain the yardstick for this ski racer in measuring toughness, her favorite attribute. Vonn praises her grandfather as a role model and says of her having raced downhill against men, "I definitely send some home crying."

Dismissive

Estee Lauder
Kim Kardashian
J. K. Rowling
Elvis Presley
Aretha Franklin
John Lennon
Amy Schumer
Jimmy Page
Bill Gates
Madonna

The Top 10 list for Dismissive is full of equally "feisty" women, to use Vonn's term for herself and others whose fighting spirit means they never surrender. I'll single out two of the women here. A natural affinity for feistiness links Aretha Franklin to Madonna, with Franklin perhaps most famous for her song "Respect". Meanwhile, Madonna's unabashedly strong, free-spirited stance is encapsulated in songs like "Express Yourself."

Buoyancy

It's an ugly truth, but no less real all the same: some people simply enjoy feeling superior to others. Whether doing so boosts or merely affirms their self-esteem makes no difference. In a good, better, *I'm-the-best* scenario, a contempt verdict imposed on others leaves these people guilt-free to enjoy their success. Then the usual smirk combines with a higher level of happiness, such as a big pleasure smile. Buoyancy is at once both a comparative and self-referential form of contempt. It reflects the spirit of *I'm having a good time savoring supremacy.*

- Buoyancy: A larger smile would fit this look better, but the smirk is definitely there. Note the tight lift of the left lip corner.

- Other emoting: A firm lower left eyelid and firmly pressed lips contribute anger. The eyes are wide and signal being on-guard.

Judy Garland

Movie producer Arthur Freed said of Judy Garland, there's "not a mean bone in her body." Yes, it's true: anger was a rare emotion for this singer and film star. Garland nevertheless had enough life experiences to soon come armed with some contempt for the situations she faced. Pushy movie studio executives and disloyal spouses made life stressful. For example, one husband threatened to seek custody of Garland's children in a divorce if she didn't keep up her heavy, money-making work load of live shows as well as TV and radio appearances.[18]

Buoyancy

John Lennon
Brian Jones
Ringo Starr
Tom Brady
Bill Gates
Ray Croc
Martha Stewart
Judy Garland
Paul McCartney
Mariah Carey

In short, Garland always had her talent and appreciative fans, but caring husbands *not so much.*

Buoyancy is about extreme confidence and finding ways to enjoy yourself. In the Top 10 list for Buoyancy is Paul McCartney, who admitted that "At the end of The Beatles, I was really done in for the first time in my life. Until then, I really was a kind of cocky sod." When you see a smirk enlivened with a strong smile, you get the sense that these are people sure they've got it made. Selling lots of records (five singers are listed here), or software (Bill Gates), or hamburgers (Ray Croc) can do that for you.

Applications for Your Life

In your own life, when might you see these four forms of contempt? How might you best react to them, given what causes people to feel contempt?

Scorched Earth: People in financial services who see this look will almost certainly be wasting their time on prospects who scorn them. The same goes for social workers hoping their clients will adopt new habits. A marketing manager who notices an expression of Scorched Earth from focus group participants

Scorched Earth

Surly
Inconsiderate
Callous
Spiteful
Frank

should realize the advertising being tested requires serious revisions. A corrections officer should be alert to danger if in physical proximity to an inmate responding in this way. In your personal life, a repeated Scorched Earth pattern means you should arrange for a marriage counselor ASAP.

When people emote like this, they're adding the venom of anger to contempt—serving up a strong emotional cocktail. You'll experience their behavior as most likely ranging from being surly to brutally frank, with little hope of respite.

Among the likely causes of this form of contempt, two possibilities stand out. First, the people with a Scorched Earth expression find others inferior and in need of correction "for their own good." Second, they've been hurt somehow and are now seeking retaliation. How best to respond? Struck by their derision, it's only natural that you might react in kind. Nothing good will come of counter-attacking, however, as it will merely lead to more conflict. Instead, affirm equal status by establishing your competency. Undermine the other party's scorn by referencing your relevant experiences, or by otherwise showing that your viewpoint is worthy of consideration. If these people still won't curb their hostility, try to arrange for the important conversations to happen when a third party is present. A larger audience may help to rein them in and act, if not in fact become more respectful.

Vindication: People showing this look have likely concluded that they were correct. You must be either up to no good or of no help whatsoever. For any front-line supervisor seeing Vindication reign on the faces of her workers, it's time for a team meeting. A management consultant seeing this expression needs to shore up rapport with a client before it's too late. A doctor seeing such a mix of contempt and sadness should fear the patient is losing hope. In your social circle, somebody flashing this signal may soon be ducking your phone calls.

Vindication

Reluctant
Grave
Peevish
Philosophical
Bitter

People expressing themselves like this feel distrust and disappointment. Odds are that from their point of view, nothing is going right and they're dubious of getting what they want. The resulting reluctance to engage with you can be casual or bitter in nature, depending on the individual's temperament and the depth of the let-down involved.

Two causes may be especially pertinent here. These people could be rejecting others as unworthy, either because of their perceived responsibility for a failure or because of an alleged transgression. As a result, people feeling Vindication are likely to go into an emotional shell. Assuaging the sadness that probably triggered the contempt is the key. Get at the basis of their disappointed reaction. What's the initial hurt that got the train rolling? Listen with care. A meal or other downtime activity together may provide a good, solid way to reconnect. Find points of affinity. Expressing admiration for these people goes hand in hand with reminding them of your own positive qualities so that you can create a sense of camaraderie.

Dismissive: The barely on-board, no-commitment spirit of this look should be taken seriously by lawyers mistakenly thinking they have the judge siding with them. Middle-school teachers will probably see the Dismissive look a lot and have to find ways to relate to, and motivate, the kids all the same. Anybody in the health care field seeing this expression from a patient should be

concerned about the degree of medical compliance the patient is actually practicing. If you're spending time with your in-laws, this kind of reaction may indicate you've got a long journey ahead of you in terms of gaining their respect.

116

A Dismissive look mingles contempt with the slightest of smiles. These people are being cool to cold, and are smug in their assumption of superiority. If nothing changes, you're on track to endure plenty of haughtiness.

What might have caused this expression? Chances are you're seen as inferior and easily excluded. Then again, maybe these people see you as somebody who "broke the rules" and should be avoided. Here are some ways to respond. The softest option is to learn what ideal behavior looks like to them and then adjust to whatever extent you deem reasonable. A second option is to implicitly challenge the contemptuous person's judgment about you by learning their supposed basis for feeling superior. The third and toughest option is to put the onus on them by directly asking: "When you treat others with contempt, how does that cycle of disrespect end?"

Buoyancy: Administrators seeing a look of Buoyancy in a colleague should expect only breezy, non-committal behavior. On the other hand, psychologists or physical therapists may now realize that a patient they've been seeing for a while is regaining his or her mojo after a debilitating setback. On a first date, a look of Buoyancy from the other party is alluring to the extent that confidence, not condescension, serves as the basis of the person's interactive style.

Buoyancy
Exuberant
Snobby
Conceited
Ostentatious
Charismatic

People feeling this way will tend to be both elated and cocky. The more that a sense of superiority overshadows their being animated by just plain old "high spirits," expect them to be pretty conceited as well as outgoing—and all but indifferent to you. In all likelihood, you won't be too far off the mark.

With this form of contempt, one cause clearly fits a feeling of Buoyancy. Look for the confidence that goes hand-in-glove with asserting power and status. How can you get them to notice you and achieve mutual respect? Play big yourself. Go big-picture by referring to the theory behind the idea you're proposing. Emphasize the uniqueness of what you're discussing with them. Make them curious. Next, appeal to their ego by soliciting their opinion, all the while playing on their desire to be seen as innovative and the purveyor of quality. This go-big, stay-positive approach best aligns with how and why the person is feeling upbeat.

Summary

Commonly defined as a mixture of disgust and anger, contempt is really more a matter of *pressure* and *pleasure*. The accepted formula of anger plus disgust equals contempt supplies the pressure. The drive to achieve and set a higher standard of conduct for oneself is frequently a big part of why a person feels contempt. In regards to pleasure, bear in mind the happiness people may enjoy in concluding that, by comparison, they're better than the object of derision. Rather than *you're okay, I'm okay*, contempt is often more a matter of *you're mediocre (at best), which means I'm right to feel pretty good about myself.*

Is there a social virtue to feeling contempt? Yes, there is because contempt can serve as a non-verbal means of warning others that so-and-so is a "bad apple." If valid, that judgment can help to protect a community by alerting its members to protect themselves from harmful, unfair people. Beyond that point, however, the virtues of contempt get cloudier. In evaluating others regarding who you think they really are, defects and all, you're most likely also affirming yourself. While the other party doesn't meet some implied standard, you do. So an ego boost of self-praise remains a big part of contempt. To display this emotion may, in effect, be a means of asserting one's greater power, status, ability, and integrity, too, relative to whomever or whatever is subject to dismissal.

Disgust

Turning Away

What Disgust Means

Billie Jean King enters the Astrodome's temporarily installed tennis court as Queen Cleopatra. Decorated with pink and white ostrich feathers, the litter holding her aloft is being carried by a team of four muscular men dressed as ancient slaves. It's September 20, 1973, and King's opponent for the evening's "Battle of the Sexes" tennis match is Bobby Riggs. He arrives in a rickshaw pulled by "Bobby's Bosom Buddies," all dressed in tight outfits.

Riggs presents King with a giant candy sucker bearing the name of his corporate sponsor, Sugar Daddy. She in turn presents him with a piglet symbolizing male chauvinism.

The match with over 30,000 live spectators and a worldwide TV audience estimated at 90 million is pageantry as well as dead-serious business. Forget the $100,000, win-

Billie Jean King

ner-take-all prize money. As the pre-match press conference confirms, there are much larger stakes involved.

A 55-year-old former Wimbledon champion, Riggs has recently beaten the world's number one ranked female player, Margaret Court, backing up his claim that the professional female tennis circuit is of inferior quality. For her part, King, age 29, and the ranking #2 female tennis player in the world, can't suppress a disgusted curl of her upper lip during the press conference. Looking over at Riggs, she vows to "put women's lib" where it belongs: in a place of honor. As King will later admit, "I thought it would set us back 50 years if I didn't win that match. It would ruin the women's [tennis] tour and affect all women's self-esteem."

Win King does, and she can laugh about subsequently appearing with Riggs in an episode of *The Odd Couple* entitled "The Pig Who Came to Dinner." For King and her fans, what doesn't change is that sexism remains morally intolerable and invites disgust: a feeling that something is either literally or figuratively akin to poison.

Like its "first cousin," contempt, disgust is a rejection-based, spurning emotion. Not a haughty feeling like contempt, disgust is in contrast a somewhat less dominant, more down-in-the-trenches emotion. Disgust isn't so much about *rising above* our circumstances as it is about simply *getting away*. Consider the emotion's lowly, immediate, visceral origins. Something physically stinks or tastes bad. Universal triggers for disgust include:[1] feces, vomit, urine, mucus, and blood. In idiomatic terms, something *grosses us out*. For the vast majority of people, after a substance leaves our own body, we find it abhorrent—and that's doubly true of what belongs to another person.

Are there exceptions? Yes, blood-splattered horror films attract fans. In pursuit of pleasure, sex depends on overcoming any reservations we might have about physically comingling. But in general, people abhor ona basic, biological level the threat of contamination and take it seriously. Unlike the case with the emotions of anger and fear, with disgust our heart rate *decreases*. We've stopped in our tracks to mull over something too "ugly" to approach more closely.

Outside of sensory threats, disgust likewise operates on a moral basis. We might find a person, idea, attitude, or specific behavior odious. What's unacceptable in those instances may qualify as offensive and repugnant, much like Riggs's chauvinism was for King in a match in which her vocation and entire gender were both under attack.

The slang term of being "fed-up" with something or someone fits this emotion well, linking the two basic modes of disgust: a momentary, visceral, sensory antipathy or a sustained, morally-infused revulsion. Further linking the two basic modes of disgust is the emotion's overall orientation. We're practicing avoidance. We have an aversive response and want to protect ourselves. Something akin to a gag reflex kicks in; feeling queasy or offended, we back off.

Given their often very tangible nature, the triggers for disgust can be very intimate. For example, a wrinkling nose may contract in order not to smell an offensive odor close at hand. Ultimately, though, disgust always leads to creating boundaries in order to keep our distance from whatever strikes us as objectionable. So in the end, (unless leavened by happiness) disgust becomes an intimacy-killing emotion likely to reduce our capacity for empathy and compassion.

Spotting Disgust

A disgusted face *recoils* as if the person has been confronted by a dead skunk. The physical essence of disgust is evasive action. More specifically, disgust appears in five ways on the face. Twice, disgust is the only emotion being shown on a person's face, as illustrated here:

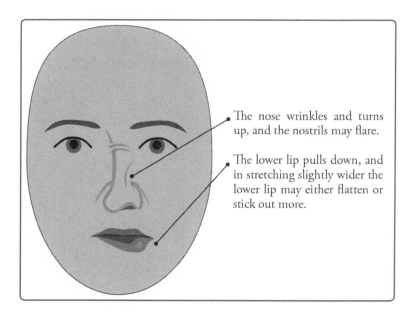

The nose wrinkles and turns up, and the nostrils may flare.

The lower lip pulls down, and in stretching slightly wider the lower lip may either flatten or stick out more.

There are also another three cases in which disgust mingles with at least one extra emotion:

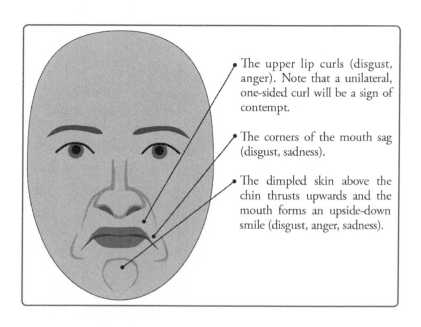

The upper lip curls (disgust, anger). Note that a unilateral, one-sided curl will be a sign of contempt.

The corners of the mouth sag (disgust, sadness).

The dimpled skin above the chin thrusts upwards and the mouth forms an upside-down smile (disgust, anger, sadness).

Most Disgust

Roger Clemens
Barack Obama
Andy Warhol
Serena Williams
Greg Norman
Hank Aaron
John McEnroe
Aaron Rodgers
LeBron James
Elvis Presley

Among the celebrities analyzed for *Famous Faces Decoded*, disgust is almost as rare of an emotion as contempt. On average, just under 4% of the emoting involves disgust. But way back in the hunter-gatherer era, you can imagine how helpful and frequent the visceral, sensory mode of disgust could be. Our ancestors had to make gut-level decisions, like whether to bypass an overly-ripe fruit or a slimy watering hole. Wrong choices could leave them incapacitated and more vulnerable to predators.

In terms of possible gender differences, the book's male celebrities reveal a small but proportionally far greater likelihood to show this feeling than their female counterparts. In the Top 10 list for Most Disgust, athletes abound. In my experience doing facial coding work in professional sports as well as for Division 1 NCAA teams, some of the greatest players are warriors whose feelings of disgust are driven by a strong, *internal* desire to constantly strive for success. Put another way, on an almost sensory basis they reject the status quo "stench" of mediocrity in favor of reaching another, higher level of physical performance.

Least Disgust

Aretha Franklin
James Dean
Estee Lauder
Edward Snowden
Martha Stewart
Kim Kardashian
Edward R. Murrow
Walt Disney
Ray Croc
Martin Luther King*
Princess Diana*
*two-way tie

In contrast, the disgust felt by Barack Obama, Andy Warhol, and Elvis Presley strikes me as more morally based and likely to reflect what they find unpleasant *around them*. In their cases, disgust might be more a matter of disengaging from what they find externally unwelcome, as in *this is dull or disagreeable, so I'm out of here.*

Among the Top 10 list for Least Disgust are celebrities less likely to dismiss possibilities or people out of hand. For instance, when asked about his sexual orientation, James Dean reportedly said: "No, I am not a homosexual. But I'm also not going to go through life with one hand tied behind my back." Likewise on this list is Martin Luther King Jr., who stayed *on-message* and *on-emotion* by continuing to advocate for nonviolent, civil disobedience despite the beatings his followers endured. It would have been *off-emotion* for him to give into disgust, thereby signaling rejection instead of the patience and enduring hope he exhibited.

How good are people at spotting disgust? Not so great, as it turns out. At 23%, disgust is in the cellar for detection accuracy, alongside surprise, sadness, and contempt. The following three photographs illustrate ways in which disgust appears, and the celebrities' emotional profiles indicate how well voters did in choosing the top two emotions that distinguish these famous people.

It's hard to look past Roger Clemens' bulldog, lips-tight expression of anger. But if you do so, you'll notice signs of disgust: a raised chin thrust, and the skin slightly lifted above the upper lip. Asked about the steroid abuse allegations then emerging, Clemens cryptically replied: "I could care less about the rules." A similar statement could probably be made to explain his pugnacious stance toward the batters he faced. Called a "headhunter" by Seattle Mariners manager Lou Piniella, Clemens rejected anything but winning and trained rigorously. Who in baseball but Clemens could win the Cy Young Award for being a top pitcher so late in his career (at the age of 38 and again at 41)?

Voted	Actual	Rare
happiness anger	disgust anger	fear

Roger Clemens

Roger Clemens is in third-place all-time in major league baseball history for his 4,672 strikeouts. No pitcher has equaled his seven Cy Young Awards for being the pitcher of the year in one of baseball's two leagues.

Done to imitate Andy Warhol's serial depictions of other celebrities like Marilyn Monroe, the basic image here is of Warhol's skin rumpled by a severe upward chin thrust. While the lip corners are faintly sagging, the folded skin below the lower lip indicates a chin area severely raised. Unwilling to meet the camera's eye with his own eyes, this is Warhol as Drella: the nickname given to the artist by associates who saw his personality as being part Dracula, part Cinderella.

Voted	Actual	Rare
sadness fear	disgust sadness	*pleasure*

Andy Warhol

Born Andrew Warhola, Andy Warhol is best known for his 1960's pop art. Warhol also created documentary films, briefly managed the rock band The Velvet Underground, starring Lou Reed, and founded *Interview* magazine.

Back stage with Ed Sullivan in 1956, Elvis Presley looks both uncon-cerned and unimpressed by his sudden fame. Besides the smile, there's the flared upper lip and a slight chin thrust. As indifferent to money as he is to fame, what's ahead for Presley is to be ripped off by his manager Colonel Tom Parker. "Elvis detested the business side of his career," Presley's first wife, Priscilla, has confirmed, adding that Presley "would sign a contract without even reading it." Parker liked that kind of behavior just fine, taking first a 25% commission and later on nearly 50% of Presley's earnings.[2]

Voted	Actual	Rare
happiness sadness	disgust acceptance	fear

Elvis Presley

Elvis Presley was a singer and actor, and is often called the "King of Rock and Roll." His record sales are estimated to exceed 600 million units worldwide. Presley won three Grammys for his gospel music, plus a Lifetime Achievement Award.

What May Cause Disgust

The essence of disgust is rejection, as we seek to distance ourselves from whatever causes an aversive reaction. Unlike the more cerebral, attitudinal emotion of contempt, with disgust it's not that we distrust or disrespect someone or something per se. Instead, it's more a matter of a gut-level abhorrence for whatever triggered our response, as the following seven causes make evident.

1. What our senses take in strikes us as unhealthy; the input is unwelcome or potentially even harmful.

By game four of the 2016 NBA finals, the Golden State Warriors' spark plug, Draymond Green, and the Cleveland Cavaliers' superstar, LeBron James, have been mixing it up repeatedly. In this game, the two players get entangled, tumbling to the floor. As James steps over Green to rejoin the play, the sprawled Warrior seems to take a swipe at James's groin region. Nerves are raw. Among the players crowded together on court during the next stoppage of play, Green is making taunts that James responds to by showing his signature disgust expression: an upside down "smile" that may resemble a pout as James objects to Green's antics.

The NBA head office decides it's seen enough, and Green gets suspended from the next game in the series. In response, Green's teammate Klay Thompson says, "It's a man's league" and, in regards to James, "I guess his feelings got hurt."[3] Thompson is indirectly referring to James' complaint that something derogatory, something that *smells bad*, got said on court after the tangle-up. Warriors fans take the hint. They bring "Cry Baby" signs to the next game, including one that names James the NBA's Most Valuable Baby. Somebody else brings a giant baby bottle to the Warriors' arena. Immune to insults meant to poison his self-esteem, James takes the Most Valuable Player award after having enabled the Cavaliers to win the championship.

2. We're bored, as if what we're experiencing has no taste at all.

Aspiring "to be plastic," to live without emotion, Andy Warhol feels like he's mirroring his early 1960's experience. Authenticity, originality, skill, and beauty are all getting washed away by commercialism. Nothing is sacred, so why pretend that it is? Warhol often shows disgust in the way the corners of his mouth droop. The art dealer Leo Castelli isn't happy, either. Warhol won't sign his Pop Art works, insisting that anonymity reinforces the message that everything is being subject to mass reproduction. As soon as Castelli threatens to exclude Warhol from his gallery, however, the artist relents. The compromise proves to be a signature stamp.[4] That way, Castelli can approach big-money collectors while Warhol can stay true to his bored-with-everything outlook as he mourns the death of individuality.

3. Concerns about death and decay typically provoke feelings of disgust because what's unhygienic may infect us.

How to explain Whitney Houston's frightening and sad fall from grace? A good place to start is Houston getting booed by some members of the audience at the 1989 Soul Train Music Awards for being an "oreo" (black only on the outside). That same night she meets Bobby Brown. It's as if Houston then decides to fight her (alleged) infection—being an "oreo"—by rejecting her positive image. Soon, the singer is telling *Rolling Stone*: "I am nobody's angel. I can get down and dirty. I can get raunchy."[5]

Proving her point, Houston becomes famous for being infamous by appearing in the reality TV series *Being Bobby Brown*, aired by Bravo in 2005. "Kiss my ass!" she snaps in one scene. The signature remark that signals Houston's refusal to "play nice" and get along with others, though, becomes "Hell to the no," a remark prominent in an episode devoted to Mother's Day. Houston renames the holiday "Hell Day," supporting her opinion by how her lower lip curls down and out in disgust. That same expression occurs again when Brown presents Houston with a bouquet of flowers. Everything, *even flowers* apparently stink if you're not enjoying your life, which is Houston's predicament.

The show gets widely panned for its many compromising situations, but bad reviews are trivial problems compared to Houston's debilitating drug habit. When the star dies of a heart attack, one of Houston's aides tells a waiting VH1 TV crew (with unintentional irony) that Houston "can't make it" to the interview because "she's dead,"[6] having just been found submerged in a bathtub upstairs in her suite at the Beverly Hilton.

4. Short of being "poisoned," we also don't want to appear weakened in any way. Our vitality is affirmed by being the opposite of a flaccid "loser".

Early in baseball's 2000 season, Rogers Clemens beans Mike Piazza with a pitch. The resulting concussion forces Piazza to miss the All-Star game.

It's hardly a freak occurence. Known for the hard-throwing, intimidating style that inspired his nickname, "Rocket" Clemens will ultimately rank 9th all-time among MLB pitchers for hitting the bodies of batters.

Now it's the World Series and Piazza is at the plate, facing the Rocket again. As Piazza swings, a fragment of his broken bat flies toward Clemens on the pitcher's mound. Picking it up, the Rocket uses a wrist-whipping motion to throw the fragment in front of Piazza running to first base. As he does so, Clemens' face becomes contorted by a strong, upward-chin-thrust expression (signaling disgust, anger, and sadness). It's as if Clemens is offended by a foreign object, Piazza's splintered bat, trying to infiltrate the kingdom of his pitcher's mound. Afterwards, Clemens claims: "I was fired up and emotional and flung the bat toward the [hitters'] on-deck circle where the batboy was. I had no idea that Mike was running."[7]

Fined $50,000 for the "inappropriate" bat toss, Clemens will also, after his retirement, face scrutiny for his alleged steroids abuse. In defense, Clemens will ascribe his enduring prowess to a regimen of strenuous work-outs, not to mention odd rituals like having searingly hot muscle liniment applied to his private parts during post-game rub-downs. (Yes, it's yet another case of true stories often being stranger than fiction.)

5. We reject what feels morally tainted, looking to protect our values and integrity.

From the start, Serena Williams's father and initial, long-time tennis coach Richard Williams sets the agenda. He prepares Serena and her sister Venus for any and all racism ahead by paying for busloads of local kids to ring the practice courts in Compton, California, and shout the foulest things possible. Serena doesn't back down. Her signature expression is how her nose wrinkles in disgust, dismissing whatever she can't abide.

Taken to extremes, that stance can lead to a mishap like the time in 2009 when Serena threatens to stuff a tennis ball down a lineswoman's throat at the U.S. Open. Most times, however, Serena doesn't lose focus. She stands alone for having won a major tournament a record three times after facing match point during a two-week schedule of matches. About the only contest that Serena hasn't won is more corporate endorsements than her less-accomplished, blonde rival Maria Sharapova. If racial bias taints the awarding of those endorsement contracts, Serena doesn't say. Instead, she sticks to readily admitting that "I play for me" while also recognizing that, as a black female role model, she battles to represent "something much greater" than herself alone.[8]

6. Defending our boundaries, we cast off what we regard as strange and atypical.

America has never seen anything like it. Donald Trump comes down an escalator inside of Trump Tower to announce his candidacy for president on June 16, 2015, and promptly denounces foreigners. Besides ISIS, the countries of China, Japan, and Iran all get described as violating America's best interests. No country gets attacked more than Mexico, though, which is allegedly "sending people that have lots of problems, and they're bringing those problems" to America. So declares Trump with his most characteristic sign of disgust: an upward thrusting chin. "They're bringing drugs," the new candidate says, adding: "They're bringing crime. They're rapists. And some, I assume, are good people."

Trump's promise to "build a great, great wall on our southern border" is really an anti-promise, a vow to disavow others. In that way, it's no aberration. A germaphobe who prefers not to shake hands and who doesn't touch booze, drugs, or cigarettes, Trump is full of dislikes. For him disgust can apply to whole classes of people, enveloping racial and religious minorities as well as America's majority: women. Trump describes Rosie O'Donnell as a "big fat pig," while Megyn Kelly has "blood coming out of her wherever." Only family members are immune.

For everyone else, there's Trump's signature phrase from *The Apprentice* (2004–2015)—"You're fired"—which constitutes yet another case of rejecting perceived impurities. Time and again, Trump's tweets read like bullying snorts of derision for others.

7. Fed-up and sick of it, we inoculate ourselves against a hostile social environment.

Sam Phillips, the owner of Sun Records in Memphis, has lately been saying: "If I could find a white man who had the Negro sound and the Negro feel, I could make a billion dollars." Living in town is a poor, as-yet-unknown young man named Elvis Presley, who happens to know and appreciate black culture.[9] Before Presley's family moved to Memphis when the future star was 13 years old, the family had lived in Tupelo, Mississippi, where Presley would bring his guitar to gatherings in the nearby "colored" section of town.

In early July, 1954, a Memphis DJ plays a newly-covered song on the radio and soon the switchboard at WHBQ is lighting up. *Who's the artist? Who's singing "That's All Right, Mama"?* Quickly tracked down in a local movie theater, Presley find himself giving his first radio interview. *Where did you go to high school, son?* The DJ is asking as a way of letting white audiences know the singer is one of them, thanks to the whites-only, segregated school that is Presley's alma mater.[10]

Acceptance won't always come so easily. After Presley's first appearance in Las Vegas in 1956, a *Newsweek* critic will deride his act as akin to "a jug of corn liquor at a champagne party." Also put off, a judge in Jacksonville, Florida, will object to Elvis-the-Pelvis's stage antics, ordering Presley to tone things down. Besides dabbling in his usual upper lip curl, Presley's response to the judge will be to wiggle his little finger very suggestively while onstage the next time he performs in Florida.

Four Forms of Disgust

One of the most notable ways that disgust's theme of rejection gets expressed is when a MLB umpire calls a batter out on a third strike.[11] Many umpires use what's been called the *Invisible Chainsaw* motion, where the arm goes out, then pulls back, as if an umpire is ripping the cord of a chainsaw or lawn mower. Other umpires throw an *Uppercut*. And a few *Pick an Apple*, as if pulling down an unseen tree branch to get the fruit. That's tough competition in terms of memorable names, but here's my take on describing four forms of disgust.

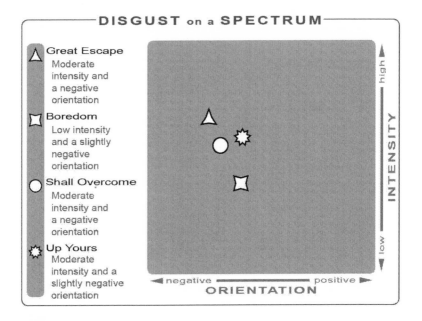

Two of these forms involve disavowing, withdrawal reactions. People displaying the Great Escape or Boredom look want to avoid whatever is distasteful. Of those two, the Great Escape is more active and Boredom more passive. In contrast, the other two forms combine disgust with the *hit*-or-*hug*, approach emotions of anger or happiness. Shall Overcome takes the anger route, while Up Yours combines disgust and mild happiness.

Great Escape

This look gets expressed in any or all of these ways: a wrinkling, upturned nose; a curling upper lip; or a lower lip pulling down and slightly outward, as if somebody is sucking on a really bitter lemon. People who exhibit such strong signals of disgust want to escape feeling contaminated. The person, object, situation, or place that triggers these kinds of reactions can't be left behind quickly enough.

- Great Escape: The one-two punch here is a raised upper lip and a slightly scrunched-up nose.

- Other emoting: This big smile verges on expressing joy.

Kate Winslet

What does Kate Winslet want to escape from? Quite a lot, as it turns out. Topics she doesn't much want to discuss with the press include: Hollywood's gender bias, which means bigger contracts for its male stars (too "vulgar" to address "out in the open"); and the actress's weight ("once a fat kid, always a fat kid").[12] Winslet might have played a socialite traveling first class in *Titanic* (1997), but "I didn't come from the fancy home, no," she freely admits in interviews laced with obscenities.

Who else is in the Top 10 list for the Great Escape? Prominent is Jimi

TOP 10

Great Escape

Hank Aaron
Roger Clemens
Jimi Hendrix
Kate Winslet
Khloe Kardashian
Elvis Presley
Will Smith
Serena Williams
Ringo Starr
Jack Nicklaus

Hendrix, who told a *Rolling Stone* reporter a year before his death: "I don't want to be a clown anymore. I don't want to be a rock and roll star."[13] Hendrix is joined by three other African-Americans. (The total climbs to fully half this list if we include Khloe Kardashian, who was fathered by O. J. Simpson,[14] at least according to Simpson's friend and former manager Norman Pardo.) Topping the list of those turned off by what they've encountered is Hank Aaron. That persevering slugger never forgot the time in his Negro League days when he heard the white restaurant staff breaking all the plates on which the team's players had just finished eating.

Boredom

In this era of entertainment, we expect to be endlessly enthralled and amused. So something dull with no taste to it is, for lots of people, likely to be even worse than something in bad taste. Indifference kills TV ratings and many a conversation. Feeling let down in this way may lead to a frown alone, or be combined with the mouth falling ever so slightly open, as if the person is suppressing a yawn.

Larry Bird

- Boredom: The mouth hanging slightly open here fits well.

- Other signs of emoting: A raised upper lip, a slight smile, and a wince round out the picture, adding anger, happiness, and sadness to the mix.

For a guy with skin described as "perpetually the color of mayonnaise," Larry Bird sure hated to have another white guy guard him. To Bird, that wasn't enough of a challenge. Consider the time the basketball star turned to Chicago Bulls coach Doug Collins, sitting courtside, and guffawed, "Are you fucking kidding me?" about the

Caucasian no-name player trying to hold down his point total. On another occasion, a bored Bird decided to shoot left-handed for a game and had 27 points after three quarters.

Bird's on-court antics prove he was no slouch when it came to fighting against the Boredom he felt. Another Boston sports legend, Ted Williams, also appears in the Top 10 list for Boredom. That baseball star's loathing for whatever disinterested him was so colorful a reporter called him "Our Hemingway. He writes our stories for us." Then there's John McEnroe, whose decision to stop playing tennis doubles with Peter Fleming was fatal to his career because of McEnroe's intolerance for doing drills. Mens' doubles matches had often been McEnroe's only real "practice" sessions for his more important singles matches, and now those warm-ups had gone away.

Boredom

Andy Warhol
Larry Bird
Adele
Jackie Robinson
Beyonce
Ted Williams
John McEnroe
Marilyn Monroe
Diane Keaton
Jane Fonda

Shall Overcome

Witness the convergence of two *don't-tread-on-me* emotions: namely, disgust and anger. An upraised chin that puckers, tightened lips, and either a wrinkled nose or a raised upper lip becomes the expressive package. This look signals a determination not to accept what is, and instead resist and overcome challenges to one's preferred outcome.

- Shall Overcome: Subtle but real, note the upraised chin and the lips pressed together, as well as the faintly raised upper lip.

- Other emoting: The lower eyelids are tight, increasing the amount of anger shown.

While Kanye West began his career as a producer using pitched-up vocal samples to enact a musical style sometimes mocked as "chipmunk soul," you wouldn't know it now. West has appeared on the cover of *Rolling Stone* wearing a crown of thorns, how appropriate for a guy who proclaims: "I'm like a vessel, and God has chosen me to be the voice and

Kanye West

the connector." If Jesus comparisons aren't enough, try Michael Jackson, Leonardo da Vinci, and Steve Jobs among the litany of greats West puts himself in league with. Then in 2016, West literally upped the ante. In a Twitter posting, the musician told Mark Zuckerberg he should "invest 1 billion dollars" in West's ideas to support the "greatest artist of all time."[15]

The Top 10 list for Shall Overcome includes some of the strongest personalities found in *Famous Faces Decoded*. There's Aaron Rogers ("I think very highly of myself"); Barry Bonds ("I like to be against the odds. I'm not afraid to be lonely at the top"); and Elton John ("There is nothing wrong with going to bed with someone of your own sex. People should be very free with sex, [though] they should draw the line at goats.") Clearly, people who combine disgust with anger have no problem being brazen.

TOP 10
Shall Overcome

Aaron Rodgers
Douglas MacArthur
Barry Bonds
Barack Obama
J. K. Rowling
Prince
Eminem
Kanye West
Elton John
George Wallace

Up Yours

In this case, a wrinkled nose or a raised upper lip merges with slight smiles frequently shown. *How strange,* you might say. *How can disgust and happiness cohabitate?* And yet it's a pretty common look. In rebellion against the status quo, some people readily blend these two emotions. Why not, when they find it satisfying to take sweet revenge on whatever they find disagreeable by turning the situation to their advantage.

- Up Yours: This smile is bigger than a classic Up Yours look, which would involve a smaller, acceptance level smile. But the raised upper lip is unmistakable and fits the look well.

Madonna

Through her stage costumes, lyrics, and the imagery in her musical videos, Madonna has always pushed boundaries. This musical artist insists on autonomy. "Papa Don't Preach" is but one illustrative song title. As to imagery, her "Like a Prayer" video showcases the erotic dream of making love to a saint, a move that brought Madonna both condemnation and publicity. When you're the best-selling female recording artist ever and second behind The Beatles on *Billboard's* Greatest of All Time list, then you've earned the right to entitle your greatest-hits album *The Immaculate Collection* (1990).

TOP 10

Up Yours

Amy Schumer
Elvis Presley
Jimmy Page
Aretha Franklin
Madonna
Jane Fonda
Khloe Kardashian
Steven Spielberg
Elizabeth Taylor
Hank Aaron

While Madonna's fluid, ever-evolving image has, at times, echoed in style Marilyn Monroe's persona, a different sex symbol in the Top 10 list for Up Yours is Elizabeth Taylor. Many of the celebrities on this list have bigger-than-life personalities, and Taylor is certainly a case in point. During the transition from childhood star to ingenue, Taylor was asked: "Elizabeth, where on earth did you ever learn how to make love like that?" That question came from Hollywood gossip columnist Hedda Hopper after she saw Taylor's performance in *A Place in the Sun* (1951).[16] Taylor was bold, concluding that people with "no vices" generally "have some pretty annoying virtues." Fast forward to Taylor leaving her fourth husband, Eddie Fisher, for Richard Burton. There again was Taylor going her own way, exhibiting behavior the Vatican would publicly condemn as constituting "erotic vagrancy."

Applications in Your Life

In your own life, when might you see these four forms of disgust? How might you best react to them, given what causes people to feel disgust?

Great Escape: If you're the sales manager of an under-performing or high turn-over staff, stay alert. Odds are you'll see the Great Escape look. As a social worker or health care specialist, a Great Escape look from a client is your heads-up that you'll never get more than lip-service answers to your queries. In your personal life, you can surely expect such expressions from your teenaged kids.

Great Escape

Impatient
Reclusive
Reluctant
Evasive
Unhelpful

People showing this form of disgust have a strong, virulent sense that something is unpleasant, even unhealthy. Because they don't want to engage, they might come across as evasive.

What causes are most likely to trigger this kind of response? Unwelcome sights, sounds, and smells constitute one possibility. Another is when people are backing off from a debilitating social situation (they're fed up with others). Whether the trigger is physical or social in nature, imagine you're the culprit. Maybe you're too sloppy? It can't hurt to tidy up a little! If it's a matter of how you're interacting with the person, examine whether the majority of the messages you deliver are the equivalent of "yuck". If so, remember that a disagreeable tone takes a toll. Research indicates that the ideal ratio of positive to negative content in interactions is five to one.[17] If you're too sweet, the compliments smack of mere flattery. Get too sour, too often, and you may be thought of by others as the equivalent of a toxic waste dump.

Boredom: For teachers, this is surely a kiss-of-death look. The instructors of students who often show this expression are effectively talking to themselves and might consider new ways to connect in their classrooms. As an accountant, indifference advertised in this way signals the moment you've gotten "too deep in the weeds" for a client to stay with you. On a first date, this look from the other party means there won't be a second date.

Those who reveal looks of Boredom are a little bit like both Droopy, MGM studio's anthropomorphic dog, and Sleepy in Disney's *Snow White*

and the Seven Dwarfs (1937). With this look, it's as if nothing in life tastes good or is worth pursuing. Listlessness and sulky indifference are the kinds of behaviors likely to be on display, at least until these people discard Boredom for diverting action.

Among disgust's set of causes, the one that fits like a glove here is that seemingly everything is bland or unsavory. On seeing this signal from otherwise good employees or struggling friends, remember that perhaps they could benefit from more rest or greater variety in their routines in order to stir things up. Introducing some amusement would be a start, but what they may need most is *a reason to care*. If they have unmet needs or wants and you're able help them realize their hopes, then step in. Otherwise, maybe your role consists of helping them brainstorm new in-depth approaches they might take.

Shall Overcome: Imagine you're a loan officer, and now you're asking a couple to provide you with more financial records to verify their solvency. Learn to recognize that this look signals strong objections. The same goes for turf-conscious managers expected to turn in detailed goals for the upcoming fiscal year. A police cop or sheriff seeing this type of expression from a stopped motorist or uncooperative pedestrian should be on guard against a potential altercation. After a divorce, this look may be your first clue that your ex-spouse isn't going to be very flexible during on-going interactions involving the kids.

People showing the Shall Overcome look are blending disgust with anger. That's a potent mix—requiring grace and respect to respond well. Testy, even disruptive behavior is likely from people feeling as if their preferences are being ignored or violated. Be ready to defuse conflicts.

Shall Overcome

Zealous
Ambitious
Cantankerous
Testy
Disruptive

Among the causes of this form of disgust, two stand out. The first is that you're with people concerned about a potential downward spiral in their lives. For people who feel like decay has set in, restoring a sense of vitality is urgent. You'll need to be seen as helping to offset whatever might be "bringing them down." The second, often related cause involves people rejecting anything strange or "foreign" because that is the easiest, defensive reflex. These people assume that whatever new, unknown idea you're proposing will imperil them. Make the case for why your intent is actually constructive and healthy—even admirable—and will serve them well. To better align with them, you might start by finding common ground based on ways you both consider the status quo to be a festering mess.

Up Yours: If you're a member of the clergy and notice this combination of disgust and a slight smile, it's likely your advice isn't being taken seriously by a member of the congregation. A public relations specialist should suspect that a client feeling this way won't abide by the new crisis management procedure. School counselors seeing this look should doubt they're connecting with a pupil in need. In your personal life, a "friend" who shows this expression may be about to blow off your next party.

People showing an Up Yours look are combining rejection with the wry version of happiness. You could say they're trying to tolerate a situation they find unacceptable. Of relevance is Elvis Costello's line: "I used to be disgusted, now I try to be amused." Expect these people to be determined to rise above the "muck" in a sassy, blunt manner.

What may cause this response? A likely trigger could be that these people don't want to be undermined or "poisoned" by hanging around "losers".

Or maybe they feel like their values are somehow being tainted by circumstances they prefer to avoid. If either cause fits the situation, re-establish rapport with these people by learning what they will and won't tolerate; in other words, *where the line is.* From that, you may infer what kind of progress is possible in your interactions with them. Always remember that while someone's lifestyle may be malleable, *values* arise from one's life experiences and deepest influences. So they won't change much. Those who show lots of disgust will be especially unlikely to yield to coaxing. All the same, point out the costs and consequence of intolerance. Then figure out how much you're willing to give ground yourself, and leave it at that.

Summary

What innately triggers disgust includes, but isn't limited to, anything physically inopportune, strange to us, or morally tainted. Something "stinks" or, alternatively, is so boring it seemingly has no taste or smell at all. Put off, we back off. Given its often sensory nature, disgust can originate as a very intimate emotion, but it always leads to creating boundaries. We like to keep our distance from whatever strikes us as repellant. Therefore, disgust reduces our capacity for empathy and compassion.

We reject what we consider bad, including anyone or anything that lands on a scale somewhere between "yucky" to "poisonous". People experience disgust on a sensory level early in life (kids tend to be finicky eaters). Then the morally based version of disgust becomes a greater factor as our beliefs and values take firm, even permanent shape as we move from being teenagers to adults. While the related emotion of contempt comes more from the head, disgust is a gut-level verdict rejecting anything that doesn't meet our tastes.

Spurning Emotions Quiz

(in answering, focus on each emotion's four forms and not the personalities involved)

1. Which of these three celebrities meets the requirements of the **Dismissive** form of contempt most accurately?

| Jennifer Lawrence | Jon Stewart | Dwight Eisenhower |

2. Who here best conveys the look of **Up Yours**?

| Peyton Manning | Joni Mitchell | Greg Norman |

3. When it's the **Shall Overcome** form of disgust, can you spot it easily? Which athlete shows **Shall Overcome** best?

| Ted Williams | John McEnroe | Aaron Rodgers |

143

ANSWERS

1. Contempt

Scorched Earth
Vindication
Dismissive
Buoyancy

Dismissive combines the happiness of either a satisfaction or acceptance smile, with contempt: an upper lip asymmetrically raised or a smirk at the corner of the mouth. Lawrence is the weakest option here, twice over. First, her smile is so big it qualifies as a pleasure smile. Second, there's some fear evident given her wide-open eyes and the uneasy nature of her smile. Although Stewart is showing happiness, it's too strong. His smirk verges on a guffaw, and he looks too giddy to be Dismissive. With Eisenhower, the mouth is perfect for this look. It's a rock-solid, low-key satisfaction level smile combined with a smirk. Note the upturned left lip corner. Yes, there are extraneous hints of fear (the raised right eyebrow), plus anger (a hard gaze), which don't match the Dismissive form. But clearly it's the look of assurance from someone who won't be deterred.

2. Disgust

Great Escape
Boredom
Shall Overcome
Up Yours

With the **Up Yours** form of disgust, either a satisfaction or an acceptance level smile should accompany one of these two disgust displays: an upturned nose or a raised upper lip. Norman is easiest to disqualify here because sadness is prevalent, instead of happiness, and disgust is entirely absent. Of the two remaining celebrities, Manning is the weaker choice; he's smiling too broadly. Mitchell is the correct answer because her modest, tepid satisfaction smile includes an upper lip curl, a key sign of disgust.

3. Disgust

Great Escape
Boredom
Shall Overcome
Up Yours

Shall Overcome is the form of disgust that also involves anger. The essence of this look is an upward chin thrust (disgust) combined with lips sealed tight (anger). The display of disgust will be accentuated by either an upturned nose or a raised upper lip. Given his surly reputation, Williams is a tempting choice. But in this photo the anger comes from his narrowed eyes, not his mouth, and disgust isn't shown much. Rodgers has an acceptance smile, instead of lips pressed in anger. So he isn't a fit, despite his upper lip curl. The strongest option is McEnroe. He's got the chin thrust that meets an immovable object: firmly pressed lips. Furthermore, note the deep disgust "pouch" either side of McEnroe's nose.

flash

Personality insights revealed by facial coding comparisons

{ parallel

careers }

Hugely successful talk show hosts who both hail from the Deep South, Ellen DeGeneres and Oprah Winfrey also have in common upbringings that
involved sexual molestation.[1] How have they come through their respective
experiences? Emotionally, the answer is on identical terms—just as voters
predicted. These two women are amazingly upbeat. Any difference between
them centers instead on which emotion they feel *least* often. For the efferves-
cent DeGeneres, who doubles as a stand-up comedian, it's sadness. In Winfrey's case, she hardly registers any contempt for others after having grown up
so poor that her dresses were humbly made of potato sacks.

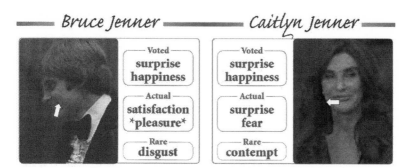

When Caitlyn Jenner was still Bruce Jenner, the 1976 Olympic decathlon
winner, he felt like he was "always telling lies" as he gave promotional
speeches while wearing panty hose and a bra under his suit.[2] In a long
career as primarily a television personality, has the new identity made
Jenner more content? The answer may be *no*. As Bruce, happiness was the
more dominant emotional note. For Caitlyn, surprise and fear have been
the most prevalent. That change is in keeping with her confession: "the
uncomfortableness of being me never leaves all day long." The good news is
that free of playing Bruce, the masculine, all-American hero, Caitlyn feels
less contempt. She's no longer living a life that feels deceitful.

Aretha Franklin · Diana Ross

Voted
happiness
sadness

Actual
acceptance
satisfaction

Rare
disgust

Voted
happiness
happiness

Actual
pleasure
acceptance

Rare
sadness

Voters saw happiness in both of these singers, but less so in Aretha Franklin. And in that, they were correct. The Queen of Soul's version of happiness wasn't as upbeat as is true of former Supremes' lead singer Diana Ross. Of greater note are the emotions qualifying as rare. It's sadness for Ross, who has never publicly regretted monopolizing the microphone when the Supremes attempted the group's first reunion. For Franklin, the answer was disgust. There was little she had the self-discipline to avoid indulging in, though she learned that "I wouldn't starve if I had one hot dog instead of two."[3]

Steve Jobs · Bill Gates

Voted
surprise
sadness

Actual
anger
surprise

Rare
sadness

Voted
happiness
happiness

Actual
contempt
satisfaction

Rare
fear

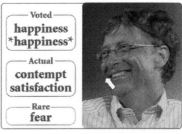

The two men were at first uneasy business allies, then bitter rivals on the way to ultimately becoming friends of a sort.[4] Besides different commercial instincts, Bill Gates and Steve Jobs also had to navigate their different styles. Most of the harder, verbal jabs exchanged between them came from Jobs. "Gates has no shame" is but one example of Jobs's anger outwardly directed. Surprise was also true of Jobs, an often times wide-eyed innovator. But the sadness voters purported to see in Jobs was actually a rare emotion for him. By comparison, Gates runs cooler than Jobs. His version of a rebuke was to call Jobs "fundamentally odd," a put-down that conveys a sense of superiority based on feeling contempt and an utter lack of fear.

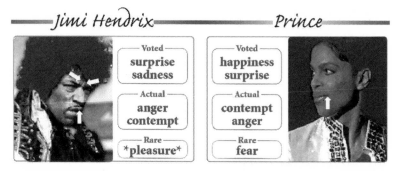

The pair of emotions that most distinguish these two legendary guitarists is interchangeably the same: anger and contempt (thereby throwing voters' choices out the window). Where the two men varied involves which emotion arose least often. For Prince, it was a lack of fear. Never one to pander, Prince turned the pinnacle of his commercial success into the moment he deconstructed the sound that got him there. In Jimi Hendrix's case, the answer is that he rarely felt pleasure. As if imprisoned by stardom, Hendrix began to quietly rebel by mumbling "etcetera etcetera" in interviews. The girlfriend he lived with remembers seeing Hendrix smile only when he was jamming and "got it right for himself, not for anyone else."[5]

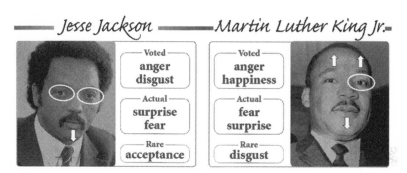

People often "see" what they expect to see, and here's a striking example. Voters saw both of these civil rights icons as predominantly *angry*. In truth, the two emotions that distinguish Jesse Jackson and Martin Luther King Jr. are surprise and fear. Does King have more of a halo around his image? Perhaps, as voters also ascribed to him the more upbeat emotion of mild happiness. For Jackson, the voters thought disgust accompanied anger. Rarely given to slight smiles, Jackson has nevertheless delivered this example of sly humor: "Poor people lie, rich people prevaricate."

Rush Limbaugh — Howard Stern

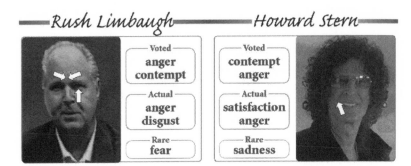

— Voted —
anger
contempt

— Actual —
anger
disgust

— Rare —
fear

— Voted —
contempt
anger

— Actual —
satisfaction
anger

— Rare —
sadness

Voters didn't see these two radio "shock jocks" as being very different, emotionally speaking, and they're correct in that anger defines both Rush Limbaugh and Howard Stern to a large degree. A big emotional difference that does exist between them, however, is hinted at by the titles of books they published a year apart: *The Way Things Ought to Be* (1992) by Limbaugh, and *Private Parts* (1993) by Stern. In the end, what does satisfaction-oriented Stern want? To have fun, sex, money, and great ratings, is surely the answer. For Limbaugh, a focus on politics leads to what supporters view as fearless, courageous, red-meat attacks on liberals. Trying to shape America's body politic is what drives Limbaugh to challenge what he finds repugnant.

Mick Jagger — Keith Richards

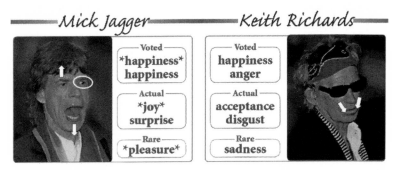

— Voted —
happiness
happiness

— Actual —
joy
surprise

— Rare —
pleasure

— Voted —
happiness
anger

— Actual —
acceptance
disgust

— Rare —
sadness

A journalist who has long covered The Rolling Stones[6] says of Mick Jagger, he's "Elvis in a gold lame jacket." In comparison, Keith Richards is "the friend who won't let you forget the promise you made under the bridge." Voters saw Jagger as happy and rightly so, given the lead singer's flashy expressions of joy and surprise. Richards is different. The guy who tagged Jagger's 2001 solo album *Goddess in the Doorway* as "Dogshit in the Doorway" after their friendship collapsed, instead favors acceptance, the lowest, most begrudging version of happiness, along with disgust.

part 3 three

reactive

emotions

Surprise

Change Is Afoot

What Surprise Means

For a few hours on November 10, 2014, Bill Cosby's public relations team posts on billcosby.com a meme generator: a free online image maker. The entry comes complete with a photograph of a grinning Cosby and the statement, "Hello my name is Bill Cosby, I am the star of the classic 90s comedy 'Ghost Dad.' Also I am a serial rapist."[1] A tweet from Cosby's account simultaneously invites response by urging, "Go ahead. Meme me!" What kind of captions Cosby expects people to add to his photo, who knows? This pair of strange postings does nothing to slow down the fast-moving transformation of Cosby's public image from beloved, cuddly funnyman to sexual predator.

To reconstruct how Cosby's image gets altered, I need to start in early 2014 with a different case, involving another celebrity, to pinpoint what indirectly initiates the change. That's when Dylan Farrow publishes a letter in *The New York Times*,

Bill Cosby

reminding readers in very personal terms of accusations that Woody Allen had raped her during her childhood over two decades ago. *What other icons might have skeletons in the closet?* Three days later, *Gawker* publishes a story about Cosby's multiple sexual assault accusations in 2004–2006, for which he's never been charged.

Before long, numerous women are presenting their own, additional allegations regarding Cosby and a time period stretching from the mid-1960s to 2008. Then the comedian Hannibal Buress develops a stand-up act that features remarks calling Cosby a "rapist". After a video of the act goes viral, Buress gets interviewed by Howard Stern. Explaining his motivation for launching the anti-Cosby routine, Buress suggests Cosby's hypocrisy for telling young black people how to live: "Yeah, but you raped women, Bill Cosby. So, brings you down a couple notches."

Following the Stern interview, Cosby's public relations team posts the meme-generator stunt. Now things really heat up. Cosby cancels an interview on the *Late Show with David Letterman*; NBC cancels its plan for a new comedy in which Cosby will play a wise grandfather; and on NPR, Cosby says literally not a single word to refute the new felony charges, despite being given multiple opportunities to do so. How perplexing. Thereby proven powerful again is surprise, an emotion about the various mysteries in life that make us pay attention.

Surprise stands alone among the seven core emotions being covered in *Famous Faces Decoded*. The other six emotions get stereotyped as simply being either positive or negative in nature, when in fact they can have both good and bad implications. Surprise belongs in a category by itself due to two qualities. The first is its *brevity*. While the other core emotions may last a few seconds, then resurface repeatedly over time based on a specific triggering detail being recalled, surprise functions like a pre-emotion. Surprise happens quickly—in a second or less, if genuinely felt. Then it's done and gone because a real surprise can't be a surprise twice over.

The second unique quality concerns surprise's *supposed neutrality*. This emotion is typically classified as neither positive nor negative. It's thought of as merely setting the stage for other emotions to weigh in. Now let me complicate that assumption of neutrality with dual examples of when a surprise might happen. Maybe your parents give you *a new car* for the holidays. Or maybe a stranger drags you into *a new car accident* on your way home from work one day. You've just experienced a good or bad surprise.

Granted, during the first nano-seconds of a surprise, your reaction might be essentially *neutral*. An emotional verdict awaits. And on occasion, after reflection, you realize that what's happened qualifies as ambiguous and, therefore, a *neutral*, mixed experience. Maybe for instance the gift of a new car comes with expectations that you'll improve your grades in college.

On balance, though, surprise encompasses two opposing instincts: *positive* curiosity and *negative* wariness. Curiosity reflects our inherent desire to uncover knowledge. The pleasure of discovery activates parts of the brain that welcome rewards. In contrast, wariness arises when we're confronted by what's puzzling or conflicts with what we thought we knew. The resulting unpleasant feeling may cause cognitive dissonance and, instead, activates parts of the brain associated with suffering.[2]

Either way, in keeping with the Nature and Frequency of Emotions chart that appears in the introduction to *Famous Faces Decoded*, surprise joins fear in being a reactive emotion. That's because, for starters, surprise is a submissive as opposed to a dominant emotion. Again, the essence of surprise is that in a flash we face the unknown. Does pleasure or pain, or a combination thereof, await us? We don't know, and the mystery has power over us rather than the other way around.

At times, people clearly welcome surprises. Good movies and novels, like anything creative, depend on an element of surprise to keep us engaged. But in daily life, most people rarely welcome surprises because of the effort required to deal with them. Left to our own devices, lots of us welcome the opportunity to lounge around like house cats, only occasionally exerting ourselves. As a result, surprise has to be classified as an avoidance rather than as an approach emotion.

To reinforce that point, consider this basic truth about human nature. Behavioral economists research the role of emotion in people's decision-making process. Their studies find that we hear bad news *twice* as loudly as good news.[3] Our survival mechanisms prompt us to be more alert and prone to letting setbacks gnaw on us, rather than relish success. So it shouldn't be a shock that surprise and fear often go hand-in-hand in the way the two emotions get expressed, as you're about to learn.

Spotting Surprise

A surprised face *elongates* as if the face's reaction to a sudden, unexpected event is getting painted on a larger canvas than normal. More specifically, surprise never appears entirely on its own. There are instead four ways in which it shows in conjunction with other core emotions:

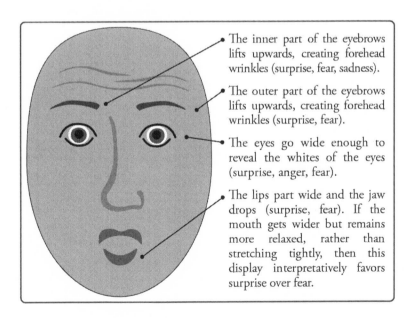

The inner part of the eyebrows lifts upwards, creating forehead wrinkles (surprise, fear, sadness).

The outer part of the eyebrows lifts upwards, creating forehead wrinkles (surprise, fear).

The eyes go wide enough to reveal the whites of the eyes (surprise, anger, fear).

The lips part wide and the jaw drops (surprise, fear). If the mouth gets wider but remains more relaxed, rather than stretching tightly, then this display interpretatively favors surprise over fear.

Now, one extra point needs to be made here regarding surprise. Sometimes being *startled* is thought of as being *surprised*, but the two responses are different. With a startle, the eyes close, the brow lowers, and the mouth tenses. A startle reaction is a physical reaction, not a feeling. You can be startled without being surprised. For example, you want to set off some firecrackers on July 4th. It's therefore hardly unexpected when a loud boom jolts you.

Among the celebrities facially coded for *Famous Faces*, on average just over 8% of their feelings involve surprise. The results also show that male celebrities have a slightly higher average than their female counterparts, and that men dominate the Top 10 list for Most Surprise.

Again, since people rarely welcome surprises, it's no wonder that surprise and fear have plenty of overlapping facial muscle movements.[4] Marilyn Monroe, Bill Cosby, Wayne Gretzky, and Jimmy Stewart also appear in the following chapter's Top 10 list for Most Fear. Of those four celebrities, only Monroe shows more surprise than fear—a finding that refutes anybody who assumes that Monroe's anxiety crippled her natural inquisitiveness.

TOP 10

Most Surprise

Marilyn Monroe
Edward R. Murrow
Bill Cosby
Wayne Gretzky
Jimmy Stewart
Ingrid Bergman
Alfred Hitchcock
Jesse Jackson
Frank Sinatra
Little Richard

As for the other six celebrities in this list, they all show more surprise than fear—an outcome that suggests that for them positive curiosity outweighs negative wariness. Of those six, the intrepid journalist Edward R. Murrow most favors surprise, followed in descending order, from more to ever less of a mix in favor of surprise over fear, by Ingrid Bergman, Alfred Hitchcock, Little Richard, and Jesse Jackson. Then finally there's Frank Sinatra, the wariest of the lot, who only just barely shows more surprise than fear.

As to the celebrities in the Top 10 list for Least Surprise, again men predominate. What makes these men different from the men most given to surprise? It's probably fair to say that many of them qualify as too self-possessed or insular to be deeply interested in what others think or feel about them. In that camp you could place, among others, the Rolling Stones' founder Brian Jones, along with radio host Rush Limbaugh.

Least Surprise

Douglas MacArthur
Brian Jones
Khloe Kardashian
David Letterman
John Bonham
Joseph McCarthy
Leonardo DiCaprio
Bill Wyman
Charles Schulz
Rush Limbaugh

How good are people at spotting surprise? At 25%, this feeling comes in fifth among the eight emotional categories in terms of detection accuracy. In order, anger, mild happiness, strong happiness, and fear are all observed more faithfully. The following two photographs illustrate ways in which surprise appears, and the celebrities' emotional profiles indicate how well voters did in choosing the top two emotions that distinguish these famous people.

You can't do much better than this photo of Frank Sinatra when it comes to depicting surprise. The eyes of "Old Blues Eyes" are wide, his outer eyebrows raised, and his mouth slightly open as if transfixed by the unexpected. That surprise is so flexible in orientation, from positive curiosity to negative wariness, fits Guy Talese's *Esquire* profile of Sinatra.[5] There, Talese writes: "The most distinguishing thing about Sinatra's face are his eyes, clear blue and alert, eyes that within seconds can go cold with anger, or glow with affection."

Voted	Actual	Rare
happiness	surprise	anger
happiness	fear	

Frank Sinatra

Born Francis Albert Sinatra, Frank Sinatra is one of the best-selling music artists ever and was highly successful in films like *From Here to Eternity* (1953) and *The Manchurian Candidate* (1962).

Seen here many years before his arrest, Bill Cosby adds to this slight smile not only wide open eyes, but also slightly raised outer eyebrows. Is Cosby a studious person? You would have to say so. It's the rare person who would earn first a master's degree, then a Doctor of Education degree in the 1970s after having already starred in the TV show *I Spy*. Add to that the comedy album *To Russell, My Brother, Whom I Slept With* (1968), which *Spin* magazine has named the number one comedy album of all-time, and you can be sure that success didn't keep Cosby from resting on his laurels.

Voted	Actual	Rare
sadness	surprise	acceptance
anger	fear	

Bill Cosby

Bill Cosby Jr. starred in *The Cosby Show*, America's number one TV program from 1984–1989. He also hosted the animated comedy TV series *Fat Albert and the Cosby Kids* (1972–1985).

What May Cause Surprise

Surprise arises from a disruption of the status quo. Whether a surprise heralds pleasure, pain, or a blend of those two outcomes, change is afoot. Unlike the case with the other core emotions in this book, here only the first four causes address surprise's sudden nature. The final three "causes" are really about making adjustments. They focus on how people handle *learning moments*, which require them to acclimate to surprises and accordingly make changes in their lives.

1. Overconfidence leads to our over-estimating the likelihood of positive outcomes. So when reality intervenes, high hopes and expectations get dashed.

A reaction of "Oh, man, I am going to die" follows on first hearing the news from The Los Angeles Lakers' team doctor.[6] Now Earvin "Magic" Johnson is largely composed as he begins his November 7, 1991 retirement press conference by declaring, "Because of the HIV virus I have obtained, I will have to retire from the Lakers today." With that opening statement, Johnson's left eyebrow rises in a look of surprise and fear. Clearly, the point guard never expected to find himself in this situation. For anyone who's a star athlete, it must be tempting to imagine you're invincible and, therefore, immune to diseases, too, regardless of how you handle your private life.

Johnson's wife Cookie is newly pregnant with their son. Will the baby be safe? Did his wife contract the disease? For how long might Johnson live? It will be another five years before the invention of a life-saving, "triple cocktail" drug therapy means an HIV infection isn't a death sentence. Much about the disease remains unknown in 1991.

As Johnson discloses his plan to "become a spokesman for the HIV virus because I want people, young people, to realize that they can practice safe sex," his eyes go wide. Still trying to reconcile himself to this HIV bombshell announcement, Johnson will try returning to the NBA next year. But plagued by weakened knees and opposition from several players who feel he poses a health hazard, he will then retire for good.

2. In behavioral economics, the principle is known as "probability blinders." In other words, some surprises wouldn't be surprises at all if only we weren't so willfully blind regarding the likely consequences of our actions.

It's July of 1972, a little over a year before U.S. troops leave Vietnam and less than three years before the war finally ends. Jane Fonda's second husband, the anti-war activist Tom Hayden, has convinced her to visit Hanoi. There and in the surrounding landscape, Fonda sees firsthand the damage American bombing has done to the country. Easily the most indelible photographs from her visit are those of the actress beside an enemy anti-aircraft gun meant to shoot down U.S. planes. The photos often show Fonda with not only a wide-eyed look, but also a cocked right outer eyebrow and her mouth hanging ajar, as if bewildered by what's going on. An intense backlash follows her return to America.

In a 2011 entry on her official website, Fonda explains that a translator said some soldiers wanted to serenade her. "I hardly even thought about where I was sitting. The cameras flashed," Fonda writes. "It is possible that it was a set-up, that the Vietnamese had it all planned. I will never know." Then in post-surprise, retrospective mode, Fonda apologizes: "If I was used, I allowed it to happen … a two-minute lapse of sanity that will haunt me forever." A reviewer of Fonda's autobiography, *My Life So Far*, ends up calling the actress "breathtakingly naive."[7]

3. Sometimes reality exceeds our expectations, leaving us feeling lucky and perhaps even downright incredulous.

Could her time on stage represent both the most extraordinarily earnest and shortest Academy Awards acceptance speech ever given? I'm talking about Audrey Hepburn winning Best Actress in 1954 for *Roman Holiday*. Here's the entire 32-second speech, which follows a stunned Hepburn reaching the stage, eyes down, at first accidentally turning away from the podium. "It's just too much," Hepburn falteringly begins, before gushing: "I want to say *thank you* to everybody who in these past months and years has helped, guided, and given me so much." A pause lets Hepburn catch her emotional breath. "I'm truly, truly grateful," the actress all but concludes. Then, as her demeanor of raised eyebrows but a downcast head gives way (at last) to a beaming, joyful smile, Hepburn adds, "and *terribly happy*." With that final verbal burst, the speech ends in hearty applause. It's affirmation once unimaginable for a woman whose frail frame is a vestige of her having nearly starved to death in her native Holland during World War Two.[8]

4. In treasuring the unexpected, our spontaneity can give rise to the unexpected being truly realized.

Who among us ever gets asked to stop singing in church? Little Richard does, for "screaming and hollering" so loudly his childhood nickname becomes "War Hawk." The boy who beats on house steps or pots and pans while singing eventually becomes the man famous for lifting one leg while playing piano, or jumping around atop the piano itself. As Little Richard ecstatically pumps his legs, often his eyebrows are shooting skyward and his mouth falls wide open, seemingly in astonishment at his own antics.

The first rock musician to use spotlights and flicker lights, the bi-sexual Little Richard takes the stage by storm, wearing makeup, colorful capes, blouses, and precious-stone-and-sequin-studded suits. The essence of experiencing Little Richard's act, however, remains hearing him *sing* in a raspy shout—*crooning*—*wailing*—*screaming*. What does it take to cover a song like "Tutti Frutti" (1956)? Paul McCartney recalls: "I could do Little Richard's voice, which is … like an out-of-body experience. You have to

162

leave your current sensibilities and go about a foot above your head to sing it."

5. There are situations whereby a surprise mixes good and bad elements, and it will take time for us to understand the balance.

For the half-time show at the 2004 Super Bowl, Janet Jackson and Justin Timberlake are performing together. They're singing "Rock Your Body" and making all sorts of brief, suggestive body contact during the duet. Two lines from the lyrics stand out. First, Timberlake sings: "No disrespect, I don't mean no harm." Then he pulls off the rubber bustier covering Jackson's right breast as he croons, "Gotta have you naked by the end of this song." Viewers find themselves witnessing "the boob seen around the world," until the CBS cameras retreat to a wide-angle shot of the stage.

What's Jackson's reaction? Just before the apparent mishap, her eyes were closed. But now as her whipping hair hides her face, she looks down over her chest. Next, she cups a hand across her exposed breast and gives Timberlake a wide-eyed, hard look. Jackson's glaring suggests she *is* in fact surprised by what's happened. For his part, Timberlake is still clutching the bustier as he momentarily closes his eyes and his eyebrows knit together, indicating dismay and concern with how the stunt has turned out.

Afterwards, attention turns to a pre-event story. The MTV website was promising "shocking moments" during Jackson's performance at the Super Bowl. Jackson's publicist insists the stunt was meant to reveal only Jackson's red lace bra. For its part, MTV admits to a rehearsal that explored the possibility of a fake skirt being ripped away. Clearly, *something* was planned, even if it went awry. Jackson's subsequent apology, exonerating CBS and the NFL from any prior knowledge or guilt, hardly resolves the scandal. Nevertheless, on balance and regardless of whatever kind of stunt was planned in advance, the outcome favors Jackson. Not only does "Janet Jackson" become the most searched term in internet history, "Nipplegate" and "wardrobe malfunction" become household words.

6. Surprises can be learning moments, but often we refuse to learn from them. We're in denial. Unwilling to adapt to change, we try to thwart what's new.

Elvis Presley releases "Heartbreak Hotel" in 1956 and quickly becomes known as "the King." Frank Sinatra's response is to give a Tipper Gore like blast attacking rock and roll, describing it as "brutal, ugly, degenerate, vicious" and "sung, played and written, for the most part, by cretinous goons." The irony is that the same swooning of teenage girls for Presley that inspired this blast by Sinatra had, a decade earlier, been true of himself. If Sinatra is merely protecting his turf, he comes by his wide-eyed, ever-alert-to-danger instinct naturally. His mother Dolly is by all accounts his biggest childhood influence. Then one day, still wanting her son to grow up to become an aviation engineer, she notices a rival influence. There are now photos of the singer Bing Crosby adorning the teenager's bedroom, to which Dolly responds by throwing a shoe at her son.[9]

7. Other learning moments are embraced. We're open to how the world really works and respond by adjusting our internal forecasting model.

His pronouncements are legendary, beginning with "Float like a butterfly, sting like a bee." But others will surprise you. Consider: "The man who has no imagination has no wings" and "It isn't the mountains ahead to climb that wear you out; it's the pebble in your shoe." Nobody should underestimate Muhammad Ali, as the younger, stronger George Foreman discovers during the famous Rumble in the Jungle heavyweight championship bout held in Zaire in 1974. Showing his imagination, the 32-year-old Ali uses an unorthodox rope-a-dope strategy that requires taking endless punches to the gut in order to tire out Foreman, the prohibitive favorite.

That's Ali the boxer, but how about Ali the man? He's no fool, judging by his remark: "At home I am a nice guy, but I don't want the world to know. Humble people, I've found, don't get very far." Ali is drawing on what he's witnessed. His father had wanted to be a fine arts painter but ended up becoming a sign painter instead.[10] His son won't settle for anything less than realizing his own dreams. Attentive and concerned, with eyes that widen and inner eyebrows that frequently lift, Ali stretches his vision. "I'm something new," says the boxer who can rightly boast of being strong, proud, handsome, and witty, all at the same time.

Four Forms of Surprise

When we throw a surprise birthday party, we look closely to note just how pleasantly surprised the recipient is. Was the party a secret? Did the person suspect something was brewing? If that person's eyes don't go wide and mouth doesn't fall open, a smile alone isn't enough to confirm that a coup was pulled off.

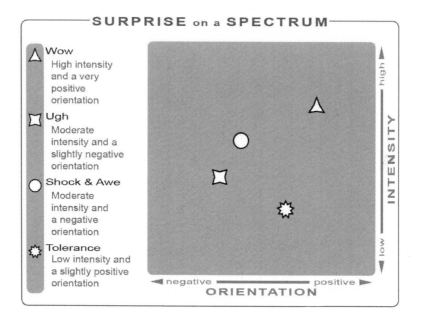

Three of the four forms of surprise revolve around what kind of emotional reaction accompanies or resolves the surprise. With a Wow surprise, it's joy. With the Tolerance version of surprise, it's the satisfaction or acceptance level of mild happiness that emerges. In contrast, an Ugh surprise involves some combination of the "negative" emotions of anger, sadness, disgust, and contempt. That leaves Shock & Awe—naked surprise—where a blatantly vulnerable quality predominates.

Wow

People who react with both joy and surprise are delighted by the unexpected. A big, true smile is joined by the eyebrows arching upwards, horizontal wrinkles appearing across the forehead, and the mouth falling wide open to create a vertically stretched face. It's a fair bet that people who often emote in this way are likely to be full of enthusiasm and cheer.

Walt Disney

Wow

Marilyn Monroe
Little Richard
Ellen DeGeneres
Larry Page
Ingrid Bergman
Magic Johnson
Mary Lou Retton
Walt Disney
Frank Sinatra
Michael Jackson

■ Wow: There's a twinkle in the eyes and the push of skin surrounding them. Complimenting those signs of joy is the surprise hinted at by a lilting left eyebrow.

Who but Walt Disney would sink to his knees on Main Street, all the better to appreciate how Disneyland's attractions are experienced from the vantage point of a six-year-old kid? Likewise, consider another example of Disney wanting to get the details right in order to create a wow. The Dodgers have moved to Los Angeles, and Goofy will throw out the first pitch in the team's new stadium. Disney insists on rehearsing the event until Goofy understands that in order to be *in-character*, he needs to be *incompetent*. As a result, Goofy realizes he must *bobble and drop* the ball the catcher tosses to the mound before he opens the season.

In the Top 10 list for Wow are some of the most magnetic performers ever: Marilyn Monroe, Magic Johnson, and Michael Jackson. There is also a pair of businessmen. Like Walt Disney, Larry Page, Google's cofounder, likes to dream big. When Eric Schmidt stepped down as Google's CEO in 2011, he famously tweeted: "Day-to-day adult supervision no longer needed."[11] A spree of far-out projects and acquisitions have followed. While these efforts are casually referred to as "other bets" in investor relations documents, within Google they're known as "moonshots".

Ugh

The opposite of Wow is Ugh, whereby people react to surprise with dismay. Any one or more of the so-called negative emotions of anger, sadness, disgust, and contempt will color their response. Large doses of these emotions linked to surprise reveal uncomfortable responses to sudden changes in the status quo.

Charles Manson

- Ugh: While the eyes are wide and the outer eyebrows flared, both signs of surprise, the lips are pressed tight together in anger. Beware.

From Timothy McVeigh and the Oklahoma City bombing to the Orlando nightclub shooting and the Sandy Hook massacre, the senseless

167

TOP 10

Ugh

Edward R. Murrow
Jesse Jackson
Johnny Cash
Hillary Clinton
Aaron Rodgers
Alfred Hitchcock
Charles Manson
Elton John
Bill Cosby
Caitlyn Jenner

killings keep piling up. Once as shocking as any of those calamities was when Charles Manson's followers murdered the actress Sharon Tate and four others in Los Angeles in 1969. According to Manson, in childhood he found himself sold by his mother for a pitcher of beer to a childless waitress, and an equally detached Manson showed no remorse while on trial for his role in the Tate killings.

Infamy defines Manson, but not the others on this Top 10 list for Ugh. What everyone here does share is that in conjunction with surprise, they rarely link that feeling to happiness. For Johnny Cash, sadness often accompanies surprise. For Hillary Clinton and Aaron Rodgers, it's contempt; and so on.

In Elton John's case, when he feels surprise he typically also feels anger. As if to break that pattern, twice in February 2016 John created happy surprises. In London, he serenaded commuters at the St. Pancras railway station with a piano medley of his greatest hits. Then in Los Angeles, a free concert announced only the night before was staged in the parking lot that once belonged to the city's Tower Records store, where John used to spend so much time perusing the latest releases.

Shock & Awe

The eyes go wide and the mouth drops wide open, exposing the teeth. Intuitively, Shock & Awe signals people so caught off guard that they completely freeze. Of note is that in this version of surprise, the eyebrows *don't* rise (thus failing to aid vision and awareness). As a result, this hard look suggests people stumbling along rather than pro-actively adapting to change.

- Shock & Awe: The eyes are wide, and the mouth hangs open (though admittedly that might be due to the in-concert setting).

Adele

- Other emoting: The mouth pulled wide, the clenched teeth, and the lowered eyebrows all combine to indicate that fear is a much stronger force here than the hint of a smile.

Known to feel homesickness if on tour, Adele doesn't welcome surprises. Few singers would turn down an opportunity to perform the halftime show at a Super Bowl. For Adele, though, it was an easy decision to stay home because "I don't dance or anything like that."[12] Adele's song "Hello" is by her own account about "making it out alive from your late teens, early twenties,"[13] a look back that reflects the British diva's view of life as a harrowing, always on-the-edge-of-your-seat journey.

TOP 10

Shock & Awe

Billy Graham
Bruce Jenner
Adele
Andy Warhol
Wayne Gretzky
Little Richard
Natalie Portman
Caitlyn Jenner
Jane Fonda
Michael Milken

The Top 10 list for Shock & Awe is full of celebrities who frequently exhibit a version of surprise that may indicate somebody struggling to absorb and learn from their experiences. With two ministers on this list—Billy Graham and Little

Richard—it's tempting to call the celebrities here *forever pilgrims*. There's often a bolt-from-the-blue, revelatory look to them that implies they retain some innocence, despite all their years of fame.

While everyone suffers bumps and bruises in life, several of these celebrities are notable for having undergone major changes. Wayne Gretzky merely changed the country he lived in as a hockey player, moving from Canada to America. Little Richard, however, went from rock star to minister; Jane Fonda from marrying the anti-war activist Tom Hayden to media mogul Ted Turner; and Bruce Jenner changed gender, appearing here twice (both as Bruce and Caitlyn). Rounding out this list: Michael Milken, a former junk bond king who has become a big-time philanthropist, giving support to medical research.

Tolerance

The inverse of Shock & Awe, Tolerance causes people to raise their eyebrows, taking in information, while they also manage satisfaction or acceptance level smiles in reaction to what they've encountered. Tolerance suits people better able to accept and assimilate novelty. Anyone sporting this look will be more likely to believe that adapting to what's new is worth the effort.

- Tolerance: This expression is embodied by the modest smile and the slightly raised left outer eyebrow (tipped off by the forehead wrinkles just above it).

Mocking himself for his well-known shy ways, Jimmy Stewart would say of his marriage proposal to his first and only wife Gloria McLean: "I, I, I … pitched the big question to

Jimmy Stewart

> ### TOP 10
> ## Tolerance
> Estee Lauder
> Aretha Franklin
> John Lennon
> Jimmy Stewart
> Steven Spielberg
> Jackie Onassis
> Walt Disney
> Marilyn Monroe
> Paul McCartney
> Elizabeth Taylor

her last night and to my surprise she, she, she said yes!" That was 1949, and Stewart had recovered. Few know that in playing George Bailey in *It's a Wonderful Life* (1946), Stewart was under the influence. No, I'm not referring to booze. Stewart's newfound capacity for giving such a raw performance came amid recovery from post-traumatic stress following his service as a pilot in World War Two.

The Top 10 list for Tolerance includes introverted celebrities like Jimmy Stewart, Steven Spielberg, and Jackie Kennedy Onassis. As for Estee Lauder, the only woman to make *Time* magazine's list of the 20 most influential business geniuses of the 20th century, she had once wanted to become an actress with her "name in lights" and her life a matter of "flowers and handsome men." If *settle* is the word, then settle Lauder did, making a fortune from selling the beauty products her uncle, a chemist, initially developed.

Applications in Your Life

In your own life, when might you see these four forms of surprise? How might you best react to them, given what causes people to feel surprise?

Wow: Want change agents joining your staff? People given to Wows could be perfect because they're

> ## Wow
> Impulsive
> Impetuous
> Playful
> Quick-witted
> Creative

"wired" for delight and, therefore, might be better able to find ways to upgrade the experiences your customers have. This look might also be a good fit when needing a sales person to handle a unique, new product line. If, on the other hand, you're seeking a bridge partner who will count cards, keep looking. In that case, dutifulness more than pursuing novelty is surely required.

People showing a Wow look are combining surprise with joyfulness. They're ecstatic about an unexpected, welcome surprise. Did they help make it happen? Characteristics like being quick-witted and creative mean the answer is quite possibly *yes*.

Likely related to this response is a pair of causes: expectations were exceeded, or else spontaneity was rewarded. It's also possible that a learning moment has opened a clear path forward. Besides celebrating people's successes, what's the best way for you to react when they feel a Wow? In a work situation, help them "grow the pie" by asking them: how can the triumph be repeated? What were the ingredients to achieving success? And finally, who all needs to be acknowledged? For momentum to be sustained, any achievement should likewise be attributed to colleagues, to avoid having them feel neglected amid the giddiness of an unexpected triumph. Ultimately, your role is to keep a person expressing a Wow hungry and humble enough to enable future success stories.

Ugh: Repeatedly shown, such a look suggests a dour, pained individual. When two companies are merging, a person prone to this look isn't likely to handle the transition well. At a party, someone expressing an Ugh isn't who you hope to be seated alongside. With your children, you will want to ensure they're as Ugh-free and nimble as possible, given a 21st-century economy increasingly about "gigs" instead of steady paychecks.

Chances are that people showing an Ugh look have been let down, perhaps by themselves most of all. Surprise coupled with anger, sadness, disgust, or contempt reflects a sorry encounter with the unexpected. You might have your hands full handling someone with such a sour, hard-to-console disposition.

What might an Ugh involve? The triggers could be either overconfidence or probability blinders. Then again, maybe a big learning moment adjustment is needed, but isn't happening, due to the stress that people experience when facing change. How best to respond? First, remember that the harsher the surprise, the kinder you want to be. Being gentle might keep these people from flinching and pulling back, shunning others, after receiving bad news. You can help by keeping people who show the Ugh expression open-minded about the necessary steps ahead. First, help them assess the situation at hand. Then figure out together how any damage recently suffered can be mitigated, before finally providing counsel as to how they might best avoid future pain. For your own sake, during this three-step process avoid fostering codependency.

Shock & Awe: Want a seasoned doctor or attorney you can rely on? Then you may want to look elsewhere; don't depend on people so evidently caught off-guard much of the time. Managers and teachers who encounter this look will want to bring along, with compassion, employees and students who may be stunned by their struggles to succeed. Coaches will find themselves

Shock & Awe

Unassuming
Naive
Unguarded
Absent-minded
Flexible

shaking their heads at players apparently shocked to receive yet another penalty for yet another bone-headed move during competition.

People caught up in Shock & Awe represent the essence of surprise. Their eyes "bug out" and they become slack-jawed. Surprise overwhelms them, which raises the question: why? Is it that they repeatedly put themselves in the way of the unexpected? That explanation would reflect a willingness to take risks in search of new worthwhile adventures. Or is it that they're naive and largely unable to absorb the lessons of previous experiences in ways that could help them better prepare for the future? The answer is probably a little of both, which helps explain their susceptibility to this form of surprise.

The two strongest, most likely causes of Shock & Awe are identical to those for Ugh: overconfidence or probability blinders. These are often people blindsided by circumstances they might have anticipated with a little more forethought. How best to respond? As clarity begins to replace ambiguity, you can assist by turning the surprise into an optimal learning moment. Explore with work colleagues and friends alike, as pertinent, whether current expectations are matching actual outcomes. Are there ways they could be better prepared? Keep the process of reflection broad, so that these people don't just focus on the bad news alone. In the end, ensuring that they get a handle on what they're "missing" and still need to know is the key.

Tolerance: Are you an executive needing to make your company's workforce more diverse? A manager expressing this look might be a good person for you to promote in order to pioneer such an initiative within the ranks. In your personal life, are you looking to adopt new hobbies

Tolerance

Inquisitive
Clever
Oblique
Resourceful
Pioneering

and activities? Someone showing Tolerance might be an innovative friend with whom to brainstorm new possibilities.

People who show Tolerance have reacted to a surprise by also summoning a low-grade version of happiness, either a satisfaction or acceptance smile. Expect them to be resourceful and probing in times of uncertainty.

One cause may best apply in this case: spontaneity has led to an unexpected reward, making the person receptive to more experimenting. If a positive learning moment likewise applies, it may be that a forecasting model has panned out. Should you encounter this look, how might you want to respond? Think in terms of *flirting*. As a manager or parent, ask yourself: how can this person's natural curiosity be rewarded in ways that build momentum? To accomplish that trick, highlight a knowledge gap and invite the two of you, together, to fill it. A crucial part of this joint effort will be deciding which procedures or habits deserve to be discarded and which, in turn, newly created. Sustain interest by emphasizing the pay-offs likely to ensue.

Summary

Remember that anybody who looks surprised for more than a second is almost certainly faking it. Often, a third of a second or less: that's how quickly this emotion moves across the face. Triggered by a sudden, unexpected event, surprise hinges on the emotional verdict that follows. If no other emotion, positive or negative, mingles with, or follows close behind the *whoosh* of a surprise, then the unexpected proved to be of no real consequence—hence no additional feelings come into play.

Since it announces a change in the status quo, a surprise look merits our attention when we see it in others. There's probably an opportunity to seize, or a painful adjustment to make. Either way, with surprise our field of vision often widens to help us gather new information. Then it's encumbent on us to make the most of every new learning opportunity.

Fear

Catching on Fire

What Fear Means

Press conferences are a staple of quarterback Tom Brady's life. That makes it easy to compare Brady's facial expressions after a regular NFL game to his expressions amid the alleged football-tampering, Deflategate scandal. The difference between the quarterback's usual post-game facial expressions and those he shows during the scandal is vast.

Normally, Brady remains the epitome of unflappable. All kinds of smiles are commonplace. The guy has enjoyed plenty of success and it shows. Over two NFL seasons, I facially coded the first two minutes of press conferences given by every starting quarterback in the NFL, after both a winning and losing game. I chose which games based on the quarterback's performance being crucial to a given victory or loss. From that process, I typically covered four games per quarterback; and from that facial

Tom Brady

coding data, I can tell you the average NFL quarterback feels *twice as much fear* as Brady reveals during regular-season press conferences.

How about the Brady of the January 22, 2015 Deflategate press conference? Suddenly, he's ill at ease. He's showing five times more fear than in a press conference after a Patriots' loss. *Five times more fear* is a lot of fear. To look at Brady's mouth pulled anxiously wide, cheeks deflated, is to see a star quarterback severely out of his comfort zone.

For instance, during the Deflategate press conference, a reporter asks: "When and how did you supposedly alter the ball?" Even as the question is being asked, Brady swallows hard and the right side of his mouth stretches laterally, back towards the ear. Then as he answers, here's what happens: (mouth pulls wider) "I didn't" (mouth widens slightly more) "you know" (both eyebrows shoot upwards) "have any, uh ..." (mouth both widens again and falls open), "I didn't hold onto the balls in any way."

With a voice quavering at times, Brady will go on to offer other, not exactly on-point denials. One example is when he says, "I didn't alter the ball in any way," which Allysia Finley recasts in a *Wall Street Journal* opinion piece[1] as follows: "Of course, you didn't. Your ball boys did. That's what flunkies are for: Doing things you don't want to get caught doing and then taking the fall."

Similarly, note Brady's careful wording when asked if he had cheated: "I don't believe so. I feel like I've always played within the rules." On Bloomberg TV just a few minutes after the Deflategate press conference ends, what kind of appraisal do I give on the air? How culpable might Brady be? Seeking a point of reference, I cite an old Second City comedy skit. In it John Belushi is playing U.S. Senator Howard Baker during the Watergate hearings. "What I want to know," Belushi drawls, "is what did the President know and when did he *stop* knowing it?"

Awaiting not only the NFL's verdict, but also how public opinion will help to define his legacy, it's inevitable that Brady feels fear. This emotion is about being confronted by risk. As Finley adds, "Of course, you don't believe you did anything wrong." The question that Brady is waiting to have answered the day of the press conference is, *now what will others believe?* In awaiting outcomes we can't control in life, we reactively experience fear as a submissive rather than dominant emotion. Faces threats that sometimes strike us as bigger than our ability to handle them, fear kicks in.

In general, fear is also an avoidance instead of an approach emotion. Other than safe, boredom-relieving exceptions like watching a scary movie or going on an amusement park ride, most people's basic orientation is *not* to approach a risk. When we're scared, more blood goes to the large muscles in our legs. It's as if nature is enabling us to run away, if we choose to do so, among the three basic options for handling fear: freeze, flight, or fight. In essence, when afraid we're driven to protect ourselves from uncertainty and possible harm. Fear is uncomfortable to feel or even contemplate feeling and adventure-seekers aside, people typically hate to experience being on-edge for very long (if at all).

One final note here: the common, kneejerk impression of fear is that it's the worst of the "negative" emotions, especially for men. The male code is to be brave, impervious to fear, but of course both men and women feel fear. Fear and survival go hand in glove. Nothing is more important than being alert to danger so that we remain safe. As neuro-scientists have learned, within our brains our "fear button" (the amygdala) is also sensitive to noting other people's faces.[2] That makes sense given our ancient, instinctive concern about distinguishing between friend and foe by both identity and facial expressions alike.

Spotting Fear

A fearful face *opens* and may also blanch or tremble, as if someone afraid has "just seen a ghost." Like surprise, fear typically involves expressions that let us take in more information through widened eyes and lifted eyebrows. Compared to surprise, however, fear involves heightened tension and a more prolonged duration, indicating greater vigilance. The compression of facial muscles is stronger with fear because this emotion prepares us to confront likely danger. *Alarm* supersedes alertness, just as *fear* supplants surprise. More specifically, there is one tell-tale way in which fear is the singular emotion being shown, plus five more ways fear gets expressed in conjunction with other core emotions:

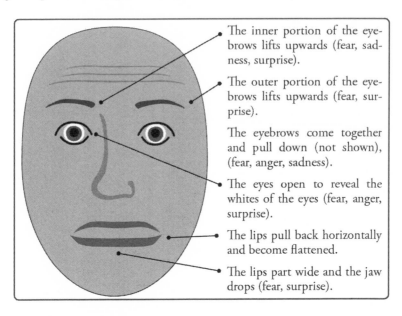

The inner portion of the eyebrows lifts upwards (fear, sadness, surprise).

The outer portion of the eyebrows lifts upwards (fear, surprise).

The eyebrows come together and pull down (not shown), (fear, anger, sadness).

The eyes open to reveal the whites of the eyes (fear, anger, surprise).

The lips pull back horizontally and become flattened.

The lips part wide and the jaw drops (fear, surprise).

From the diagram, it's obvious that fear and surprise often overlap. To distinguish between them, here are three tips for knowing when the emotion is likely to be fear, not surprise. First, look to see if both the inner and outer eyebrows are raised simultaneously. If that's true and the eyebrows are also taut and straight (rather than more gently rounded in shape), then the odds favor fear over surprise. Second, the odds again favor fear over surprise if the eyelids stay raised longer (rather than only very briefly). Third, the odds yet again favor fear over surprise if, when the mouth falls open, it's tense (rather than being relatively more relaxed).[3]

After anger and sadness, fear is the third most versatile emotion in terms of the many ways it shows on people's faces. Fear also comes in third, far behind happiness and anger, in frequency. Among the celebrities analyzed for *Famous Faces Decoded*, on average almost 10% of their expressions involve fear. For the male celebrities in this book, the average amount of fear is higher, by a small but clear margin, than is true of their female counterparts.

The Top 10 list of the celebrities who are Most Fearful features such "manly men" sports stars as Wayne Gretzky, Cam Newton, and Jackie Robinson. (Not far off this Top 10 list appear other prominent athletes like Larry Bird, Willie Mays, Jack Nicklaus, and Muhammad Ali.) Also notable here is the White House pairing of Ronald Reagan and his vice president, George H. W. Bush. In contrast, there are just two women on this list. While Marilyn Monroe's source of alarm (childhood neglect) is crystal clear, Natalie Portman's remains obscure.

Finally, there's a special case. An aspect of fear is shyness: a social anxiety that makes people avoid saying or doing what they prefer. Extreme shyness affects an estimated 15% of Americans. Shyness may be why, for instance, Jimmy Stewart needed tutoring from Margaret Sullavan, the ex-wife of his best friend, Henry Fonda. Only then could Stewart keep his gawky, halting mannerisms from inhibiting his career.

Are there disadvantages to rarely feeling fear? Yes, there are because fear can help us maintain focus and gives us a jolt of energy helpful in tackling a challenge. Usually, however, there is more upside to eluding fear. People relatively free of fear won't tend to panic, be timid, or easily intimidated. While fear might motivate us, it's also true that remaining on "battle alert" for too long can cause chronic stress, which ultimately fatigues us.

Prominent on the Top 10 list for Least Fearful are two of the bold, self-promoting Kardhashian sisters: Khloe and Kim. The other four women on this list consist of a pair of hugely successful female business leaders, Martha Stewart and Estee Lauder; the billionaire author J. K. Rowling; and, intriguingly enough, Jennifer Aniston.

If the tabloids are to be believed, Aniston has been an emotional wreck seemingly *forever*. Although she played the role of a fairly neurotic Rachel Green on *Friends* (1994–2004), in real life Aniston emerges as among this book's least fearful celebrities. That result aligns with Aniston's approach to romance, which she has described in an interview as "Love just shows up and you go, 'Oh, wow, this is going to be a hayride and a half.'"[4] A low level of fear likewise fits the actresses's admission that whereas she "used to loathe confrontation,"[5] she no longer cringes like before.

How good are people at spotting fear? At 33%, this emotion comes in just below the average for accuracy detection, which is again 34.5%. Despite the likely advantage of being aware of this emotion in others you may have to fight, detecting fear therefore appears not to be a commonly held skill. The following three photographs illustrate ways in which fear appears, and the celebrities' emotional profiles indicate how well voters did in choosing the top two emotions that distinguish these famous people.

The single strongest, stand-alone mark of fear is when the mouth pulls wide, as it does here in Natalie Portman's case. Then add the actress's wide eyes as another clue signaling fear. (Meanwhile, her upper and lower lips have curled in opposite directions, indicating plenty of disgust.) An understudy by age ten for the off-Broadway show *Ruthless!* (1992), Portman has said, "We all have phases of not feeling so great about ourselves." As I'll be discussing, Portman may, in fact, be her own worst critic.

──Voted──	──Actual──	──Rare──
happiness *happiness*	fear acceptance	satisfaction

Natalie Portman

Born Neta-Lee Hershlag, Natalie Portman has augmented her *Star Wars* appearances by winning a slew of awards for her role in *Black Swan* (2011), including an Academy Award for Best Actress. In 2015 she directed her first film, *A Tale of Love and Darkness.*

Joe DiMaggio wanted his new wife to become a quiet homemaker, but Marilyn Monroe longed for the limelight. Divorce was all but inevitable.[6] Observe Monroe filing the divorce papers, determined yet fearful, as revealed by her raised left outer eyebrow and a mouth slightly ajar.

──Voted──	──Actual──	──Rare──
sadness fear	surprise fear	anger

Marilyn Monroe

After hits like *Gentlemen Prefer Blondes* (1953), Monroe objected to being typecast and underpaid. Following a contract dispute, she appeared in the movie *Some Like It Hot* (1959), which won her a Golden Globe for Best Actress.

Is Wayne Gretzky emotionally as cold as ice? Hardly, as shown in this photo in which there's a wealth of emotions. Fear is evident in Gretzky's raised eyebrows, his wide open eyes, and a mouth stretched wide. Also evident is a smile invaded by a smirk, and lips pressed tight in anger. Captured on camera at a film festival event with his wife, the actress Janet Jones, the shy Gretzky hardly appears to be enjoying himself. Discomfort is instead the basic feeling being conveyed.

─Voted─	─Actual─	─Rare─
happiness *happiness*	fear surprise	contempt

─ Wayne Gretzky ─

Wayne Gretzky is the leading scorer in NHL history, with the most goals as well as assists ever. On retirement, he held 61 NHL records and is a five-time winner of the Lady Byng Memorial Trophy for sportsmanship and performance.

What May Cause Fear

To describe fear as akin to catching on fire deliberately invites ambiguity. Both positive and negative connotations apply. The phrase's upside is that in sports or the fine arts arena, for instance, athletes or artists "catching on fire" are red-hot and doing well. They're in the flow, the zone; they're *feeling it.* Conversely, catching on fire is in the most literal sense a disaster. Your body is burning, and the adrenaline rush you feel is due to summoning your willpower to survive. As this list of six likely causes of fear will show, the risks involved include both physical and emotional danger.

1. We face a threat of physical pain, immediate or pending.

"Growing up, I was always the small guy," Wayne Gretzky recalls, a reality that forces him to be resourceful. At age six, his jersey hangs down so low his hockey stick gets caught in its hem as he skates around the rink. At age ten, Gretzky is a four-foot, four-inch tall center the season he scores an amazing 378 goals to go along with 120 assists. Nor are the physical threats confined to hockey rinks. Aware that local parents feel their kids are being overshadowed by Gretzky's growing fame, a local baseball coach tells the youngster: "You won't live to see Christmas."

Even on turning pro in 1978, Gretzky finds the physical challenges never end. While he might be nicknamed The Great One, he's certainly not The Big One. He weighs 30 pounds less than the average NHL player. Whenever he and his Edmonton Oiler teammates have to take a strength test, Gretzky comes in dead last. To overcome those limitations, he skates to "where the puck is going to be" rather than where it is. Given the variety of ways he shows the emotion, most notably wide eyes and a mouth that stretches outward, it figures that Gretzky admits, "My whole sports life I've played in fear."[7]

2. We believe either grave physical or psychological harm is imminently possible, whether from our fellow human beings or otherwise.

Often wide-eyed, with inner eyebrows whose lift likewise indicates fear, Michael Phelps has had a nearly life-long inability to say the word "snake".[8] The back-story begins prior to Phelps's parents divorcing when he was nine years old. One day a young Phelps picks up a rock out in the yard and comes face-to-face with a hissing snake. Ever after, Phelps has suffered reoccurring nightmares involving snakes. Following an arrest for drunk driving in 2014, Phelps is now enrolled at a Phoenix-area trauma and addiction center. There, the swimmer comes to a realization: "whenever I was angry with my father or if anything about my father would come up, I'd have a dream about a snake that week."

Since his parents divorced, Phelps's interactions with his father Fred have been rare and almost always unsatisfying. Shaken by understanding the link between the nightmares and his dad, Phelps adds Fred to a list of guests welcome to visit him at the rehab clinic. Soon they're bonding (symbolically enough) over putting puzzles together. Coach Bob Bowman has always been Phelps's male mainstay. As the 2016 summer Olympics approach, Phelps suddenly has both his "dads" in his corner and feels mentally ready to become the most decorated Olympic athlete in history.

3. Psychological pain can include doubts that lead to self-loathing. Under pressure, we suffer through an internal drama.

Natalie Portman becomes a vegetarian by the age of eight, and while attending Harvard University tells *The New York Post*: "I don't care if [college] ruins my career. I'd rather be smart than a movie star." By then, Portman is already halfway through her participation in three *Star Wars* movies (1999, 2002, 2005). Of them, she says: "Everyone hated my performances" and "thought I was a terrible actress." This is no one-off instance of self-flagellation[9] from an actress whose signature expressions of fear involve her mouth pulling wide to match open-eyed looks. "I often feel insecure and don't believe in myself," Portman admits in a different media interview.

Where might Portman's "not feeling so great" about "almost every performance" of hers come from? The movie star's own words offer the best clues. That her family moved to America from Israel isn't everybody's experience in life, but seems rather benign. The same can't be said for the part of her childhood story where Portman confesses: "I have no clear memories from before I was around 12," and "I don't even remember who my friends were before I was nine."

Why might Portman's early childhood have been seemingly erased, at least within her own mind? A possible explanation emerges from Portman's reflection that as an only child, "You really learn to function as an adult." Could the stress of acting older than your age have been a factor in Portman's case? And how about the possible role of high expectations fostered early in life? Could demanding parents (perhaps her father, who's a well-published doctor) be behind Portman's admission that "Doubting yourself too much can also become like a sickness"? If so, then Portman's striving for excellence, even perfection, may explain her frequent, harsh self-scrutiny.

4. The loss of social support from others, especially those we love, can leave us feeling deeply undermined.

From an unsettled childhood, what does Marilyn Monroe remember most painfully? That would be getting relegated by her mother, Gladys, in 1935 to the Los Angeles Orphans Home in Hollywood. There, the nine-year-old girl still known as Norma Jeane Mortenson vehemently protests: "But I'm not an orphan." Monroe's second husband, Arthur Miller, notes in his autobiography, *Timebends: A Life*, Monroe's "unrelenting uncertainty."[10] The fear she expresses most clearly by raising her outer eyebrows is a force Miller ultimately can't cope with any more than she can. As with her previous marriage to Joe DiMaggio, Monroe leaves Miller, too, and at age 36 is found dead of a barbiturate overdose.

5. A loss of status or power becomes a source of embarrassment for us and sets off alarm bells.

An estimated 95 million people are watching the world's suddenly most famous motor vehicle. A white Ford Bronco is being driven by a friend of O. J. Simpson as the ex-football star sits in the back seat, leading police on a low-speed chase along the #405 freeway in Los Angeles on June 17, 1994. Less well known[11] is that the evening before the chase, Simpson stays at the house of another friend: Robert Kardashian. From there the former running back nicknamed Juice escapes before the police can arrive. Left behind is what might have been a suicide note, which Kardashian reads on live TV in an apparent bid to garner support for his friend.

"I have nothing to do with Nicole's murder," Simpson has written. Kardashian then concludes by sharing with viewers the note's final words:

"Don't feel sorry for me. I've had a great life, great friends. Please think of the real O. J. and not this lost person. Thanks for making my life special. I hope I helped yours. Peace and love. O. J."

What's changed in Simpson's life? His former wife Nicole Simpson is dead, her throat having been brutally slit. Nicole had left Juice, probably having taken up again with Marcus Allen, O. J.'s protégé, close friend, and somebody 15 years younger than himself and closer in age to Nicole. A friend of hers says Nicole's attitude was, *"You have lost me OJ. Watch me run."*[12] Now in the Bronco, the former running back has $8,000 in cash, a passport, a fake goatee, extra clothes, family photos of the children the former couple had together, and the .357 Magnum he's holding to his temple. What you can't see on TV is whether, once again, O. J.'s eyebrows are flashing upwards, as they so often do when he's feeling fear.

6. We face vague, unknown threats that endanger our future and leave us on unfamiliar, unsettled ground.

What must it feel like to be Jackie Robinson in his first MLB season in 1947? Given his many admirers, Robinson may not be the most hated man in the world, but he's certainly one of the most isolated. Film footage shows Robinson sitting alone in the Brooklyn Dodgers' dugout, eyes wide open, as he darts glances around the stadium as if alert to looming danger. By now he has already experienced plenty of abuse from bigots. First, Enos Slaughter tried to get his St. Louis Cardinals teammates to strike in protest of Robinson joining the league. Months later, Slaughter put a seven-inch gash in Robinson's leg by deliberately spiking the Dodgers' first baseman with his cleats on reaching the bag.

Where the next insult or threat will come from, Robinson never knows. His goal is to persevere with dignity. Not even all of his fellow players can be counted on. Putting down a brewing rebellion in the Dodgers' clubhouse, manager Leo Durocher curtly tells the squad (with no need to directly refer to Robinson): "I do not care if the guy is yellow or black, or if he has stripes like a fuckin' zebra. I'm the manager of this team, and I say he plays."

Four Forms of Fear

In general, the more a person's facial muscles stretch, the greater the likelihood you're witnessing somebody feeling fear. Now let's move to specifics. Like the Homeland Security Advisory System—with its color-coded terrorism threat levels from "low" (green) to "severe" (red)—what are the four forms of fear that identify various responses to experiencing duress?

Fear expressions run the gamut from someone terrified (Egads); to concerned (Worry Warting); then merely watchful (Tuned-In); and finally, to a counter-response (Hereby Resolved). Of these fearful looks, Egads is utter fright. It's fear nakedly expressed. The other three forms feature an accompanying emotion that indicates the behavior likely to ensue. With Worry Warting, expect contemplation because sadness is also present. Tuned-In suggests a search for additional information because surprise

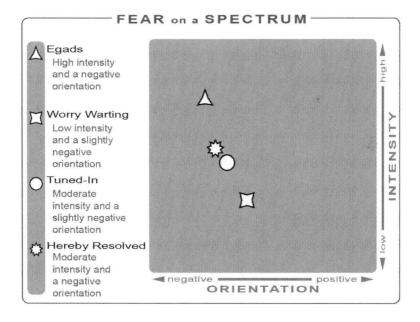

figures prominently. Last but not least, Hereby Resolved is about fighting back against fear because the added emotion is anger.

Egads

Such intense fear means you'll see people's eyes go wide and their lips pull back laterally, elongating the mouth. People who feel this degree of fear may not necessarily panic, however. Think of how animals often find value in freezing, hoping not to be noticed when a predator is lurking.

Jesse Jackson

- Egads: The open eyes and a mouth pulled ever so slightly wide suggest this look. A mouth more severely stretched would better exemplify Egads.

- Other signs of fear: The outer eyebrows are raised some, and the mouth has fallen barely open.

TOP 10

Egads

Natalie Portman
Wayne Gretzky
Andy Warhol
Jane Fonda
Adele
Caitlyn Jenner
Billy Graham
Diana Ross
Joni Mitchell
Jesse Jackson

Jesse Jackson has often had an uneasy time of it in life. Experiences that have shaped him include: getting taunted by other kids regarding his out-of-wedlock birth; growing up under Jim Crow segregation laws in Greenville, South Carolina; and (perhaps) having Martin Luther King Jr. die in his arms (a claim disputed by King's other aides). "When we change the race problem into a class fight between the haves and the have-

190

nots, then we are going to have a new ball game," Jackson observed in 1969, as he became King's heir apparent. Jackson's Rainbow Coalition solidified his stature thanks to respectable vote totals in running for president in 1984 and 1988. On the other hand, moments like calling New York City "Hymietown" and criticizing Barack Obama for "acting like he's white" have dented Jackson's stature.

Intense fear cuts through the clutter like nothing else, and the anticipation of pain makes feeling fear worse. Among those on the Top 10 list for Egads is Jane Fonda.[13] Her accomplishments range from award-winning movie roles to a series of best-selling exercise videos. Alongside those accomplishments, though, is a string of marriages to domineering men that has caused Fonda to wonder, "How was it that a seemingly strong woman could so thoroughly and repeatedly lose herself?" Could the answer be found in Fonda's relationship with her father, Henry Fonda? "I would try to be perfect" Jane has written of her dad, who Katherine Hepburn described as "cold, cold, cold," after working with father and daughter to film *On Golden Pond* (1981).

Worry Warting

The inner eyebrows shoot upwards and simultaneously knit together, creating vertical wrinkles that form a crease. People prone to this look may fret without reducing or eliminating the threat that caused it. These people may also be more susceptible than others to what is known in behavioral economics as *loss aversion*: a focus on potential losses rather than gains whenever a change occurs.

George H. W. Bush

- Worry Warting: Fear and sadness are especially evident from these deep forehead wrinkles, the result of eyebrows pinched together and an inwardly raised left eyebrow.

- Other emoting: While the ever-so-slightly stretched mouth shows another version of fear, the puckered chin adds a note of sadness.

TOP 10

Worry Warting

George H. W. Bush
Humphrey Bogart
Yogi Berra
Jay-Z
Marlon Brando
Cary Grant
Jackie Robinson
Clint Eastwood
Ronald Reagan
George W. Bush

Pressed by a friend to articulate the overarching purpose of his prospective presidency in 1987, George H. W. Bush responded in exasperation: "Oh, the vision thing." More of a pragmatic caretaker by nature than a fierce partisan, Bush once said, "I have opinions of my own, strong opinions, but I don't always agree with them." Credit that self-effacing hesitancy to the influence of Bush's patrician mother, who liked to remind him that nobody wanted to hear from the *Great I Am*.[14] Pulling together a coalition to fight the Iraq War was quintessential Bush. His childhood nickname was *Have-Half*, due to his preference for building social ties by splitting any candy or other treats evenly with friends.

The Top 10 list for Worry Warting is at times a matter of one-degree-of-separation from George H. W. Bush. Both his son George and the president he served under (Ronald Reagan) join him here. This entirely-male list showcases many contemplative, even brooding types. Outside of politics, note the inclusion of a pair of athletes from baseball: a sport that gives you plenty of time to think.

Tuned-In

In this form, people's eyebrows lift and their eyes go wide. Their lips also pull back horizontally. Safety is first on almost everyone's intuitive checklist, a frame of mind typified by the habit of looking both ways before one crosses the street. People who frequently show a Tuned-In expression honor the human tendency to often doubt what's new and unfamiliar, and accordingly remain hyper-alert to danger as they make their way forward in life.

Ingrid Bergman

■ Tuned-In: The signs in place consist of the raised outer eyebrows; plus the right eye, in particular, being fairly wide open. What would suit Tuned-In perfectly would be a mouth pulled much wider and with more force.

> TOP 10
>
> ## Tuned-In
>
> Wayne Gretzky
> Bill Cosby
> Edward R. Murrow
> Marilyn Monroe
> Jesse Jackson
> Frank Sinatra
> Larry Ellison
> Jimmy Stewart
> Little Richard
> Natalie Portman

■ Other emoting: Taken together, the set lips and the slight tension under the eyelids suggests a bit of anger.

These days Ingrid Bergman's scandal seems quaint. The married heroine of movies like *Notorious* (1946) was denounced on the floor of the U.S. Senate in 1950 for bearing a child out of wedlock with Italian film director Roberto Rossellini. Why the romantic spark? Bergman admired Rossellini's daring work at a time when both her marriage to a dentist and the roles she was being offered in Hollywood felt stifling. Described by producer David O. Selznick as "the most completely conscientious actress" he ever had the pleasure to work with, Bergman could be wary but not craven. By 1950, she had already played a nun and a virgin saint on screen, building an image strong enough to keep the public rooting for her despite the scandal.

In the Top 10 list for Tuned-In appears a new name that may best give you the spirit of this look: Larry Ellison. He's a two-time college dropout who, in getting ahead, saw threats to his success lurking everywhere. At least once, a sign of the animosity the rapacious, ever-on-guard Ellison has spurred by trash-talking about competitors was *literally* a sign. A business rival of Ellison's had a "Caution Dinosaur Crossing" street sign installed near the offices of Ellison's company, Oracle, during the 1990s, invoking Silicon Valley's most dreaded put-down: you're obsolete.[15]

Hereby Resolved

As striking as any mix of emotions is fear that incorporates anger. The fear part involves the lips pulling wide. The anger part can get expressed with firm lips, tightened lower eyelids, or even both of those expressions at the same time. The resulting look indicates the willingness to handle a threat. People who show this form of fear will most likely react to danger as if it's a speed bump. They might be slowed down, but definitely won't be kept from moving ahead. If any-

Tom Brady

thing, they may even relish the excitement of a risky situation.

Hereby Resolved

Douglas MacArthur
Eminem
John Bonham
Ronald Reagan
Leonardo DiCaprio
Angelina Jolie
Khloe Kardashian
Sandra Bullock
Robert Redford
Kanye West

■ Hereby Resolved: On display is a mouth pulled wide in fear, plus a lower lip tight with anger. The hard-eyed glare also reveals anger.

■ Other emoting: Other indications of fear are the raised outer eyebrows wrinkling the forehead. As to more anger, note the raised chin.

"Let's go! Let's show some fight! Let's play harder! Harder! Tougher! Everything!" That's what Tom Brady was yelling on the sidelines to his teammates when they were down 28-3 in Super Bowl 51.[16] Never had the 39-year-old Brady taken so many line-of-scrimmage snaps in a game (99) as he did against the Atlanta Falcons. Overcoming the biggest deficit in Super Bowl history on the way to his fifth championship ring, Brady didn't choke. Instead, when cornered, he fought off the threat of losing with incredible composure.

Among the Top 10 list for Hereby Resolved, let's focus on two examples of grit and fortitude. In reviewing the movie *Gravity*, a reporter for *The New York Times* calls Sandra Bullock "arguably Hollywood's gutsiest A-list actress."[17] Similarly, what does Peggy Noonan believe was Ronald Reagan's defining characteristic? Courage. While trailing Gerald Ford for the 1976 Republican nomination, Reagan tells his staff: "I don't care if I lose every damn primary" prior to taking the fight with Ford to the party's convention. Noonan remembers that moment as confirming Reagan's "warmly ruthless" nature.[18]

Applications in Your Life

In your own life, when might you see these four forms of fear? How might you best react to them, given what causes people to feel fear?

Egads: Management consultants showing this look may believe your company is doomed. Greenhorn sales people expressing themselves in this way aren't likely to persevere. Conflict-avoidant managers will en-counter even more problems if their staff notices them feeling insecure along these lines. Marriage counsel-

ors may have this look in facing a couple they realize should have sought help long ago, before the couple's problems became embedded.

People showing Egads come the closest to being entirely gripped by fear. Pressure combined with uncertainty can, in the extreme, leave people aghast, which is why nobody wants to see such fear on a colleague or team member's face. An Egads look carries the weight of an existential threat.

Among the most likely causes triggering this response in others is a struggle for survival against aggressors, or else a seemingly irreparable loss of status and power. How best to respond? Intense fear invites flight to evade danger. So start by restoring a sense of safety through unity. Move the conversation gently from what's understood and agreed on, to what-if scenarios for limiting the threat. If people caught in the web of Egads defensively flinch at the prospect of exploring solutions, help them understand that the story they're telling themselves may be bleaker than reality. Where might they be imagining problems that don't really exist? Dilute their fear with plausible hope, reducing their sense of vulnerability with a promise that they will get the support they need.

Worry Warting: Perfectionists often display this look. They might be ideal additions to a staff while being *exactly* who many of us don't want for a boss, knowing that micro-managing will ensue. Another possible dichotomy concerns nervous financial advisors, who may save you from your lack of planning by crisply summarizing

Worry Warting

Pensive
Reluctant
Apprehensive
Timid
Hesitant

your options or, unfortunately, drown you with too many details. In your personal life, you might notice this look from people struggling to get out of their comfort zone and make new friends. In parenting, adults with a Worry Warting tendency may find it hard to bestow care without being seen by their kids as smothering.

People exhibiting this expression add sadness to fear and will tend to use memories of adversity and previous disappointments as benchmarks in navigating an uncertain future. Fretful by nature, they will probably need to be coaxed into overcoming concerns that leave them hesitant to address problems.

What's likely to trigger Worry Warting involves not only doubts that border on self-dismissal, but also a foreboding concern that a stable future is in jeopardy. People prone to this form of emoting can best be reassured by a pair of approaches. One is through visualizations: steer them toward creating images in their own heads that demonstrate their ability to re-solve issues. The other approach involves creating comfort. Offer advice for how these people can outline a decision-making process they can rely on as a familiar tool in handling each new crisis over time.

Tuned-In: An excellent focus group moderator will be the epitome of Tuned-In. A little fear of coming up empty-handed in the search for insights can constructively mix with an aptitude for staying alert.

Attentive private-equity investors know that while many factors are quantifiable, gauging the honesty, resiliency, and receptivity to advice of a start-up company's leadership team is a harder read. A first date means watching for warning signs, including overly-eager availability.

People who exhibit the Tuned-In look will be watchful and wary, mixing surprise with fear. The causes most likely to trigger this reaction include either having to deal with the aggressive behavior of others, or a sudden loss of social support. Both of those triggers reflect ever-shifting social alliances that undercut a desire for stability and assurance.

How best to respond to people who may be so vigilant and on-edge that they may be slow to cooperate with others, or suffer from paralysis-by-analysis? Don't let them abandon faith in social ties. Guide them toward opportunities to collaborate easily, and warn them against prejudicing the outcome with excessive doubts. The way forward could be to encourage Tuned-In types to participate in group efforts, which will eliminate the risk of a lone individual letting them down.

Hereby Resolved: Expect this look from people who transform fear into fuel for getting things done. Many an all-star athlete reveals this expression and will be a stalwart player if coached correctly. At an advertising agency, seeing this look on a client's face could signal their willingness to sign-off on innovative, breakthrough

concepts. At a neighborhood watch meeting, the guest instructor giving the community safety advice may suggest this look is a home-owner's best bet for intimidating an intruder.

People given to a Hereby Resolved display blend anger with fear. Chances are they're going to be pro-active in resolving their anxiety, whether it's been caused by the threat of physical pain or is due to their fighting to recover from a perceived loss of power and status. Being both motivated and stoical, these people could well qualify as *least* in need of help when struck by fear. In response to risk, they will tend to show courage and, with any luck, will be magnanimous in proving their prowess.

Summary

It's time to retire the pejorative notion that feeling fear means you're a "spineless wimp." The emotion's impact isn't so certain. Facing a threat can either arm or disarm people, depending on however they handle the challenge. The prospect of pain causes some people to tackle a situation, whereas others avoid even acknowledging discomfort. Social support can make a difference as to which course of action people follow.

An affirmative example of fear spurring on greatness is the story of Muhammad Ali, the former heavy-weight boxing champion of the world. For Ali, *running scared* got transformed into dancing around the ring. What did Ali dread?[19] In the summer of 1955, his dad showed him photographs of Emmett Till's mutilated corpse. That African-American teenager from Chicago had been lynched after supposedly whistling at a white woman in a grocery store while visiting cousins in Mississippi. Ali would later recall lying "awake scared, thinking about somebody getting cut up or being lynched." Soon a white policeman coaching at a nearby gym turned Ali's thoughts to boxing instead. From that suggestion, Ali's dread was eclipsed by a new reality: Ali dominating his chosen profession in a way that made "Black Power" awe-inspiring to watch.

Reactive Emotions Quiz
(in answering, focus on each emotion's four forms and not the personalities involved)

1. Look for someone secure yet wary. Can you spot which celebrity here best exhibits the **Tolerance** form of surprise?

Woody Allen

Alfred Hitchcock

Jackie Kennedy Onassis

2. Being determined despite inner doubts characterizes the **Hereby Resolved** form of fear. Who shows that look most faithfully?

Ronald Reagan

Cher

Tiger Woods

3. **Worry Warting** is a potent mixture of sadness and fear. Who has this form down pat?

Marlon Brando

Robert De Niro

Meryl Streep

Answers

The first box says "1. Surprise"

1. Surprise
Wow
Ugh
Shock & Awe
Tolerance

The signs for **Tolerance** are surprise (eyebrows raised) along with happiness (a satisfaction or acceptance level smile). Hitchcock is a director who didn't like somebody else's camera turned on him. So while his eyebrows are up, there's no smile and, instead, anger emerges given his piercing eyes, firm lips, and upraised chin. In Allen's case, the raised eyebrows indicate fear more than surprise because they're more taut than rounded. Moreover, Allen's smile is awfully slight and there are hints of sadness: skin pulled up against the left eye and a downward gaze. He's out, too. The best fit here is Onassis, with eyes wide and alert, raised outer eyebrows, and a slight but definite smile.

2. Fear
Egads
Worry Warting
Tuned-In
Hereby Resolved

Hereby Resolved involves a blend of mouth-pulled-wide fear, and one of two signs of anger: lips firmly pressed together or eyes narrowed with tight lower eyelids. Cher shows anger due to lips firmly pressed together, but the fear element is weak. While her eyes are wide and alert, a stretched mouth isn't shown. Reagan's resolute expression has the necessary anger; his lips are firmly pressed and his chin is pushed upwards. But his mouth is barely stretched, despite a hint of fear in the raised eyebrows. Woods is the best choice. Fear is clearly present in his stretched mouth and there's the requisite anger given the fiercely narrowed eyes.

3. Fear
Egads
Worry Warting
Tuned-In
Hereby Resolved

Worry Warting is a combination of fear and sadness. The inner eyebrows rise, creating forehead wrinkles, and the eyebrows pull together to form a vertical crease between them. Therefore, the ideal option here isn't Streep. Only her *outer* eyebrows are up, and sadness isn't evident. Her eyebrows aren't pinched together, nor are the inner eyebrows raised. Instead, she's showing happiness (an acceptance level smile) and a trace of anger (her pressed lips). The best choice could be a tie between DeNiro and Brando. Both have the between-the-eyebrows wrinkle. But DeNiro's eyebrows are raised, whereas Brando's are pushed down severely, supporting sadness, so Brando deserves the nod.

Epilogue

On Lying

Can You Spot Deceit?

In the comedy *Liar, Liar* (1997), Jim Carrey stars as a self-aggrandizing, dishonest Los Angeles lawyer. His ashamed son asks, as a birthday wish, that his dad would stop lying for a day. Instantly, that wish comes true and the lawyer begins blurting out all sorts of offensive, painful truths certain to destroy both his career and private life.

In reality as opposed to a movie, it's estimated that 42% of people tell up to five lies a day and 11% of us over five lies daily.[1] Those are just the lies known to us, the lies we tell *others*. What about the lies we're only dimly, half-aware of telling *ourselves*?[2] (Examples might range from "What's the harm of taking home some of my company's office supplies?" to "My spouse starts all the fights.") If those private lies—sometimes the biggest lies—are included, the actual amount of lying could be much higher. After all, people are like a fun house of mirrors. We embody our own contradictions. We're not bred to be truth machines because our top priorities in life are to attract allies (survival) and to feel good about ourselves (pleasure).[3]

As Carrey's *Liar, Liar* predicament illustrates, lying isn't always bad any more so than the "negative" emotions covered in *Famous Faces Decoded* are always bad. Polite lies can douse the flames of what could otherwise be a lot of contentious encounters with people. Overall, though, as little as 7% of the lies we tell are considered to be altruistic. In comparison, 44% of them are meant to promote ourselves and another 34% are meant to protect us. (The other 13% of our lying involves ambiguous motives, maliciousness, or even pathological dishonesty.[4])

From the other perspective, being the deceived party rarely, if ever feels good—*especially* if the stakes are high. Many lies involve important information that's been hidden or diverted away from us. Remember Oprah Winfrey's outrage on finding out that one author she was championing, James Frey, had made up much of his memoir? As we try to size up others, knowing whether we're dealing with a "liar" or not is of vital interest to us. The number one question I get asked after a speech has long been: does knowing facial coding mean you can "tell when people are lying?"

If only it were that simple.

There is no single facial muscle movement or signature expression that betrays a lie. If there were, believe me, somebody would have "bottled it" by now. Law enforcement officers, oversight committees, and suspicious spouses would all have an easier time confirming or disproving their doubts than is actually the case. That said, some clues exist.

Possible Tells

You might think the surest way to spot lying is to look for fear. You're only partially correct. Habitual liars or simply very good liars may not show any fear, or show it so subtly you won't notice. In this camp are liars who believe their own lies *are* the truth, making those instances among the hardest ones to detect.

204

Then again, there's Richard Nixon—a terrible liar. In 1977, an often fearful Nixon sat down with David Frost for a series of interviews that inevitably focused on the Watergate scandal. The footage reveals Nixon's eyelids nervously fluttering, his voice quavering at times, and plenty of faltering word choices. But it's how often and strongly Nixon's outer eyebrows shoot up, and how much his mouth pulls wide as he insists there wasn't a cover-up, that should draw your attention. Nixon's face is spontaneously *leaking* the truth. The guy is profoundly uncomfortable with many of the assertions he's making in giving his version of the scandal, including most famously: "When the President does it, that means that it's not illegal."

Despite Nixon's example, more than fear should be on your radar screen in trying to spot a liar. Let's cover the other emotions, starting with anger. Self-righteous indignation is a technique often resorted to by people engaged in lying, as in *how dare you impugn my integrity.*

Lance Armstrong

When interviewed at length by Oprah Winfrey in 2013, a combative Lance Armstrong showed almost no fear but often two of anger's four forms: Thunderstorm and Battle Ready. Yes, the seven-time Tour de France cycling champion was no longer maintaining that he had "never doped." Despite his new-found honesty, however, Armstrong wasn't backing down much during the interview. He remained angry and defiant in answering Winfrey's questions, painting himself as unfairly persecuted in a sport awash with fellow cheaters and hypocritical reformers pursuing their own agendas.

Alongside fear and anger, another emotion sometimes implicated in lying is sadness. Typically in these cases, the liars are disappointed in themselves for engaging in deception. In 1960, an American U-2 spy plane was shot down over the Soviet Union. President Dwight Eisenhower's administration initially denied having engaged in espionage, calling the CIA plane a NASA aircraft and releasing a photograph of a U-2 plane repainted in NASA's colors. But when the Russians let it be known that they had the pilot, Gary Powers, in captivity, Eisenhower then belatedly gave a face-saving, tell-*some* (not all) press conference. A mixture of hesitant words and sadness-laden signals followed, with Eisenhower saying America had now "uh" (a long pause, head down, and a wince) "publicly admitted" (eyes lowering) "that the U-2 belonged to us and was on a reconnaissance mission" (head drooping again). Then the anguish Eisenhower felt in private[5] about having lied became obvious for all to see.

Contempt (and occasionally disgust) can likewise figure into a lie. When you don't respect yourself for lying or, instead, don't respect who you're lying to, contempt may make an appearance. Here again, Eisenhower serves as an example because he also smirked during the passage just cited. Given that sadness was accompanying a sign of contempt, odds are good that a dejected Eisenhower also disrespected *himself* for lying.

In contrast, consider the case of Bernie Madoff. Arrested in 2008 for bilking investors like Steven Spielberg, Sandy Koufax, and Zsa Zsa Gabor out of a combined $65 billion—based on promising them steady, eye-popping returns that defied reason—Madoff is likely an example of people who easily lie to others they denigrate as gullible.

What might merit that conclusion? Two details are noteworthy in regards to Madoff's emoting. First, he's prone to combining a smirk with a smile. In those cases, one side of the upper lip rises more quickly, reaches higher, and comes down more slowly than the other, smiling lip corner. That smile-and-smirk combination is often the mark of relishing one's scorn of others. Second, when not showing that combination, Madoff usually has a poker face. There's little to no emotion shown, worrisome in itself because our emotions most reliably turn on *when* we *care about others*, including how they feel about us.

The good news about lie detection is that the so-called negative emotions I've just discussed are hard for most people to fake.[6] The bad news is that anger aside, the other "negative" emotions of fear, sadness, contempt, and disgust don't occur frequently. Moreover, those five emotions, including anger, often get *squelched* in social settings. That verb refers to when people try to suppress a reaction they suspect they're showing, or else quickly deploy a social smile to either cover up a negative feeling or soften a snide comment.

What's the next best fallback if spotting "negative" emotions doesn't help catch a liar? Once again, don't rely on words. Always remember the Russian leader Joseph Stalin's cynical observation: A "diplomat's words must have no relations to actions.... Sincere diplomacy is no more possible than dry water or iron wood."

A better approach to lie detection is to broaden your focus to include smiles, most notably satisfaction level "social smiles." Those polite smiles may mask true feelings. Throw a smile on your face and you've made happiness into a commodity. The always-smiling, whether feeling happy or not character of Smiler in *The Emoji Movie* (2017) is a case in point. Yes, smiles can defuse anger and relieve sadness—and constructively so. Smiles may, however, also become a tool for manipulation and outright deception.

To explore smiles (meant to deceive others) more deeply, we need to consider terms like *onset* and *offset* as well as *duration*.[7] As my sidebar chart on the next page illustrates, the usual smile—and indeed any natural expression—should have timing that resembles a wave hitting the shore. Look for the expression to rise, have a peak, then break and dissipate. As a cheat sheet to help you spot a lie or merely somebody faking a feeling of happiness, here are some tips for when smiles are part of the action.

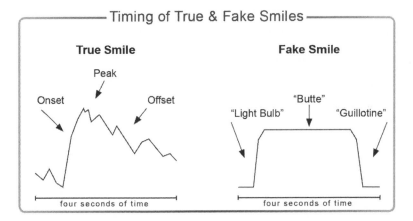

Oddly Timed Smiles: With inauthentic emoting, it's hard to get the timing right. In this pair of diagrams, entitled the Timing of True & Fake Smiles, notice the rhythm of the three separate stages of an expression (which often unfold within a four-second duration or less):

- The onset stage of a true smile can instead become the launch pad for an abrupt fake smile—namely, a fake *Light Bulb Smile*. This kind of smile turns on with unnatural speed and brightness. Example: In the 2012 vice presidential debate, a folksy Joe Biden offered up so many sudden, flashing grins that pundits and viewers alike doubted their veracity. Then four years later, a smiling Biden was asked by a reporter (after meeting with the new Vice President:) "Are you smiling right now because you genuinely like Mike Pence?" Biden's reply, "No, I'm not," reinforced the idea that not all of Biden's quick-to-flash grins are genuine.[8]

- The peak stage of a true smile can instead become a bulldozed mountaintop that signals a fake smile. A fake *Butte Smile* forgoes a peak of greatest intensity in favor of a flat-topped, overly long smile. Example: I've called Mitt Romney the Energizer Bunny of Social Smiles because his smooth, even unctuous smiles tend to go on *and on*, well past the more natural outer limit of one to two seconds of sustained intensity.

- The offset stage of a true smile can instead become the all-too-sudden closing act of a fake smile—namely, a fake *Guillotine Smile* that's here, then gone, rather than naturally fading away. This type of fake smile takes its name from the way a guillotine blade makes a rapid descent. Example: When Rachel Dolezal, the NAACP's Spokane, Washington chapter president, was exposed as actually being white in June of 2015, she was interviewed by Matt Lauer. During the segment, her every smile quickly ebbed in response to yet another probing question.[9]

Directly Contradicted Smiles: A second way to look for suspect smiles is when a display of happiness is contradicted by its opposite emotion, namely, sadness. During an *Embarrassed Smile*, people's smiles intensify at *exactly* the same time that their heads pitch down and tilt one way or the other in a sign of slumping sadness. Example: A very modest version of this look came during Ronald Reagan's Oval Office address on the Iran-Contra Affair. Just after a slightly smiling Reagan hid behind the excuse that he hadn't been kept "fully informed" about the goings-on within his own administration, he broke eye contact with the camera, looking sheepishly down at his notes.[10]

Incongruous Smiles: Finally, there are three types of incongruous smiles that lack consistency:

- The classic, words-based version of incongruity is the *Say-Feel Gap Smile*. In these cases, a sign of potential lying is that what the person is saying doesn't fit the emoting. You might hear "I'm so relieved," but you're seeing fear or sadness linger on the person's face. Example: former Ohio governor John Kasich may be as honest as any politician, but often times while Kasich's message is hopeful, his dour, "barbed-wire" smiles suggest his dreams for America will be hard to achieve.

- The physical version of incongruity is the *Lopsided Smile*. In these cases, the smile will be uneven across the face. These are smiles that give the

Lopsided Smile

appearance of having been *willed* onto the face, as a self-conscious display that everything is supposedly fine with the speaker. Example: Many a carved pumpkin ends up with a crooked smile. Here, notice how the smile is slightly higher on the right side.

- Most intriguing may be the subtle, psychological version of incongruity[11] that could be called the *Cookie Jar Smile*. These people have been caught with their hands in a cookie jar, so to speak, but they're so pleased with themselves that you just know they'll be back for more. Example: As the Whitewater investigation morphed into a probe of his affair with Monica Lewinsky, Bill Clinton found himself deposed under oath. Asked if it's true that "there is no sexual relationship" between Lewinsky and himself, Clinton gives a slight smile and a little tug on his lower lip, a small sign of defiance, in replying that his answer "depends on what your definition of 'is' is."

Caution in Drawing Conclusions about People

Facial coding provides a strong, viable opportunity to gauge others through the actions evident on their faces, and on-going usage will make the tool that much sharper in your own hands. That said, remember that facial coding can tell you what somebody is *feeling* at a specific moment in time, but not what they're *thinking*. So it's a tool to be utilized carefully. Anyone who promises you can "speed read" others, quickly profiling them, is being entirely too facile. Yes, you can use facial coding to gauge somebody's emotions in the moment and, *over time,* look for patterns. But context matters, with multiple and seemingly contradictory impulses and emotions frequently involved.

To quote the Danish philosopher Soren Kirkegaard: "Out of the twisted timber of humanity, no straight thing was ever made." People are complicated, so take account of the "knots" in the wood and don't rush to judgment. Nobody needs a return to the 19th and early 20th century physiognomy movement,[12] when an emphasis on *fixed* facial *features* (like hooked noses) aided and abetted racism.

In contrast, facial coding is at its heart about flexibility, humanity, and seeking better, sustained rapport with others in your professional and personal life. As I have shown in *Famous Faces Decoded*, even with happiness, the simplest of the emotions in terms of its display, variety exists along a continuum regarding the strength of a smile and the four forms of expression involved. There is no single template per emotion but, rather, diverse ways in which facial coding's seven core emotions get shown, with often two or more emotions being signaled by a look.

Furthermore, there are many instances involving the 173 celebrities in this book where emotionally complex people may often show two contradictory emotions at the same time. Such people aren't easily classified, nor should they be. To call them "two-faced" (liars), for instance, would be an injustice.

At times, someone's most characteristic emotions may land in opposing places on the dimensions of approach versus avoidance and dominant versus submissive. Notice how in John McEnroe's case, for instance, feeling disgust means he's pulling away at the same time that he longs to be hugged, given the sadness he often also feels. Those two emotions fall in opposite quadrants, creating an inevitable tension. Ellen DeGeneres,

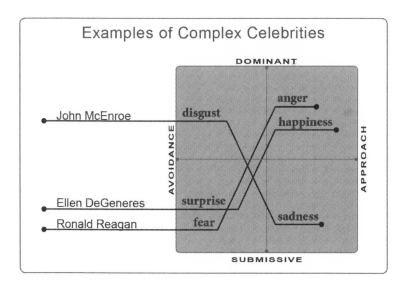

in turn, is sparklingly happy yet remains alert to whatever may change quickly around her, given her propensity for surprise. Finally, in terms of Ronald Reagan's expressions, his two most characteristic emotions were fear and anger. While Reagan "came on strong," exhibiting lots of anger, he might well have been have been seeking to "control the narrative," either in spite of or due to an underlying sense of insecurity that simultaneously caused him to feel fear.

Recognizing and relating well to individuals with complex emotions stands in contrast to resorting to terms like "hot head," "sad sack," and "chicken". Those epithets are one-dimensional, pejorative ways of describing people who tend to feel anger, sadness, and fear, respectively, and need to be replaced with a richer, more nuanced, and empathetic approach. My use of four forms per emotion is, by comparison, meant to give you, my reader, an easy handle by which to grasp the emotional nuances involved, without devolving into stereotypes.

In *Famous Faces Decoded* I've tried to take you through the journey I started two decades ago. Sure, I knew terms like "happiness" or "anger (management)." Up until that point in my life, however, I hadn't realized that emotions could be examined systematically or that a visual playbook existed for spotting them in others.

People can be fascinating or frustrating, depending on circumstance. What remains consistent is that by using emotional intelligence to navigate situations in life, we'll benefit from a feedback loop. Only then can we get out of our own heads and into the hearts of others. Thanks to facial coding, a means exists to understand what people are feeling and how they're responding to us. Even better, with practice that feedback loop can operate spontaneously, right in the moment, when it's not too late to adjust our behavior and achieve a better outcome.

There's a wealth of great quotes that could be relevant to applying the learnings available in this book. Henry James's adage, "Never say you know the last word about any human heart," comes to mind. So does Yogi Berra saying, "You can observe a lot by just watching." But I decided to open *Famous Faces Decoded* by invoking a trio of less familiar quotes by Oscar Wilde, George Orwell, and Erica Jong instead.

People's tendency to see without seeing informs Wilde's remark. His reference to *appearances* isn't an endorsement of physiognomy or merely a nod to matters like clothing style and grooming. After all, Wilde's only novel deals with how our recurring experiences in life both inform and alter our feelings. Orwell's quote gets more specific, pointing out how the sum of our previous experiences can leave their imprint on our faces due to muscle memory.

Finally, Jong echoes James's adage by noting how poorly we comprehend others, no matter how famous. Hardly anything is truly known in life. Facial coding serves to shed some light, as dim as that or any light may be, given the difficult and on-going goal of understanding people—ourselves included.

Facial Coding Explained

The face is where humans best reflect and communicate their emotions. While the correlation of expressions-to-emotions isn't, of course, beyond doubt, in an imperfect world facial coding offers a viable means to readily assess the feelings of others. Supporting explanations and credentials follow.

Darwin's Realizations:

The facial coding tool originated with Charles Darwin, who first noted in his travels on The Beagle that facial expressions may be evolved behaviors meant to express emotion.

1. Universal: Even a person born blind has the same expressions. These signals are "hard-wired" into the brain.

2. Spontaneous: The face is the only place in the body where muscles either attach to a bone and tissue or tissue only, enabling quicker, real-time reflexes shaped by pulses from the brain. (Other muscles in the body connect to two bones.)

3. Abundant: People have more facial muscles than any other species.

Ekman's Refinement:

- Along with colleague Wally Freisen, Dr. Paul Ekman codified the Facial Action Coding System (FACS) from 1965-1978, with refinements added in 2002.

- FACS is based on over 40 facial muscles and 23 movements that correspond to seven core emotions.

- Ekman was named one of *Time* magazine's 100 Most Influential People in 2009, and is ranked as the 16th Most Influential Psychologist of the 21st Century by Scientific Psychology.

16. Paul Ekman | Social Psychology, Biological Psychology

"Darwin was more than just a close and careful observer, he was an explainer. For each and every expression, Darwin asks and answers the question of why a particular movement occurs with a particular emotion."

—Paul Ekman on Charles Darwin

Facial Coding in the Mainstream

"The face is an enormously rich source of information about emotions."
—Malcolm Gladwell, *Blink*

"We make snap judgments about personality from people's faces and other tells in fractions of a second, usually showing remarkable consensus in judgment."
—Matthew Hertenstein, *The Tell*

"By the 1980s, psychologists had largely accepted as a 'fundamental axiom of behavioral science' the link between faces and emotions. Emotion therefore explains facial behavior, and facial behavior is an objective index of emotion."

WHEELS

The New York Times

Soon, Your Car May Be Able to Read Your Expressions

By JOHN R. QUAIN   APRIL 6, 2017

Facial Coding Goes Mainstream

From Silicon Valley to China, the automation of facial coding is well under way. Especially as linked to AI (artificial intelligence), the many uses of facial coding are likely to explode in the years ahead – with its application to motor vehicles but one of many ways that facial coding will enter people's lives. It's no wonder *The Economist* has referred to an emerging "facial-industrial complex" that will transform both the business world and society at large.

—Russell & Fernandez-Dols, *The Psychology of Facial Expressions*

PERSPECTIVES
on
Psychological
Science

(Vol. 1, 2016)

The Science of Facial Coding

"In a survey of 246 quantitative research experts on emotion, 88% agree that there are universal emotions, and 80% agreed that there are universal facial signals for emotions."

- Dr. Paul Ekman

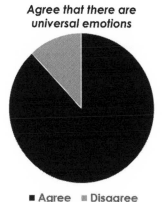

Agree that there are universal emotions

■ Agree ▦ Disagree

Agree that there are universal facial expressions

■ Agree ▦ Disagree

There are 23 expressions that correspond to seven emotions:

Two Decades of Facial Coding in Business

Dan Hill's company, Sensory Logic, has received seven U.S. patents related to facial coding including:

- Method and Report Assessing Consumer Reaction to a Stimulus by Matching Eye Position with Facial Coding

- Method of Assessing People's Self-Presentation and Actions to Evaluate Personality Type, Behavioral Tendencies, Credibility, Motivations and Other Insights Through Facial Muscle Activity and Expressions

 peg

Facial Action Coding System Final Test

Dan Hill

Your scores on the FACS Final Test show you have

PASSED

this test of skill in scoring facial actions.

From the authors of FACS
Paul Ekman, Wallace V. Friesen, Joseph C. Hager

Catalog of Facial Expressions

About one-third of the facial muscle movements that reveal people's emotional reactions occur in the upper face: they involve the eyes, eyebrows and nose. The other two-thirds occur in the lower face: they involve the cheeks, mouth, chin and jaw.

Upper Face

Eyebrows

The inner part of one or both eyebrows lifts upwards, often creating forehead wrinkles.
(fear, sadness, surprise)

Eyebrows

The outer part of one or both eyebrows lifts upwards, often creating forehead wrinkles.
(fear, surprise)

Eyebrows

The eyebrows come together and pull down, creating a vertical crease between the eyebrows.

(anger, fear, sadness)

Eyes

The eyes go wide as the upper eyelids rise.

(anger, fear, surprise)

Eyes

Activity around the eyes almost suggests joy. But instead of a twinkle appearing, with sadness the eyes often lose focus.

(sadness)

Eyes

For about half a second, both eyes close. Due to timing and the use of photos (meaning one doesn't know if fatigue instead of sadness may be the cause), this expression isn't part of my book's data.

(sadness)

Eyes

The eyes narrow and the lower eyelids tighten and rise, narrowing the eyes.

(anger)

The nose wrinkles and turns up, and the nostrils may flare.

(disgust)

Lower Face

Cheeks & Mouth

The upper lip curls, the nostrils flare, and the skin pouches alongside the nose.

(anger, contempt, disgust)

Cheeks

The furrows that angle down and away from the nose nostrils deepen and pull upwards, creating an often very subtle wince. The upper lip simultaneously pulls upward and slightly sideways.

(sadness)

Eyes, Cheeks & Mouth

The highest level of happiness is joy, which can't be faked. When you're exuberantly happy, the muscle around the eyes constricts, causing not only twinkling eyes but also the skin around the eyes to bag, wrinkle, and change their shape. Another change is that crow's feet often emerge at the outer corner of the eyes. All of this activity is accompanied by a smile and usually a pronounced lifting of the cheeks.

(happiness - joy)

Cheeks & Mouth

The second highest level of happiness is pleasure. In this case, there's no gleam in the eye but there's still a big (often toothy) grin that lifts the cheeks until they touch or almost touch the eye sockets.

(happiness - pleasure)

Cheeks & Mouth

The third level of happiness is satisfaction. These are either subdued, genuine smiles or social smiles: instances where people may not feel very happy but manage a smile when told to say "Cheese". With these smiles, the cheeks will only rise slightly. The satisfaction version of happiness requires looking for how the corners of the mouth lift just enough to clearly signal a smile.

(happiness - satisfaction)

Mouth

The lowest level of happiness is acceptance. While the cheeks barely move, if at all, one or both corners of the mouth rise ever so slightly. An acceptance-level smile still signals happiness, but of the grimmest sort.

(happiness - acceptance)

Mouth

A lip corner will tighten and often rise a little, pulling the skin slightly inward while also narrowing that lip corner. A wrinkle or bulge will form at that same lip corner and may create a small dimple or cavity in the cheek.

(contempt)

―――――――――― **Mouth** ――――――――――

The corners of the mouth sag.
(disgust, sadness)

―――――――――― **Mouth** ――――――――――

The lower lip pulls down and, in stretching slightly wider, the lower lip may either flatten or stick out more.
(disgust)

―――――――――― **Mouth & Chin** ――――――――――

The chin's dimpled skin rises and the mouth forms an upside-down smile.
(anger, disgust, sadness)

―――――――――― **Mouth & Chin** ――――――――――

The lips pull back horizontally and become flattened, as does the skin above the chin.
(fear)

Mouth

Mild anger: the lips narrow or compress and will also purse together.
(anger)

Intense anger: the lips narrow even more and a bulge forms below the middle of the lower lip.
(anger)

Extreme anger: very taut lips part and form a horizontal funnel, exposing the teeth.
(anger)

Mouth & Jaw

The lips part and the jaw drops. Two degrees of response are shown here, moving from angular lip corners (upper photo) to an active stretching of the mouth that includes rounded corners and also the flattening and stretching of the cheeks and chin (lower photo). Whenever the mouth gets wider but remains more relaxed, rather than stretching tightly, then this facial display interpretively favors surprise over fear.
(fear, surprise)

Jaw & Chin

The entire jaw pushes forward and the chin sticks out.
(anger)

WHAT EMOTIONS MEAN

"POSITIVE" EMOTIONS	DISPLAY	MEANING	UPSIDE	DOWNSIDE
JOY (strongest happiness)	big smile, eyes twinkle	*happiness* robust fulfillment	creative, open-minded	too carefree, unfocused
PLEASURE (2nd-level happiness)	big smile			
SATISFACTION (3rd-level happiness)	slight smile	happiness modest fulfillment	appreciative, receptive	hold back, fail to embrace
ACCEPTANCE (4th-level happiness)	smile hint			

NEUTRAL EMOTION	DISPLAY	MEANING	UPSIDE	DOWNSIDE
SURPRISE	face elongates	attentive	alert, on-guard	hesitant, puzzled

"NEGATIVE" EMOTIONS	DISPLAY	MEANING	UPSIDE	DOWNSIDE
ANGER	face contracts	lack control, hit back	assertive, solve problems	hot-headed, resentful
FEAR	face opens	at risk, discomfort	self-protective	freeze, choke
SADNESS	face wrinkles	irrevocable loss	empathetic, reflective	feel helpless, lose hope
DISGUST	face recoils	rejection	avoid "poison"	overly detached
CONTEMPT	smirk	superiority, disrespect	confident	isolated, dismissive

227

Comprehensive Results

Presented here are all of the Voted surveyed results, and the Actual facial coding results. Voted results came from a market research survey conducted in late 2016. Actual results came from a research study of those same celebrities via facial coding, thereby making comparisons possible.

Name	Highest Voted	2nd Voted	Highest Actual	2nd Actual	Rare
Hank Aaron	*Happiness*	Happiness	Disgust	Contempt	Acceptance
Adele	*Happiness*	Happiness	Disgust	Sadness	Satisfaction
Muhammad Ali	Anger	Happiness	Surprise	Fear	Acceptance
Woody Allen	Sadness	Surprise	Surprise	Fear	*Pleasure*
Jennifer Aniston	Happiness	*Happiness*	Satisfaction	*Joy*	Fear
Neil Armstrong	*Happiness*	Happiness	Contempt	Sadness	Surprise
Ingrid Bergman	Happiness	Sadness	Surprise	Fear	Anger
Yogi Berra	*Happiness*	Surprise	*Pleasure*	Sadness	Anger
Chuck Berry	Happiness	Sadness	Satisfaction	Surprise	Disgust
Beyonce (Knowles)	*Happiness*	Happiness	*Joy*	Acceptance	Contempt
Jeff Bezos	*Happiness*	Contempt	Sadness	Surprise	Acceptance
Larry Bird	*Happiness*	Happiness	Fear	Surprise	Contempt
Humphrey Bogart	Sadness	Anger	Fear	Sadness	Satisfaction
Barry Bonds	Anger	Sadness	Disgust	*Joy*	Satisfaction
John Bonham	*Happiness*	Anger	Anger	Acceptance	Surprise
Tom Brady	Happiness	*Happiness*	Contempt	*Pleasure*	Acceptance
Marlon Brando	Happiness	Sadness	Sadness	Fear	*Pleasure*
Garth Brooks	Happiness	*Happiness*	Acceptance	Contempt	Sadness
Sandra Bullock	*Happiness*	Happiness	Acceptance	Anger	Sadness
George H. W. Bush	Happiness	Surprise	Fear	Sadness	Satisfaction
George W. Bush	Happiness	Surprise	Fear	Contempt	Satisfaction
Jeb Bush	Sadness	Anger	Satisfaction	Anger	Fear
Mariah Carey	Happiness	Sadness	*Pleasure*	*Joy*	Anger
Johnny Cash	Happiness	Contempt	Sadness	Anger	Satisfaction
Cher	Surprise	Happiness	Acceptance	Surprise	*Joy*
Julia Child	*Happiness*	Happiness	*Joy*	*Pleasure*	Contempt
Roger Clemens	Happiness	Anger	Disgust	Anger	Fear
Patsy Cline	Happiness	Sadness	*Pleasure*	Satisfaction	Fear
Bill Clinton	Surprise	Happiness	Sadness	Disgust	Acceptance
Hillary Clinton	Happiness	Anger	Sadness	Contempt	Acceptance
Kurt Cobain	Sadness	Anger	Anger	Sadness	*Joy*
Bill Cosby	Sadness	Anger	Surprise	Fear	Acceptance
Ray Croc	Surprise	Happiness	Satisfaction	*Pleasure*	Disgust
Walter Cronkite	Happiness	Anger	Acceptance	Satisfaction	Disgust
Tom Cruise	Surprise	Happiness	Anger	Contempt	Acceptance
Bette Davis	*Happiness*	Happiness	Surprise	Acceptance	Contempt
Robert De Niro	Anger	Happiness	Sadness	Fear	*Pleasure*
James Dean	Anger	Sadness	Sadness	Anger	Disgust
Ellen DeGeneres	*Happiness*	Happiness	*Joy*	*Pleasure*	Sadness

229

Name	Highest Voted	2nd Voted	Highest Actual	2nd Actual	Rare
Princess Diana	Sadness	Fear	Acceptance	Anger	Disgust
Leonardo DiCaprio	Happiness	*Happiness*	Anger	Acceptance	Surprise
Joe DiMaggio	*Happiness*	Happiness	Surprise	Contempt	Disgust
Walt Disney	*Happiness*	Surprise	Surprise	Satisfaction	Anger
Bob Dylan	Anger	Sadness	Anger	*Pleasure*	Fear
Clint Eastwood	Anger	Happiness	Contempt	Fear	Surprise
Dwight Eisenhower	Happiness	Surprise	Contempt	Sadness	Acceptance
Larry Ellison	Happiness	Disgust	Surprise	Satisfaction	Acceptance
Eminem	Anger	Contempt	Anger	Fear	Satisfaction
Jane Fonda	Happiness	*Happiness*	Acceptance	Fear	Anger
Jodie Foster	Happiness	Surprise	Acceptance	Contempt	Sadness
Aretha Franklin	Happiness	Sadness	Acceptance	Satisfaction	Disgust
Joe Frazier	Anger	Disgust	Surprise	Fear	Acceptance
Judy Garland	Sadness	Happiness	*Pleasure*	Satisfaction	Anger
Bill Gates	Happiness	*Happiness*	Contempt	Satisfaction	Fear
Billy Graham	Happiness	*Happiness*	Fear	*Pleasure*	Acceptance
Cary Grant	Happiness	Surprise	Sadness	Fear	Satisfaction
Wayne Gretzky	Happiness	*Happiness*	Fear	Surprise	Contempt
Tom Hanks	*Happiness*	Happiness	Anger	Fear	*Pleasure*
George Harrison	Happiness	Sadness	*Pleasure*	Satisfaction	Acceptance
Hugh Hefner	*Happiness*	Happiness	Satisfaction	Contempt	Surprise
Jimi Hendrix	Surprise	Sadness	Anger	Contempt	*Pleasure*
Jim Henson	Happiness	*Happiness*	*Joy*	Satisfaction	Anger
Audrey Hepburn	Happiness	*Happiness*	Acceptance	Fear	Anger
Katharine Hepburn	Happiness	*Happiness*	*Joy*	*Pleasure*	Contempt
Alfred Hitchcock	Surprise	Fear	Surprise	Fear	Satisfaction
Dustin Hoffman	Happiness	*Happiness*	Acceptance	Anger	Satisfaction
Whitney Houston	Sadness	Fear	*Pleasure*	Disgust	Anger
Janet Jackson	Surprise	Happiness	Fear	*Joy*	Anger
Jesse Jackson	Anger	Disgust	Surprise	Fear	Acceptance
Michael Jackson	Sadness	Fear	Surprise	Fear	Anger
Mick Jagger	*Happiness*	Happiness	*Joy*	Surprise	*Pleasure*
LeBron James	*Happiness*	Happiness	Disgust	Sadness	Satisfaction
Bruce Jenner	Surprise	Happiness	Satisfaction	*Pleasure*	Disgust
Caitlyn Jenner	Surprise	Happiness	Surprise	Fear	Contempt
Steve Jobs	Surprise	Sadness	Anger	Surprise	Sadness
Elton John	Happiness	Sadness	Acceptance	Anger	*Joy*
Magic Johnson	Happiness	*Happiness*	*Joy*	*Pleasure*	Anger
Angelina Jolie	Anger	Sadness	Acceptance	Anger	*Pleasure*
Brian Jones	Happiness	*Happiness*	Satisfaction	Contempt	Fear
Janis Joplin	Sadness	Anger	Sadness	*Joy*	Anger
Jay Z (Carter)	*Happiness*	Contempt	Sadness	Fear	Satisfaction
Michael Jordan	*Happiness*	Surprise	Disgust	Fear	Satisfaction
Jackie Joyner-Kersee	*Happiness*	Surprise	*Pleasure*	*Joy*	Contempt
Khloe Kardashian	Sadness	Happiness	Anger	Acceptance	Fear

230

Name	Highest Voted	2nd Voted	Highest Actual	2nd Actual	Rare
Kim Kardashian	Happiness	Surprise	Satisfaction	Contempt	Fear
Kourtney Kardashian	Happiness	Sadness	Acceptance	Anger	Fear
Diane Keaton	Happiness	*Happiness*	*Joy*	Satisfaction	Anger
J. Kennedy (Onassis)	Happiness	Surprise	Surprise	Satisfaction	Sadness
John F. Kennedy	Happiness	Surprise	Satisfaction	Sadness	Surprise
Robert F. Kennedy	Happiness	*Happiness*	Sadness	Acceptance	Contempt
Billie Jean King	Happiness	Surprise	Disgust	*Joy*	Acceptance
Martin Luther King	Anger	Happiness	Fear	Surprise	Disgust
Estee Lauder	Happiness	*Happiness*	Satisfaction	Acceptance	Sadness
Jennifer Lawrence	Happiness	*Happiness*	Acceptance	*Joy*	Fear
John Lennon	Happiness	Sadness	Satisfaction	*Pleasure*	Anger
David Letterman	Happiness	Surprise	*Joy*	Contempt	Surprise
Rush Limbaugh	Anger	Contempt	Anger	Disgust	Fear
Douglas MacArthur	Disgust	Contempt	Anger	Acceptance	Satisfaction
Bernie Madoff	Anger	Contempt	Acceptance	Sadness	Satisfaction
Madonna	Happiness	*Happiness*	Acceptance	*Pleasure*	Fear
Peyton Manning	Happiness	*Happiness*	Sadness	Contempt	*Joy*
Charles Manson	Anger	Contempt	Anger	Surprise	Satisfaction
Mickey Mantle	Happiness	Surprise	*Pleasure*	Anger	Contempt
Willie Mays	Happiness	*Happiness*	Fear	*Pleasure*	Anger
Joseph McCarthy	Contempt	Anger	Anger	Contempt	Surprise
Paul McCartney	Happiness	*Happiness*	*Pleasure*	Satisfaction	Anger
John McEnroe	Anger	Contempt	Disgust	Sadness	*Joy*
Michael Milken	Fear	Contempt	*Pleasure*	*Joy*	Satisfaction
Joni Mitchell	Happiness	Sadness	Acceptance	Disgust	Anger
Marilyn Monroe	Sadness	Fear	Surprise	Fear	Anger
Joe Montana	*Happiness*	Happiness	*Joy*	Satisfaction	Sadness
Eddie Murphy	*Happiness*	Surprise	Surprise	*Joy*	Sadness
Edward R. Murrow	Happiness	Sadness	Surprise	Fear	Satisfaction
Elon Musk	*Happiness*	Happiness	Disgust	Contempt	Surprise
Cam Newton	Disgust	Anger	Fear	Contempt	*Joy*
Jack Nicholson	Happiness	Anger	Disgust	Surprise	Anger
Jack Nicklaus	Happiness	Contempt	Disgust	Contempt	Surprise
Richard Nixon	Anger	Contempt	Sadness	Anger	Surprise
Greg Norman	*Happiness*	Sadness	Disgust	*Pleasure*	Satisfaction
Barack Obama	Happiness	*Happiness*	Disgust	Contempt	Satisfaction
Jimmy Page	Happiness	*Happiness*	Acceptance	Anger	Fear
Larry Page	Happiness	Surprise	Surprise	Satisfaction	Anger
Ross Perot	Surprise	Happiness	Satisfaction	Fear	Acceptance
Michael Phelps	Happiness	*Happiness*	Surprise	*Joy*	Satisfaction
Brad Pitt	Sadness	Happiness	Satisfaction	Anger	Fear
Robert Plant	Happiness	*Happiness*	Contempt	Acceptance	*Pleasure*
Natalie Portman	Happiness	*Happiness*	Fear	Acceptance	Satisfaction
Elvis Presley	Happiness	Sadness	Disgust	Acceptance	Fear
Prince	Happiness	Surprise	Contempt	Anger	Fear

231

Name	Highest Voted	2nd Voted	Highest Actual	2nd Actual	Rare
Ronald Reagan	Happiness	Surprise	Fear	Sadness	Acceptance
Robert Redford	Happiness	Surprise	Anger	Satisfaction	Disgust
Mary Lou Retton	*Happiness*	Surprise	*Joy*	*Pleasure*	Anger
Little Richard	*Happiness*	Surprise	Surprise	*Joy*	Satisfaction
Keith Richards	Happiness	Anger	Acceptance	Disgust	Sadness
Jackie Robinson	Sadness	Happiness	Fear	Sadness	Acceptance
Aaron Rodgers	Happiness	Disgust	Contempt	Disgust	*Joy*
Eleanor Roosevelt	Happiness	Sadness	*Pleasure*	Satisfaction	Surprise
Diana Ross	*Happiness*	Happiness	*Pleasure*	Acceptance	Sadness
J. K. Rowling	Happiness	*Happiness*	Contempt	Satisfaction	Fear
Charles Schulz	*Happiness*	Surprise	*Joy*	*Pleasure*	Anger
Amy Schumer	*Happiness*	Surprise	Acceptance	Anger	Fear
Tupac Shakur	Anger	Contempt	Surprise	Acceptance	Satisfaction
O. J. Simpson	Anger	Disgust	Surprise	Fear	Acceptance
Frank Sinatra	Happiness	*Happiness*	Surprise	Fear	Anger
Will Smith	*Happiness*	Happiness	*Pleasure*	*Joy*	Sadness
Edward Snowden	Anger	Contempt	Anger	Acceptance	Disgust
Steven Spielberg	Happiness	Surprise	Acceptance	Surprise	*Joy*
Bruce Springsteen	Happiness	Anger	*Pleasure*	Acceptance	Surprise
Ringo Starr	*Happiness*	Happiness	Satisfaction	*Pleasure*	Anger
Gloria Steinem	Anger	Disgust	Satisfaction	*Joy*	Sadness
Howard Stern	Contempt	Anger	Satisfaction	Anger	Sadness
Jimmy Stewart	*Happiness*	Happiness	Surprise	Fear	Anger
Jon Stewart	Sadness	Anger	Contempt	Surprise	Acceptance
Martha Stewart	Happiness	Contempt	*Pleasure*	Satisfaction	Sadness
Meryl Streep	Happiness	*Happiness*	Acceptance	Anger	*Pleasure*
Taylor Swift	Happiness	*Happiness*	Acceptance	Anger	Surprise
Elizabeth Taylor	Happiness	*Happiness*	Acceptance	Satisfaction	Anger
J. Timberlake	*Happiness*	Happiness	Anger	Contempt	Surprise
Donald Trump	Disgust	Contempt	Sadness	Disgust	Satisfaction
Ivanka Trump	Contempt	Happiness	Disgust	Contempt	Sadness
Lindsey Vonn	Happiness	Surprise	Satisfaction	Contempt	Sadness
George Wallace	Disgust	Anger	Anger	Disgust	Satisfaction
Andy Warhol	Sadness	Fear	Disgust	Sadness	*Pleasure*
Charlie Watts	Happiness	Sadness	Acceptance	Contempt	Sadness
Jack Welch	Happiness	*Happiness*	*Joy*	Anger	Acceptance
Kanye West	Anger	Disgust	Anger	Disgust	Satisfaction
Serena Williams	Happiness	Anger	Disgust	Contempt	*Joy*
Ted Williams	Happiness	Surprise	Disgust	Anger	Fear
Venus Williams	Happiness	Surprise	*Joy*	Sadness	Contempt
Oprah Winfrey	*Happiness*	Happiness	*Joy*	*Pleasure*	Contempt
Kate Winslet	Happiness	*Happiness*	Disgust	Anger	Sadness
Tiger Woods	Sadness	Happiness	Sadness	*Pleasure*	Satisfaction
Bill Wyman	Happiness	Sadness	*Joy*	Anger	Sadness
Mark Zuckerberg	Happiness	*Happiness*	*Joy*	Anger	Fear

Photo Credits

While the range of options per celebrity wasn't always optimal for showing a specific expression of an emotion, the existence of the Creative Commons proved a godsend for finding photographs free of charge to illustrate facial expressions. I thank all involved for establishing and contributing to that generous initiative.

Introduction

Ryan Leaf: *Great Falls Tribune* photo reprinted with permission. Cropped, background simplified and desaturated from original.

Anger

Cary Grant: 1949 studio publicity photo. https://commons.wikimedia.org/wiki/File:Cary_Grant_-_publicity.jpg. (Public Domain). Cropped from original.

Eminem: Eminem in Munich 1999 by Mikael 'Mika' Väisänen. https://upload.wikimedia.org/wikipedia/commons/c/cd/Eminem-01-mika.jpg. CC BY-SA 3.0 (https://creativecommons.org/licenses/by-sa/3.0/deed.en). Cropped, background simplified, exposure altered and desaturated from original.

Angelina Jolie: Angelina Jolie 2 June 2014 (cropped) by the British Foreign and Commonwealth Office. https://commons.wikimedia.org/wiki/File:Angelina_Jolie_2_June_2014_(cropped).jpg. CC BY 2.0 (https://creativecommons.org/licenses/by/2.0/); excerpt of original photo: https://www.flickr.com/photos/foreignoffice/14217374639/. Cropped, background simplified, exposure altered and desaturated from original.

George Wallace: Ex-Governor Wallace of Alabama news conference - stating he is a presidential candidate [i.e., candidate] on the 3rd party ticket. US News & World Report Collection at US Library of Congress uploaded by Tilden76. https://commons.wikimedia.org/wiki/File:George_C_Wallace.jpg. (Public Domain – No known copyright restrictions). Cropped from original.

Hillary Clinton: Former Secretary of State Hillary Clinton speaking with supporters at a "Get Out the Caucus" rally at Valley Southwoods Freshman High School in West Des Moines, Iowa by Gage Skidmore. https://www.flickr.com/photos/gageskidmore/24338774540. CC BY-SA 2.0 (https://creativecommons.org/licenses/by-sa/2.0/deed.en). Cropped, background simplified, and desaturated from original.

Joseph McCarthy: Library of Congress (Public Domain – no copyright notice). https://commons.wikimedia.org/wiki/File:Joseph_McCarthy.jpg. Cropped, background simplified, exposure altered and desaturated from original.

Tom Hanks: Tom Hanks Recites Lincoln Portrait by U.S. Navy (Public Domain). https://commons.wikimedia.org/wiki/File:TomHanksJan2009.jpg. Cropped, background simplified, exposure altered and desaturated from original.

Taylor Swift: Taylor Swift performing Red Tour in St. Louis, Missouri, 25 March 2013 by Jana Beamer. https://c1.staticflickr.com/9/8525/8588016225_01796fbf12_b.jpg. CC BY 2.0. Cropped, background simplified, exposure altered and desaturated from original.

Happiness

Ellen DeGeneres: On set of her show in September 2008 by ronpaulrevolt2008. https://www.flickr.com/photos/33170765@N04/3371640116. CC BY 2.0. Cropped, background simplified and desaturated from original.

Sadness

Photo Credits

creativecommons.org/licenses/by-sa/2.0/deed.en). Cropped, background simplified, exposure altered and desaturated from original.

Johnny Cash: Sony-BMG Wall, Dufferin, South of King St., Toronto @ August 8, 2006 by alexindigo. https://www.flickr.com/photos/alexindigo/213186630/. CC BY 2.0 (https://creativecommons.org/licenses/by/2.0/). Cropped and exposure altered from original.

Elon Musk: Quote and photo by Get Everwise. https://www.flickr.com/photos/geteverwise/14965850224. CC BY-SA 4.0 (https://creativecommons.org/licenses/by-sa/4.0/deed.en). Cropped, background simplified, exposure altered and desaturated from original.

Mariah Carey: Mariah Carey at Edwards Air Force Base in Dec. 1998 by U.S. Air Force (Public Domain). https://commons.wikimedia.org/wiki/File:Mariah_Carey3_Edwards_Dec_1998_cropped.jpg. Cropped, background simplified, and desaturated from original.

Quiz, Part One

Joe Montana: On set with ESPN at Super Bowl week, February 3, 2006 by Phil Hull. https://www.flickr.com/photos/philhull/94840983/in/set-72057594057652681/. CC BY-SA 2.0 (https://creativecommons.org/licenses/by-sa/2.0/deed.en). Cropped, background simplified, exposure altered and desaturated from original.

Jack Welch: Head shot by Hamilton83, May 13, 2012. https://commons.wikimedia.org/wiki/File:JackWelchApril2012.jpg. CC BY-SA 3.0 (https://creativecommons.org/licenses/by-sa/3.0/deed.en). Cropped, background simplified, exposure altered and desaturated from original.

Katharine Hepburn: Extracted from original image with Spencer Tracy; uploaded by Kate Gabrielle (classic film scans). https://www.flickr.com/photos/slightlyterrific/5350785107. CC BY 2.0 (https://creativecommons.org/licenses/by/2.0/). Cropped and background simplified from the original.

George Harrison: During a press conference at Schiphol Airport; May 6th, 1964 by Natianal Archief. https://en.wikipedia.org/wiki/File:The_Beatles_arrive_at_Schiphol_Airport_1964-06-05_-_George_Harrison_916-5132_cropped.jpg. CC BY-SA 3.0 (https://creativecommons.org/licenses/by-sa/3.0/deed.en). Cropped, background simplified, exposure altered and desaturated from original.

Leonardo DiCaprio: Leonardo DiCaprio at the premiere of the film "Shutter Island" at the 60th Berlin International Film Festival by Siebbi. https://commons.wikimedia.org/wiki/File:Leonardo_DiCaprio_(Berlin_Film_Festival_2010)_2_(cropped).jpg. CC BY 3.0 (https://creativecommons.org/licenses/by/3.0/deed.en). Cropped, background simplified, and desaturated from original.

Barry Bonds: Barry heads to left field after driving in 2 with a single in the 3rd inning on July 19, 2007 by John (guano). https://www.flickr.com/photos/guano/865468282/. CC BY-SA 2.0 (https://creativecommons.org/licenses/by-sa/2.0/). Cropped, background simplified, exposure altered and desaturated from original.

LeBron James: In a game vs. Washington Wizards, November 2009 by Keith Allison. https://www.flickr.com/photos/keithallison/4116892286. CC BY-SA 2.0 (https://creativecommons.org/licenses/by-sa/2.0/deed.en). Cropped, background simplified, exposure altered and desaturated from original.

Princess Diana: Princess Diana opens The Paisley Centre and pays a visit to the Accord Hospice by John MacIntyre. https://commons.wikimedia.org/wiki/File:Princess_Diana_at_Accord_Hospice.jpg. CC BY 2.0 (https://creativecommons.org/licenses/by/2.0/). Cropped, background simplified, and desaturated from original.

Patsy Cline: I-40 Rest Area photograph by William Allen. https://www.flickr.com/photos/woodpainter/8319346102. CC BY-SA 2.0 (https://creativecommons.org/licenses/by-sa/2.0/deed.en). Cropped and background simplified from original.

Flash Portraits

John & Jackie Kennedy: President John F. Kennedy, First Lady Jacqueline Kennedy, and their children John, Jr. and Caroline, at their summer house in Hyannis Port, Massachusetts by Cecil W. Stoughon, Courtesy of Kennedy Presidential Library (Public Domain). https://commons. wikimedia.org/wiki/File:JFK_and_family_in_Hyannis_Port,_04_August_1962.jpg. Cropped, background simplified and desaturated from original.

Robert F. Kennedy: Cabinet Room, White House, Washington, DC. January 28, 1964 by the Executive Office of the President of the United States (Public Domain). https://commons. wikimedia.org/wiki/File:Robert_F._Kennedy_1964.jpeg.

Serena Williams: 2015 Australian Open by Tourism Victoria. https://www.flickr.com/photos/ visitmelbourne/16351695926/. CC BY 2.0 (https://creativecommons.org/licenses/by/2.0/). Cropped, background simplified, exposure altered and desaturated from original.

Venus Williams: at Taste of Tennis New York on June 30, 2016 by ayssports. https://commons.wikimedia. org/wiki/File:Venus_Williams_1.png. CC BY-SA 4.0 (https://creativecommons.org/licenses/by-sa/4.0/ deed.en). Cropped, background simplified, exposure altered and desaturated from original.

Janet Jackson: Checking her mic at 2006 press conference by Dan Ingram. https://www.flickr. com/photos/84754704@N00/317264401/. CC BY 2.0 (https://creativecommons.org/licenses/ by/2.0/). Cropped, background simplified, exposure altered and desaturated from original.

Michael Jackson: Michael Jackson with two fans at the Kahala Hilton Hotel in February 1988 by Alan Light (extracted/cropped from original). https://commons.wikimedia.org/wiki/ File:Michaeljackson_(cropped).jpg. CC BY 2.0 (https://creativecommons.org/licenses/by/2.0/). Cropped, background simplified, exposure altered and desaturated from original.

Joe DiMaggio & Marilyn Monroe: Marilyn Monroe and Joe DiMaggio from the cover of the January 1954 issue of Now magazine (Public Domain – copyright not renewed). https:// commons.wikimedia.org/wiki/File:Marilyn_Monroe_Joe_DiMaggio_January_1954.jpg. Cropped, background simplified and desaturated from original.

Kardashians: NYC Kardashian Konfidential Book Signing 11.30.10 by Faye Harris (extracted/ cropped from original). https://www.flickr.com/photos/vivalafayemous/5221196365/in/photolist-bJsTcF-8XnZLZ-8XnYZv-8Xo1sg. CC BY 2.0 (https://creativecommons.org/licenses/by/2.0/). Cropped, background simplified, exposure altered and desaturated from original.

Brad Pitt: Brad Pitt (cropped) by the British Foreign and Commonwealth Office. https://commons. wikimedia.org/wiki/File:Angelina_Jolie_2_June_2014_(cropped).jpg. CC BY 2.0 (https:// creativecommons.org/licenses/by/2.0/); excerpt of original photo: https://www.flickr.com/photos/ foreignoffice/14217374639/. Cropped, background simplified, exposure altered and desaturated from original.

Jennifer Aniston: Jennifer Aniston and Andres Useche image 2. https://commons.wikimedia. org/wiki/File:Jennifer_Aniston_and_Andres_Useche_image_2.jpg. CC BY-SA 2.0 (https:// creativecommons.org/licenses/by-sa/2.0/deed.en). Cropped, background simplified, exposure altered and desaturated from original.

Angelina Jolie: at the World Economic Forum in Davos, Switzerland, January 26, 2006 by World Economic Forum. https://commons.wikimedia.org/wiki/File:JoliePitt.png. CC BY-SA 2.0 (https:// creativecommons.org/licenses/by-sa/2.0/deed.en). Cropped, background simplified, exposure altered and desaturated from original.

Bill Clinton: December 16, 2008 by Venl. https://www.flickr.com/photos/veni/3114495652. CC BY 2.0 (https://creativecommons.org/licenses/by/2.0/). Cropped, background simplified, exposure altered and desaturated from original.

Hillary Clinton: Former Secretary of State Hillary Clinton speaking with supporters at a "Get Out the Caucus" rally at Valley Southwoods Freshman High School in West Des Moines, Iowa.by Gage Skidmore. https://commons.wikimedia.org/wiki/File:Hillary_Clinton_(24552133881).jpg.

Contempt

Lindsey Vonn: Lindsey Vonn at the Quicken Loans National Pro-Am June 25, 2014 by keithallison. https://flic.kr/p/o6Nvxm. CC BY-SA 2.0 (https://creativecommons.org/licenses/by-sa/2.0/deed. en). Cropped, background simplified and desaturated from original.

Judy Garland: A publicity still of Judy Garland from MGM used in conjunction with promotion of The Harvey Girls (1946) by Eric Carpenter (Public Domain – copyright not renewed). https:// commons.wikimedia.org/wiki/File:Judy_Garland_The_Harvey_Girls_MGM_Publicity_still.jpeg. Cropped and background simplified.

Disgust

Billie Jean King: Billie Jean King modeling in The Heart Truth's Red Dress Collections at New York's Fashion Week, 2007 courtesy of the Executive Office of the President (Public Domain). https:// commons.wikimedia.org/wiki/File:Billie_Jean_King_(1).jpg. Cropped, background simplified, exposure altered and desaturated from original.

Roger Clemens: by Keith Allison. https://www.flickr.com/photos/keithallison/2414814127. CC BY-SA 2.0 (https://creativecommons.org/licenses/by-sa/2.0/deed.en). Cropped, background simplified and desaturated from original.

Andy Warhol: Four Warhols by qthomasbower. https://www.flickr.com/photos/ qthomasbower/7774554176/. CC BY-SA 2.0 (https://creativecommons.org/licenses/by-sa/2.0/deed. en). Cropped, exposure altered and desaturated from original.

Elvis Presley: Ed Sullivan with Elvis during rehearsals for his second appearance on the Ed Sullivan Show, CBS Publicity Photo, October 26, 1956 (Public Domain – see permission on provided link). https://commons.wikimedia.org/wiki/File:Elvis_Presley_and_Ed_Sullivan_October_1956. jpg. Cropped, background simplified, and exposure altered from original.

Kate Winslet: Palm Springs Film Festival 2007 by Maggiejumps. https://www.flickr.com/ photos/38494596@N00/352236334/in/set-1803041/. CC BY 2.0 (https://creativecommons.org/ licenses/by/2.0/). Cropped, background simplified, and desaturated from original.

Larry Bird: Cardinal Law, Larry Bird and Boston's Mayor Raymond L. Flynn by Boston Mayor's Office – City Photographer (Public Domain). https://www.flickr.com/photos/ cityofbostonarchives/9519694234. CC BY 2.0 (https://creativecommons.org/licenses/by/2.0/). Cropped, exposure altered and desaturated from original.

Kanye West: Kanye before a show in Chicago on August 4, 2007 by darkroom demons. https://www.flickr.com/photos/98609527@N00/1027053347/. CC BY-SA 2.0 (https:// creativecommons.org/licenses/by-sa/2.0/deed.en). Cropped, background simplified, exposure altered and desaturated from original.

Madonna: Madonna leaving the press conference for "Filth And Wisdom" in Berlin February 13, 2008 by Siebbi. http://www.ipernity.com/doc/siebbi/1399089. CC BY 3.0 (https://creativecommons.org/ licenses/by/3.0/deed.en). Cropped, background simplified and desaturated from original.

Quiz, Part Two

Jennifer Lawrence: At the 2013 Golden Globes by jdeeringdavis. https://www.flickr.com/photos/ hayesandjenn/8379852580/. CC BY 2.0 (https://creativecommons.org/licenses/by/2.0/). Cropped, background simplified, and desaturated from original.

Jon Stewart: With U.S. Marine Gen. James E. Cartwright at the USO Metro Awards in Arlington, Va., March 25, 2008, photo by Air Force Tech. Sgt. Adam M. Stump (Public Domain). https:// commons.wikimedia.org/wiki/File:Stewart_-_USO-Metro_Merit_Awards.jpg. Cropped, background simplified, exposure altered and desaturated from original.

Dwight Eisenhower: General Services Administration. National Archives and Records Service (Public Domain). https://commons.wikimedia.org/wiki/File:Photograph_of_Dwight_D._Eisenhower_-_ NARA_-_518138.jpg. Cropped from original.

Photo Credits

Peyton Manning: On the field Super Bowl week for team photo; February 3, 2010 by Ian Ransley. https://www.flickr.com/photos/11154980@N04/4341315308. CC BY 2.0 (https:// creativecommons.org/licenses/by/2.0/). Cropped, background simplified, and desaturated from original.

Joni Mitchell: Joni Mitchell performing in concert, August 1974 by Paul C Babin. (Public Domain – author choice). https://commons.wikimedia.org/wiki/File:Joni_mitchell_1974.jpg. Cropped from original.

Greg Norman: Greg Norman signs autographs for Sailors aboard the USS John F. Kennedy, October 11, 2004. U.S. Navy photo by Photographer's Mate Airman Tommy Gilligan (Public Domain). https://commons.wikimedia.org/wiki/File:Greg_Norman_Oct._11_2004.jpg.

Ted Williams: Portrait of Boston Red Sox legend Ted Williams: Sarasota, Florida, 1949 by Florida Memory. (Public Domain – No known copyright.) https://www.flickr.com/photos/31846825@ N04/8640360344.

John McEnroe: At the 2009 US Open on September 7, 2009 by Edwin Martinez. https://www. flickr.com/photos/22705753@N06/3899871438. CC BY 2.0 (https://creativecommons.org/ licenses/by/2.0/). Cropped, background simplified, exposure altered and desaturated from original.

Aaron Rodgers: In-game December 2008 by Mike Morbeck. https://www.flickr.com/ photos/33494452@N05/5483358737. CC BY-SA 2.0 (https://creativecommons.org/licenses/by-sa/2.0/deed.en). Cropped, background simplified, exposure altered and desaturated from original.

Flash Portraits

Oprah Winfrey: Oprah at "Life You Want" in Miami, October 25, 2014 extracted from original photo by Aphrodite-in-nyc. https://www.flickr.com/photos/aphrodite-in-nyc/15628835471/. CC BY 2.0 (https://creativecommons.org/licenses/by/2.0/). Cropped, background simplified, exposure altered and desaturated from original.

Ellen DeGeneres: Ellen in 2009 by Tulane Public Relations. https://commons.wikimedia.org/wiki/ File:Ellen_DeGeneres-2009.jpg. CC BY 2.0 (https://creativecommons.org/licenses/by/2.0/). Cropped, background simplified, and desaturated from original.

Bruce Jenner: Official White House photo by Ricardo Thomas courtesy of the Ford Presidential Library (Public Domain). https://upload.wikimedia.org/wikipedia/commons/f/fc/Bruce_Jenner_ greets_Gerald_Ford_and_William_Tolbert_in_1976.jpg. Cropped and background simplified from original.

Caitlyn Jenner: Samantha Power interviews Caitlyn Jenner about LGBT rights for Human Rights Day by US Dept. of State (Public Domain). https://commons.wikimedia.org/wiki/File:Caitlyn_ Jenner.jpeg. Cropped, background simplified, exposure altered and desaturated from original.

Aretha Franklin: by AustinMini 1275 (Public Domain). https://www.flickr.com/photos/14639118@ N03/27464305590. Cropped from original.

Diana Ross: by Linda Bisset. https://commons.wikimedia.org/wiki/File:Diana_Ross.jpg. CC BY-SA 2.0 (https://creativecommons.org/licenses/by-sa/2.0/deed.en). Cropped, background simplified, exposure altered and desaturated from original.

Steve Jobs & Bill Gates: All Things Digital 2007 Interview by Joi Ito. https://www.flickr.com/ photos/35034362831@N01/522695099/. CC BY 2.0 (https://creativecommons.org/licenses/ by/2.0/). Excerpted/cropped, background simplified, exposure altered and desaturated from original.

Jimi Hendrix: Jimi Hendrix at the amusement park Gröna Lund in Stockholm, Sweden, May 24, 1967 (Public Domain). https://upload.wikimedia.org/wikipedia/commons/a/af/ Jimi_Hendrix_1967_uncropped.jpg. Cropped, background simplified, exposure altered and desaturated from original.

Prince: Performing at Coachella in 2008 by Micahmedia. https://commons.wikimedia.org/wiki/ Category:Prince_(musician)#/media/File:Prince_at_Coachella_001.jpg. CC BY-SA 3.0 (https://

creativecommons.org/licenses/by-sa/3.0/deed.en). Cropped, background simplified, and exposure altered.

Jesse Jackson: Speaking during an interview July 1, 1983 by Warren K. Leffler from Library of Congress (Public Domain). https://en.wikipedia.org/wiki/File:Jesse_Jackson,_half-length_portrait_of_Jackson_seated_at_a_table,_July_1,_1983_edit.jpg.

Martin Luther King Jr.: Receiving Medallion from Mayor Wagner. By Phil Stanziola NYWT&S Staff Photographer courtesy of Library of Congress (Public Domain). https://commons.wikimedia.org/wiki/File:Martin_Luther_King_Jr_with_medallion_NYWTS.jpg. Cropped from original.

Rush Limbaugh: Speaking to CPAC via satellite by Gage Skidmore. https://commons.wikimedia.org/wiki/File:Rush_Limbaugh_(4377537515).jpg. CC BY-SA 2.0 (https://creativecommons.org/licenses/by-sa/2.0/deed.en). Cropped, background simplified, angle corrected, and desaturated from original.

Howard Stern: In New York on May 10, 2012 by Bill Norton (blnk8). https://www.flickr.com/photos/blnk8/7196242502/. CC BY 2.0 (https://creativecommons.org/licenses/by/2.0/). Cropped, background simplified, exposure altered and desaturated from original.

Mick Jagger & Keith Richards: At the Berlinale Filmfestspiele 2008 Berlin by Der Pfalzgraf. https://www.flickr.com/photos/derpfalzgraf/3166497114/. CC BY-SA 2.0 (https://creativecommons.org/licenses/by-sa/2.0/deed.en). Cropped, background simplified, exposure altered and desaturated from original.

Surprise

Bill Cosby: Public Service Announcement by National Science Foundation, 1988 (Public Domain). https://commons.wikimedia.org/wiki/File:Bill_Cosby_Reminds_Us_That_We_Can_All_Be_Scientists.jpg. Cropped from original.

Frank Sinatra: Frank Sinatra on set of "Our Town" by NBC (Public Domain – no copyright notice). https://upload.wikimedia.org/wikipedia/commons/1/13/Frank_Sinatra_in_1955.jpg. Cropped from original.

Bill Cosby: Publicity photo of Bill Cosby from the television program I Spy by NBC (Public Domain – no copyright notice). https://commons.wikimedia.org/wiki/File:Bill_Cosby_1965.jpg. Cropped from original.

Walt Disney: Photo of him shaking hands with Robert Taylor by Alan Fisher (World-Telegram) from US Library of Congress (Public Domain – no known copyright). https://commons.wikimedia.org/wiki/File:Walt_Disney_NYWTS.jpg. Cropped from the original.

Charles Manson: San Quentin mugshot January 25, 1971 (Public Domain). https://commons.wikimedia.org/wiki/File:Charles-mansonbookingphoto.jpg.

Adele: Adele at Genting Arena holding tea cup by Egghead06. https://commons.wikimedia.org/wiki/File:Adele_with_tea_cup.jpeg. CC BY-SA 4.0 (https://creativecommons.org/licenses/by-sa/4.0/deed.en). Cropped and desaturated from original.

Jimmy Stewart: Stewart meets an attractive actress (Chanin Hale) while appearing on The Jimmy Stewart Show. https://meta.wikimedia.org/wiki/File:Jimmy_Stewart_Show_1972.jpg. (Public Domain – No known copyright restrictions.) Cropped from original.

Fear

Tom Brady: Photo by Keith Allison; December 4, 2007. https://www.flickr.com/photos/keithallison/2310900973. CC BY-SA 2.0 (https://creativecommons.org/licenses/by-sa/2.0/deed.en). Cropped, background simplified, and desaturated from original.

Natalie Portman: Portman at "The Seventh Fire" premiere in Berlin by Siebbi. https://commons.wikimedia.org/wiki/File:Natalie_Portman_Berlin_2015_2.png. CC BY-SA 3.0 (https://creativecommons.org/licenses/by-sa/3.0/deed.en). Cropped, background simplified, exposure altered and desaturated from original.

Photo Credits

Marilyn Monroe: Marilyn Monroe with her attorney Jerry Giesler at courthouse October 28, 1954 by LA Times Photographic Library, UCLA (Public Domain – Copyright not renewed). https://commons. wikimedia.org/wiki/File:Marilyn_Monroe_and_Jerry_Giesler_3.jpg. Cropped from original.

Wayne Gretzky: Janet & Wayne Gretzky at the 27th American Cinematheque Award Benefit by Mingle Media TV. https://www.flickr.com/photos/minglemediatv/11357350304/. CC BY-SA 2.0 (https://creativecommons.org/licenses/by-sa/2.0/deed.en). Cropped, background simplified, and desaturated from original.

Jesse Jackson: Jesse Jackson speaking during an interview from Library of Congress's Prints and Photographs Division (Public Domain). https://upload.wikimedia.org/wikipedia/commons/5/59/ Jesse_Jackson,_half-length_portrait_of_Jackson_seated_at_a_table,_July_1,_1983_edit.jpg. Cropped from the original.

George H. W. Bush: Former President George H.W. Bush aboard USS George H. W. Bush by U.S. Navy (Public Domain). https://commons.wikimedia.org/wiki/File:US_Navy_100714-N-3885H-208_Former_President_George_H.W._Bush_watches_flight_operations_from_the_ landing_signal_officer's_platform.jpg. Cropped, background simplified from original.

Ingrid Bergman: Ingrid Bergman at age 14 (Public Domain {PD-1996}). https://commons.wikimedia.org/ wiki/File:Ingrid_Bergman_at_age_14.jpg. Cropped from the original.

Tom Brady: Game photo by Jeffrey Beall. https://www.flickr.com/photos/denverjeffrey/6566852021//. CC BY-SA 2.0 (https://creativecommons.org/licenses/by-sa/2.0/deed.en). Cropped, background simplified, and desaturated from original.

Quiz, Part Three

Woody Allen: January 9, 2006 by Colin Swan. https://www.flickr.com/photos/cswan/87743769. CC BY-SA 2.0 (https://creativecommons.org/licenses/by-sa/2.0/deed.en). Cropped and desaturated from original.

Alfred Hitchcock: Alfred Hitchcock, profile. Unknown origin. http://prettycleverfilms.com/ files/2012/04/hitchcock-profile.jpg. Cropped.

Jackie Kennedy: President & First Lady Kennedy with Chief Justice Earl Warren & Mrs. Warren, Judicial reception, November 20, 1963. Courtesy of National Archives and Records Administration (Public Domain). https://commons.wikimedia.org/wiki/File:President_%26_ First_Lady_Kennedy_with_Chief_Justice_Earl_Warren_%26_Mrs._Warren,_circa_1962.jpg.

Ronald Reagan: President Ronald Reagan speaking at a Rally for Senator Durenberger in Minneapolis, Minnesota, 1982 courtesy of National Archives (Public Domain). https://commons. wikimedia.org/wiki/File:President_Reagan_speaking_in_Minneapolis_1982.jpg. Cropped and background simplified from original.

Cher: Original publicity photo from Light Show by Casablanca Records (Public Domain – no copyright notice). https://commons.wikimedia.org/wiki/File:Cher_-_Casablanca.jpg. Cropped from original.

Tiger Woods: At the 2014 Quicken Loans National in Bethesda, MD by Keith Allison. https:// www.flickr.com/photos/keithallison/14319849299. CC BY-SA 2.0 (https://creativecommons. org/licenses/by-sa/2.0/deed.en). Cropped, background simplified, and desaturated from original.

Marlon Brando: Civil Rights March on Washington, D.C. August 28, 1963 by US Information Agency (Public Domain). https://commons.wikimedia.org/wiki/File:Marlon_Brando_1963.jpg. Cropped and background simplified from original.

Robert De Niro: Robert De Niro at the Toronto International Film Festival, September 10, 2011 by Tony Sheck (GabboT). https://www.flickr.com/photos/tonyshek/6929603255/. CC BY-SA 2.0 (https://creativecommons.org/licenses/by-sa/2.0/deed.en). Cropped, background simplified, exposure altered and desaturated from original.

Meryl Streep: Head shot by Jack Mitchell, 1976. https://commons.wikimedia.org/wiki/File:Meryl_ Streep_by_Jack_Mitchell_(cropped_bw).jpg. CC BY-SA 4.0 (https://creativecommons.org/licenses/ by-sa/4.0/deed.en). Cropped, background simplified, exposure altered and desaturated from original.

Epilogue

Lance Armstrong: American cyclist Lance Armstrong giving a talk in 2007 by U.S. Army Cpl. William Howard (Public Domain). https://commons.wikimedia.org/wiki/File:Armstrong,_Lance_ (December_2007).jpg. Cropped, background simplified, exposure altered and desaturated from original.

Pumpkin: Jack-o'-lantern photo taken October 26, 2010 by Toyah (Public Domain–author's choice). https://commons.wikimedia.org/wiki/File:Pumpkin_lantern.jpg. Cropped, exposure altered and desaturated from original.

Sources & Notes

Besides my benefiting from numerous Wikipedia entries, and drawing on Google Images and YouTube videos for facial coding, other specific sources are cited below.

Introduction

1. Mike Foss, "Peyton Manning Was the No. 1 Pick Because Ryan Leaf Sabotaged the Draft Process," *USA Today*, January 20, 2014, available at http://ftw:usatoday.com/2014/01/how-ryan-leaf-convinced-the-colts-to-draft-peyton-manning. Also check out Kevin Armstrong, "How Ryan Leaf, NFL's Biggest Draft Bust, Turned His Life Around," *The New York Daily News*, May 4, 2016, available at http://www.nydailynews.com/sports/football/ryan-leaf-nfl-biggest-draft-bs-turned-life-article-1.2624679.

2. John Sullivan, ERE Recruiting Conference speech, October 2016. Specifically, Sullivan cited hiring rate failures of 45% for general employees, 40-60% for managers, and 50% for executives. A Heidrick & Struggles 2009 study cites a 40% failure rate for executive hires, lower than the 50-70% rate cited by the Corporate Executive Board. The last two sources are referenced in David Perry's book, *Hiring Greatness: How to Recruit Your Dream Team and Crush the Competition* (New York: Wiley, 2016).

3. Kevin Randall, "Teams Turn to a Face Reader, Looking for That Winning Smile," *The New York Times*, December 26, 2014.

4 . Reading faces has two phases, starting with face recognition. The release of the new Apple's iPhoneX with its ability to unlock the screen by "swiping" the user's face belongs to phase one, but is merely a part of something now hitting the big time. Facial recognition software enables everything from tracking church-go'ers attendance, to spotting past shoplifters, and permitting tourists to enter attractions. The Chinese company Megvii already has over 300,000 clients utilizing its face-recognition technology, named Face++, and is the world's first billion-dollar start-up in what *The Economist* has dubbed the "facial-industrial complex." Capturing "faceprints" will become a tidal wave changing business and society at large, whether always welcome or not given the privacy implications. Phase two is emotion recognition, which will also prove transformative. To read more, check out https://www.economist.com/news/leaders/21728617-life-age-facial-recognition-what-machines-can-tell-your-face, and https://www.economist/com/news/business/21728654-chinas-megvil-has-used-government-collected-data-lead-sector-ever-better-and-cheaper.

5. Travis Bradberry and Jean Greaves based their conclusion on results from what they call "the world's most popular EQ test," utilizing a reported online sample of over 500,000 participants to date (San Diego: TalentSmart, 2009).

6. Charles Darwin, *The Expressions of the Emotions in Man and Animals*, reprint of original 1872 edition by John Murray (Oxford: Oxford UP, 1998).

7. Perhaps the most striking detail in support of the universality of facial expressions is that even somebody born blind expresses their feelings the same way that people who can see do. Facial expressions are innate. They're "hard-wired" into the brain, rather than learned. Further evidence is that a child by nine months of age will display all of the seven core emotions covered in this book. In contrast, body language is affected by gender and by culture. For instance, a hand gesture that is just fine in Belgium may get you killed in Sicily. Body language can also be often more easily deployed in manipulative fashion. Presidential debates, for example, are rife with hand gestures that look "faked," as if made on the advice of a debate coach or consultant.

8. Paul Ekman Group, Facial Action Coding System, available at http://www.paulekman.com/product-category/facs/. Other facial coders who have been a resource over the years include: Jeffrey Cohn, a psychology professor at the University of Pittsburgh; and Maggie Pazian, who studied under Ekman's close associate Mark Frank.

9. Paul Ekman, "What Scientists Who Study Emotions Agree About," *Perspectives in Psychological Science* (January 2016). In a survey of 246 quantitative research experts on emotion, 88% agreed that there are universal emotions and 80% agreed that there are universal facial signals for emotions. A contrary voice is Lisa Feldman Barrett, author of *How Emotions Are Made* (Boston: Houghton Mifflin Harcourt, 2017). She argues that the FACS model is overly-simplistic in arguing for uniform "fingerprints" per emotion. She rightly attacks instances where test subjects around the world were shown a series of photos involved a single posed expression per photo and given a slate of six emotions (minus contempt) to choose from in identifying a correct answer. There is, indeed, as Barrett writes, no single "anger" or "fear" look, as blends of emotions and variations per emotion are commonplace (as illustrated in this book). The odd thing, however, is that FACS documents the "widely varying facial movements" she affirms in her own book. The original 1978 FACS model already listed a variety of complex combinations of facial muscle movements to qualify as showing an emotion, often three or more movements at once, an often unrealistic standard because in daily life people don't always show that much emotion in a single expression. When I began facial coding after my orientation from Ekman, I quickly went to a simpler, per-facial-muscle-activity model that anticipated the version of FACS scoring Ekman changed to in 2002, thereby negating much if not all of Barrett's call for sufficient flexibility.

10. Malcolm Gladwell, *Blink: The Power of Thinking Without Thinking* (New York: Little Brown, 2005).

11. Some examples of wide-ranging media coverage of development-stage versions of automated facial coding software becoming part of the business landscape are available at http://www.wired.com/2016/01/apple-buys-ai-startup-that-reads-emotions-in-faces, https://theintercept.com/2016/08/04/microsoft-pitches-technology-that-can-read-facial-expressions-at-political-rallies/, and http://www.fastcompany.com/3057283/what-happens-when-video-games-can-read-your-face.

12. This conclusion is based on a variety of tests. Some involved facial coding automators asking us to vet their software by sending us video of people whose reactions were coded by them, so my company could then compare their results to ours. In other cases, we've worked from published results and sought to replicate those results by using the same TV spots, but different test subjects, in order to compare the outcomes. In still other cases, third-party comparison studies on accuracy have been run as competitions by academic institutions or organizations. Finally, anecdotally one highly-respected business practitioner with a strong academic background in biometrics admitted in a conversation with me that to date his company relies on the automation software only for the two most obvious emotions: happiness and surprise, having found the data not sufficiently reliable for the emotions of anger, fear, sadness, disgust, and contempt. Issues with automation can include: not being able to detect quick microexpressions, not distinguishing adequately between smiles and smirks (contempt), and over-reporting the amount of activity on people's faces. The latter problem was dramatized by a U. K. researcher who put a plastic doll in front of a web cam to learn what the software would report. The outcome: supposedly lots of varied facial muscle activity from the doll in response to watching a TV commercial!

13. Albert Mahrabian, *Silent Messages* (Belmont, CA: Wadsworth, 1981).

14. See "The Ability Model of Emotional Intelligence: Principles and Updates," *Emotion Review*, 2016, a collaborative article by John D. Mayer, David R. Caruso, and Peter Salovey. Together, Mayer and Salovey invented the concept of EQ (also known as EI) in 1990, prior to it being popularized by Daniel Goleman in *Emotional Intelligence: Why It Can Matter More than IQ* (New York: Bantam, 1995). Goleman and others have made strong claims for the likely impact of EQ, with extensive research finding a more modest yet solid incremental advantage for those with higher EQ abilities. Besides the many scholarly writings of Mayer and Salovey, readers interested in this topic may also want to explore Daniel Pink's *A Whole New Mind: Why Right-Brainers Will Rule the Future* (New York: Riverhead, 2005)."

15. Peter Mayle, *Up the Agency: The Funny Business of Advertising* (New York: St. Martin's, 1994).

16. Two examples that build on this model as it relates to specific emotions are Reginald B. Adams, Jr., Nalini Ambady, C. Neil Macrea, and Robert E. Kleck, authors of "Emotional Expressions Forecast Approach-Avoidance Behavior," published online by Springer Science+Business Media in 2006; and Sandeep Gautam, author of "Emotions and Motivations," available at https://www.psychologytoday.com/blog/the-fundamental-four/201205/emotions-and-motivations. As is true of many, even most topics being debated in academia, however, the notion of exactly how many primary emotions there might be, and how best to define them, remain subject to on-going debate. The same can also, in fairness, be said of whether sadness can ever be definitively classified as an approach emotion.

17. In my choosing the 173 celebrities who appear in this book, several filters were used. First, I looked for notable, mostly American born-and-raised celebrities based on their appearing on critics' lists of the greatest achievers in their field, though great commercial success was also a factor at times. Third, I then culled the possible options by running my list by several dozen people to learn which options sparked interest because of a celebrity's personality, biography, or a trend in society he or she has exemplified. Finally, I sought diversity in terms of gender, race, and which era and professional field the celebrities came from.

18. The Voted results reflect an average of 39.5 votes per celebrity. The Actual results are based on an average of 89 facial muscle movements (Action Units) per celebrity, and typically involved facially coding 40-50 photographs per celebrity. As to the risk of selection bias, I strived to avoid it by working from expressions captured by a variety of photographers on a variety of occasions, working from viable options for facial coding purposes as sequentially available via Google Images except for when the same look had been captured during the same occasion. Naturally, it's impossible, however, to entirely eliminate selection bias even with those precautions in so far as the photographs are taken in public as opposed to private settings, with the presence of the observer (the photographer and likely others also present) meaning that to some, unverifiable degree a celebrity's branded, public persona may influence everyone involved.

Anger

1. Geoffrey Wansell, "The Cary Grant That Nobody Knows," available at http://www.carygrant.net/articles/nobody%20knows.html.

2. How myths do hold on, making the negative impact of venting an evergreen news story. Almost 25 years ago this realization got coverage in the Science section of *The New York Times:* Jane Brody, "Venting Anger May Do More Harm than Good," March 8, 1983. NPR, Fox, *Fast Company* and *The Wall Street Journal* have all covered this "news" in the years hence. A recent entry is by Fiona MacDonald, "Sorry, but Venting Online Just Makes You Angrier, Scientists Find," August 15, 2015, available at https:www.sciencealert.com/sorry-but-venting-online-just-makes-you-angrier-scientists-find.

3. This aspect of anger gets touched on by Paul Ekman, *Emotions Revealed* (New York: Henry Holt, 2003). Elevated to hate, it's the focus of an editorial by Anna Fels, "The Point of Hate," *The New York Times,* April 14, 2017.

4. Penelope Gilliatt, "Her Own Best Disputant," *The New Yorker,* December 25, 1978, available at http://www.newyorker.com/magazine/1978/12/25/her-own-best-disputant.

5. Anthony Bozza, "Eminem Blows Up," *Rolling Stone*, November 5, 2009, available at http://www.rollingstone.com/music/news/eminem-blows-up-20091105.

6. James McWilliams, "John McEnroe and the Sadness of Greatness," *PS Magazine,* September 23, 2013, available at https://psmag.com/john-mcenroe-and-the-sadness-of-greatness-7217ee89a9da#.qnxz05syw.

7. Two separate pieces, four years ago, tell a similar story. The first is Chris Houston, "Blasphemy: The Truth about Michael Jeffrey Jordan," *Bleacher Report*, September 23, 2010, available at http://bleacherreport.com/articles/471875-blasphemy-the-truth-about-michael-jeffrey-jordan/page/2. The second is Jon Wu, "Top 10 Instances of Michael Jordan Being

Just Plain Mean," *Bleacher Report,* January 31, 2014, available at http://bleacherreport. com/articles/1943095-top-10-stories-of-michael-jordan-being-the-greatest-jerk-of-all-time/ page/2.

8. Anne Helen Petersen, "Scandals of Classic Hollywood: Robert Redford, Golden Boy," *The Hairpin*, May 22, 2013, available at https://www.thehairpin.com/2013/05/scandals-of-classic-hollywood-robert-redford-golden-boy/.

9. James A. Russell may have been the first scholar to apply numerical values, on a limited basis, to some of the facial muscle activities documented by Ekman in FACS. See "Emotions from and into Faces: Resurrecting a Dimensional-Contextual Perspective," in *The Psychology of Facial Expression*, edited by James A. Russell and Jose Miguel Fernandez-Dols (Paris: Cambridge UP, 1997). As best I know, however, I was first to assign numerical values to all of the facial muscle activities in FACS that correspond to emotions, a task that involved some refinements as I began applying the facial coding tool to week-in, week-out research projects for my *Fortune* 500 clients.

10. Joe Klein, *Primary Colors* (New York: Random House, 1996).

11. Hadley Freeman, "Tom Hanks on His Diabetes, Pirates and Rapping with Dan Aykroyd," *The Guardian*, October 10, 2013, available at https://www.theguardian.com/film/2013/ oct/10/tom-hanks-diabetes-captain-phillips-interview.

12. Eells, Josh, "The Reinvention of Taylor Swift," *Rolling Stone*, September 8, 2014, available at http://www.rollingstone.com/music/features/taylor-swift-1989-cover-story-20140908.

Happiness

1. Malinda Loon, "Back in the Day: Coming Out with Ellen," April 9, 2005, available at http:www/afterellen.com/tv/34682-back-in-the-day-coming-out-with-ellen. For additional perspective, consider Erik Adams, Donna Bowman, Phil Dyess-Nugent, Genevieve Koski, Ryan McGee, David Sims and Todd Van DerWerff, "The Episode That Liberated—Then Destroyed Ellen," August 14, 2013, available at http://www.avclub.com/article/the-episode-that-liberated-then-destroyed-ellen-101551.

2. Daniel McNeil, *The Face: A Natural History* (Boston: Little, Brown, 1998).

3. Marianne LaFrance, *Why Smile: The Science Behind Facial Expressions* (New York: W. W. Norton, 2013).

4. Thomas Hardy, "Neutral Tones" in *Selected Poems* (London: Penguin, 1994).

5. Helena de Bertodano, "Diane Keaton Interview: 'I'm Going to Say What I Think,'" *The Telegraph*, May 30, 2013, available at http://www.telegraph.co.uk/culture/10073120/Diane-Keaton-interview-Im-going-to-say-what-I-think.html.

6. David Michaelis, *Schulz and Peanuts: A Biography* (New York: HarperCollins, 2008).

7. "Mariah Carey Never Played Monroe Piano," available at https:www.msn.com/en-ph/entertainment/celebrity/mariah-carey-never-played-monroe-piano/ar-BBuWMCM.

8. Mark, Lewisohn, *Tune In: The Beatles – All These Years (Vol. 1)*, (New York: Crown, 2013).

9. Laura Jacobs, Laura, "Our Lady of the Kitchen," *Vanity Fair*, August 2009, available at http://www.vanityfair.com/culture/2009/08/julia-child200908. Also check out Ruth Reichl, "Julia Child's Recipe for a Thoroughly Modern Marriage," *Smithsonian Magazine*, June 2012, available at http://www.smithsonianmag.com/history/julia-childs-recipe-for-a-thoroughly-modern-marriage-86160745/?no-ist.

10. Nicolaus Mills, "Gloria Steinem's 'A Bunny Tale' - 50 Years Later," *The Guardian*, May 26, 2013, available at https://www.theguardian.com/commentisfree/2013/may/26/gloria-steinem-bunny-tale-still-relevant-today. Another source is Evelyn Wang at http://www. dazeddigital.com/fashion/article/32834/1/that-time-gloria-steinem-went-undercover-as-a-playboy-bunny.

11. Coverage of Beyonce's childhood and later life includes: http://perezhilton.com/2008-12-30-beyonce-talks-smack-about-the-jacksons#WW9M61Tyu70, http://www.houstonpress.com/music/five-things-we-learned-from-that-beyonc-documentary-on-hbo-6778177, and https://www.forbes.com/forbes/2009/0622/celebrity-09-jay-z-sasha-fierce-inside-beyonce-empire.html.

12. Kim Kardashian, *Selfish* (New York: Rizzoli, 2015).

13. Vanessa Grigoriadis, "Kim Kardashian: American Woman," *Rolling Stone*, July 27, 2015, available at http://www.rollingstone.com/culture/features/kim-kardashian-american-woman-cover-story-20150727.

14. Jonathan Van Meter, "Amy Schumer Doesn't Care If You Like Her—She's Changing the Game," *Vogue*, June 16, 2016, available at http://www.vogue.com/tag/celebrity/amy-schumer.

15. Jon Mooallem, "Inside the Mind of Steven Spielberg, Hollywood's Big, Friendly Giant," *Wired*, July 2016, available at http://www.wired.com/2016/06/steven-spielberg-the-bfg/.

16. Antonio Garcia Martinez, *Chaos Monkeys* (New York: HarperCollins, 2016).

Sadness

1. Library of Congress, "Forty Years Ago: Nixon's Farewell Remarks to the White House Staff," *Readers Almanac*, (August 7, 2014), available at http://blog.loa.org/2014/08/forty-years-ago-nixon-farewell-remarks.html.

2. Often the eyebrows will rise as part of "speech emphasis." In other words, the person is moving their inner or outer eyebrows to dramatize or illustrate what they're saying. For example, the person might say, "What do you think?" while simultaneously raising their eyebrows. In those cases, it's likely that no emotion is being signaled. Other artifacts that could lead to misinterpreting facial muscle movements include: sucking in one's lips isn't the same as lips pressed together in anger; a movement that comes after people touch their faces isn't likely to signal emotion(s); people stretching their jaws aren't likely to be signaling surprise; and eyes that widen might not signal anything more than a person struggling to stay awake. Getting a baseline, or norm, of a person over time will also help you distinguish between what's likely to be a real sign of emoting versus non-verbal "noise." That's why for interviewing a job candidate, as in dating, getting a feel for someone likely benefits from more than a single meeting.

3. Guy Winch, "The Important Difference between Sadness and Depression," *Psychology Today*, October 2015, available at https://www.psychologytoday.com/blog/the-squeaky-wheel/201510/the-important-difference-between-sadness-and-depression.

4. Paul Hendrickson, "Janis Joplin: A Cry Cutting Through Time," *The Washington Post*, May 5, 1998, available at http://www.washingtonpost.com/wp-srv/style/features/joplin.htm. Also check out Ellen Willis, "Janis Joplin on Her Own Terms," *Rolling Stone*, November 18, 1976, available at http://www.rollingstone.com/music/news/janis-joplin-on-her-own-terms-9761118.

5. Dan P. McAdams, "The Mind of Donald Trump," *The Atlantic*, June 2016, available at https://www.theatlantic.com/magazine/archive/2016/06/the-mind-of-donald-trump/480771/; and "Harvard Psychologist Explains Trump Is 'Dangerous' Because He's Literally a Narcissistic Psychopath," *Counter Current News*, February 27, 2016, available at https://www.columbiapsychiatry.org/news/harvard-psychologist-explains-trump-dangerous-because-hes-literally-narcissistic-psychopath.

6. Nick Bilton, "Is Donald Trump's Insecurity a National Security Threat?" *Vanity Fair*, January 22, 2017, available at http://www.vanityfair.com/news/2017/01/is-donald-trumps-insecurity-a-national-security-threat.

7. Joe McGasko, "Remembering Johnny Cash: 10 Things You Might Not Know About Him," *Bio,* September 12, 2013, available at http://www.biography.com/news/johnny-cash-10-interesting-facts.

8. Henry Blodget, "I Asked Jeff Bezos the Tough Questions," *Business Insider,* December 2014, available at http://www.businessinsider.com/amazons-jeff-bezos-on-profits-failure-succession-big-bets-2014-12.

9. Peter Sheridan, "Marlon Brando: A Tormented and Misunderstood Star," *The Telegraph,* June 2014, previously available at http://s.telegraph.co.uk/graphics/projects/marlon-brando/index.html. Also check out Stevan Riley, "Marlon Brando's Secret History," *The Telegraph,* October 16, 2015, available at http://s.telegraph.co.uk/graphics/projects/marlon-brando/index.html.

10. David Fricke, "Kurt Cobain, The Rolling Stone Interview: Success Doesn't Suck," *Rolling Stone,* January 27, 1994, available at http://www.rollingstone.com/music/news/kurt-cobain-the-rolling-stone-interview-19940127.

11. Stephen Galloway, "The Woody Allen Interview (Which He Won't Read)," *The Hollywood Reporter,* May 4, 2016, available at http://www.hollywoodreporter.com/features/woody-allen-interview-he-wont-889678.

12. "Book Reveals Johnny Cash Sick, Grief-Stricken," Associated Press, August 15, 2004, available at http://www.foxnews.com/story/2004/08/15/book-reveals-johnny-cash-sick-grief-stricken.html.

13. Chris Heath, "How Elon Musk Plans on Reinventing the World (and Mars)," *GQ,* December 12, 2015, available at http://www.gq,com/story/elon-musk-mars-spacex-texla-interview.

Flash Portraits

1. Larry Tye, "Reintroducing Bobby Kennedy and His Legacy," *Prospect,* June 21, 2016, available at http://prospect.org/article/reintroducing-bobby-kennedy-and-his-legacy.

2. "Watching Serena and Venus Williams' Dad Predict the Outcome of His Daughters' Great Tennis Rivalry in This 1992 Clip," *The Week,* available at http://theweek.com/speed-reads/576003/watch-serena-venus-williams-dad-predict-outcome-daughters-great-tennis-rivalry-1992-clip.

3. Michael Jackson, *Moonwalk* (New York: Doubleday: 1988).

4. Iona Kirby, "Brad Pitt Reveals He Was 'Wasting' His Life Away while Married to Jennifer Aniston," *The Daily Mail,* May 21, 2013, available at http://www.dailymail.co.uk/tvshowbiz/article-2328477/Brad-Pitt-reveals-wasting-life-away-married-Jennifer-Aniston.html.

5. "Hillary Clinton's Strengths and Anger in White House Revealed" by Alex Seitz-Wald, Nov. 26, 2014, see http://www.msnbc.com/msnbc/hillary-clintons-strengths-and-anger-white-house-revealed. Also discussed in George Stephanopoulos's autobiography, *All Too Human: A Political Education* (Boston: Little, Brown, 1999).

6. Hannah Al-Othman, "Trump Jokes He Has 'Sex' in Common with Daughter Ivanka in Bizarre Wendy Williams Interview," *The Daily Mail,* October 25, 2016, available at http://www.dailymail.co/uk/news/article-3870754/the-thing-common-sex-bizarre-interview-Donald-Ivanka-Trump-resurfaces-three-years-later.html.

7. "Beyonce: Marriage to Jay-Z 'A Power Struggle,'" *Access Hollywood,* December 30, 2008, available at https://www.accesshollywood.com/articles/beyonce-marriage-to-jay-z-a-power-struggle-66881/.

Contempt

1. Maureen Orth, "Scientology: What Katie Didn't Know," *Vanity Fair,* October 2012, available at http://www.vanityfair.com/hollywood/2012/10/katie-holmes-divorce-scientology.

2. Jade Watkins, "Matt Lauer Admits Cold War Period After Tom Cruise Called Him Glib in Infamous Interview," *The Daily Mail*, June 21, 2013, available at http://www.dailymail.co.uk/tvshowbiz/article-2345978/Matt-Lauer-admits-cold-war-period-Tom-Cruise-called-glib-infamous-interview-reveals-actor-wanted-rant-removed-from-air.

3. A. H. Fischer and I. J. Roseman, "Beat Them or Ban Them: The Characteristics and Social Functions of Anger and Contempt," *Journal of Personality & Social Psychology*, 93, 2007.

4. Malcolm Gladwell, *Op. Cit.*

5. Tina Brown, "Diana's Final Heartbreak," *Vanity Fair,* July 2007, available at http://www.vanityfair.com/news/2007/07/diana200707.

6. Ian Parker, "Mugglemarch: J. K. Rowling Writes a Realistic Novel for Adults," *The New Yorker*, October 1, 2012, available at http://www.newyorker.com/magazine/2012/10/01/mugglemarch.

7. James Hansen, "The Truth About Neil Armstrong," *Space*, August 23, 2013, available at http://www.space.com/22510-neil-armstrong-astronaut-icon-remembered.html.

8. Coverage of Hillary Clinton's post-defeat demeanor includes, perhaps most prominently, David Remnick's piece at https://www.newyorker.com/magazine/2017/09/25/hillary-clinton-looks-back-in-anger. Also check out: Peggy Noonan at http://www.peggynoonan.com/hillary-lacks-remorse-of-conscience/. Among Clinton's 2008 campaign coverage is "The Tears Over Coffee That Turned Round Poll" at https://www.theguardian.com/world/2008/jan/10/hillaryclinton.uselections20082. Relevant conference appearance highlights include: https://www.youtube.com/watch?v=pXE2qEfhIDY for the interview with CNN's Christiana Amanpour at the 2017 Women for Women International luncheon, and https://www.youtube.com/watch?v=KgdJlzuaJ6k for Clinton being interviewed at the Code 2017 conference.

9. Jason Heller, "12 Wildest Prince Moments," *Rolling Stone*, April 22, 2016, available at http://www.rollingstone.com/music/lists/12-wildest-prince-moments-20160422.

10. Steve Kettmann, "The World's Richest Crybaby: How Bill Gates' Arrogance Led to His Decline and Fall," *SF Gate*, February 11, 2001, available at http://www.sfgate/com/books/article/the-World's-Richest-Crybaby-How-Bill-Gates-2953310.php.

11. Simon Davis, "Bill Gates Arrogant as Napoleon, Says Judge," *The Telegraph*, January 9, 2001, available at http://www.telegraph.co.uk/news/worldnews/1314005/Bill-Gates-arrogant-as-Napoleon-says-judge.html.

12. Ian Parker, *Op. Cit.*

13. Scott Wilson, "Obama, the Loner President," *The Washington Post*, October 7, 2011, available at https://www.washingtonpost.com/opinions/obama-the-loner-president/2011/10/03/gIQAHFcSTL_story.html?utm_term=.e61327fcf1d7.

14. Maureen Dowd, *The Year of Voting Dangerously: The Derangement of American Politics* (New York: Hatchette, 2016). To learn the depth of the intransigent, hard-ball manuevering Obama faced check out Jane Mayer's *Dark Money: The Hidden History of the Billionaires Behind the Rise of the Radical Right* (New York:Doubleday, 2016).

15. "Oral History: Prince's Life, as Told by the People Who Knew Him Best," *The Minneapolis Star-Tribune*, April 29, 2016, available at http://www.startribune.com/the-life-of-prince-as-told-by-the-people-who-knew-him/376586581/#1.

16. Roger Ebert, "Hugh Hefner Has Been Good for Us," October 24, 2010, available at http://www.rogerebert.com/rogers-journal/hugh-hefner-has-been-good-for-us. For unsavory details related to the demise of Hefner's estate, look up Brooks Barnes's story, "Behind Glamour of the Playboy Mansion Lurked a Sometimes Ugly Reality," *The New York Times*, September 29, 2017, B6.

17. Mike Larkin, "Tiger Woods Put Her Off Marriage! Champion Skier Lindsey Vonn Admits Troubled Love Life Made Her Wary of Getting Wed on Running Wild," *The Daily Mail*, September 6, 2016, available at http://www.dailymail.co.uk/tvshowbiz/article-3775530/Lindsey-Vonn-reveals-Tiger-Woods-marriage-Running-Wild-Bear-Grylls.html.

18. John Fricke, *Judy: A Legendary Film Career* (New York: Running Press, 2011).

Disgust

1. Mandy Van Deven, "The Science Behind Disgust," *Salon*, July 24, 2011, available at http://www.salon.com/2011/07/24/disgust_interview/.

2. "Elvis Presley Bio," *Rolling Stone*, available at http://www.rollingstone.com/music/artists/elvis-presley/biography.

3. Marc Berman, "Ayesha Curry, Klay Thompson Pile on LeBron: He's a Crybaby," *The New York Post*, June 12, 2016, available at https://nypost.com/2016/06/12/ayesha-curry-klay-thompson-pile-on-lebron-hes-a-crybaby/.

4. Benjamin Genocchio, "When 'Delinquents' Infiltrated Art," *The New York Times*, May 11, 2003.

5. Anthony DeCurtis, "Whitney Houston Opens Up About Her Marriage, Fame," *Rolling Stone*, June 10, 1993, available at http://www.rollingstone.com/music/news/whitney-houston-opens-up-about-her-marriage-the-pressures-of-fame-and-more-20120212.

6. Mark Seal, "Inside Whitney Houston's Final Days—And Her Troubled Relationships," *Vanity Fair*, May 3, 2012, available at https://www.vanityfair.com/culture/2012/05/whitney-houston-final-days-mark-seal.

7. Erick Fernandez, "15 Years Ago, Roger Clemens Infamously Tossed a Bat Toward Mike Piazza," *The Huffington Post*, October 22, 2015, available at http://www.huffingtonpost.com/entry/roger-clemens-throws-bat-mike-piazza_us_562828a4e4b02f6a900f9486.

8. Claudia Rankine, "The Meaning of Serena Williams," *The New York Times*, August 25, 2015, available at https://www.nytimes.com/2015/08/30/magazine/the-meaning-of-serena-williams.html.

9. A long-standing rumor is that Elvis Presley supposedly said, "The only thing Negroes can do for me is buy my records and shine my shoes." It's claimed Presley said so at a concert in Boston before he'd ever visited that city, and the quote was later explicitly disavowed by Presley himself. There's likewise plenty of evidence of Presley's support of black culture from his friendships with James Brown, Ike Turner, B. B. King, Cissy Houston, and Muhammad Ali, among others. That said, Presley and the topic of white musicians appropriating African-American songs is a long-standing, complex issue more fully explored in sources like https://www.thedailybeast.com/the-truth-about-elvis-and-the-history-of-racism-in-rock, and http://www.newsweek.com/elvis-presley-40-years-later-was-king-rock-n-roll-guilty-appropriating-black-651911.

10. Phil Picardi, "On This Day in 1954, Elvis Is Heard on the Radio for the First Time," Minnesota Public Radio, July 8, 2014.

11. Grant Brisbee, "MLB Umpires and the Classification of Strike-Three Calls," *SB Nation*, July 9, 2012, available at http://www.sbnation.com/2012/7/9/3142348/mlb-umpire-strike-three-calls.

12. Krista Smith, "Isn't She Deneuvely?" *Vanity Fair*, December 2008, available at http://www.vanityfair.com/news/2008/12/winslet200812.

13. Sheila Weller, "Jimi Hendrix: "I Don't Want to Be a Clown Anymore,'" *Rolling Stone*, November 15, 1969, available at http://www.rollingstone.com/music/news/jimi-hendrix-i-dont-want-to-be-a-clown-anymore-19691115.

14. Lili Anolik, "How O. J. Simpson Killed Popular Culture," *Vanity Fair*, June 2014, available at https://www.vanityfair.com/style/society/2014/06/oj-simpson-trial-reality-tv-pop-culture.

15. Amy Reyes, "Kanye West's Five Weirdest (and Greatest) Stories of 2016 (So Far)," *Miami*, September 14, 2016, available at http://www.miami.com/miami-news/kanye-wests-five-weirdest-and-greatest-stories-of-2016-so-far-22169/.

16. Anne Helen Petersen, "Scandals of Classic Hollywood: Elizabeth Taylor, Black Widow," *The Hairpin*, July 25, 2011, available at https://www.thehairpin.com/2011/07/scandals-of-classic-hollywood-elizabeth-taylor-black-widow/.

17. Richard Conniff, *The Ape in the Corner Office: Understanding the Workplace Beast in All of Us* (New York: Crown, 2005).

Flash Portraits

1. Ashleyvr, "Oprah Winfrey vs. Ellen Degeneres," available at https://oprahwinfrey12.wordpress.com2012/12/10/oprah-winfrey-vs-ellen-degeneres.

2. Buzz Bissinger, "Caitlyn Jenner: The Full Story," *Vanity Fair,* July 2015, available at http://www.vanityfair.com/hollywood/2015/06/caitlyn-jenner-bruce-cover-annie-leibovitz.

3. Rob Hoerburger, "Long Live Aretha, the Queen of Soul," *The New York Times Magazine*, July 8, 2011, available at http://www.nytimes.com/2011/07/10/magazine/long-live-aretha-the-queen-of-soul.html.

4. Matt Weinberger, "The Strange Love-Hate Relationship between Bill Gates and Steve Jobs," *Business Insider*, March 10, 2016, available at http://www.businessinsider.com/the-bill-gates-steve-jobs-feud-frenemies-2016-3/#gates-wasnt-particularly-impressed-with-what-he-saw-as-a-limited-platform.

5. Ed Vulliamy, "Jim Hendrix: 'You Never Told Me He Was That Good,'" *The Guardian*, August 7, 2010, available at https://theguardian.com/music/2010/augu/08/jimi-hendrix-40th-anniversary-death.

6. Rich Cohen, "Inside Mick Jagger and Keith Richard's Five-Decade Bromance," *Vanity Fair,* April 2016, available at http://www.vanityfair.com/culture/2016/03/mick-jagger-keith-richards-rich-cohen.

Surprise

1. Kate Aurthur, "18 Moments That Led to Bill Cosby's Stunning Downfall," *Buzzfeed*, November 21, 2014, available at https://www.buzzfeed.com/kateaurthur/18-moments-that-led-to-bill-cosbys-stunning-downfall?utm_term=.pilknLGNE#.kb74NkVDz.

2. John Williams asks authors five questions in his columns, in this case of Mario Livio, the author of *Why: What Makes Us Curious.* See https://www.nytimes.com/2017/07/16/books/mario-livio-why-what-makes-us-curious.html for further details.

3. Daniel Kahneman, *Thinking, Fast and Slow* (New York: Farrar, Straus and Giroux, 2011).

4. Three tips worth bearing in mind favor the verdict being surprise rather than fear. First, a mouth that falls open stays relaxed and the lips aren't tense. Second, should the eyelids rise, they do so more briefly than if fear is involved. Third, the raised eyebrows will be less tense and more rounded. This same rules apply in reverse, of course, when the verdict favors fear.

5. Gay Talese, "Frank Sinatra Has a Cold," *Esquire*, April 1966, available at http://www.esquire.com/news-politics/a638/frank-sinatra-has-a-cold-talese/.

6. Sarah Moughty, "20 Years After HIV Announcement, Magic Johnson Emphasizes: 'I Am Not Cured,'" *PBS*, November 7, 2011, available at https://www.pbs.org/wgbh/frontline/article/20-years-after-hiv-announcement-magic-johnson-emphasizes-i-am-not-cured/.

7. Maureen Dowd, "'My Life So Far': The Roles of a Lifetime," *The New York Times*, April 24, 2005, available at http://www.nytimes.com/2005/04/24/books/review/my-life-so-far-the-roles-of-a-lifetime.html.

8. Sarah Bibel, "6 Lesser-Known Facts about Audrey Hepburn," *Bio*, May 3, 2015, available at http://www.biography.com/news/audrey-hepburn-facts-biography.

9. Gay Talese, *Op. Cit.*

10. Mikel Gilmore, "How Muhammad Ali Conquered Fear and Changed the World," *Men's Journal*, June 2016, available at https://www.mensjournal.com/featureshow-muhammad-ali-conquered-fear-and-changed-the-world-20130205.

11. Steve Tobak, "Alphabet CEO Larry Page Needs Adult Supervision," Fox Business, August 15, 2016, available at http://www.foxbusiness.com/features/2016/08/15/alphabet-ceo-larry-page-needs-adult-supervision.html.

12. Justin Bariso, "Adele Turning Down the Super Bowl Teaches All of Us a Major Lesson," *Inc.*, August 6, 2016, available at https://www.inc.com/justin-bariso/adele-turning-down-the-super-bowl-teaches-all-of-us-a-major-lesson.html.

13. Brian Hiatt, "Adele: Inside Her Private Life and Triumphant Return," *Rolling Stone*, November 3, 2015, available at http://www.rollingstone.com/music/news/adele-inside-her-private-life-and-triumphant-return-20151103.

Fear

1. Allysia Finley, "What Bill and Hillary Could Tell Tom Brady," *The Wall Street Journal*, May 8, 2015, available at https://www.wsj.com/articles/what-bill-and-hillary-could-tell-tom-brady-1431040303. To view Brady's deflategate press conference, check out https://www.youtube.com/watch?v=lhslsyH3PlY.

2. Alexander Todorov, *Face Value: The Irresistible Influence of First Impressions* (Princeton, NJ: Princeton UP, 2017). The fusiform face area (FFA), the amgygdala, and the hippocampus (involved in memory functions) are all key components employed in the brain's neural systems in order to help us understand others.

3. Kasia and Patryk Wezowski, *The Micro Expressions Book for Business* (Belgium: New Vision, 2012).

4. Jonathan Van Meter, "Jennifer Aniston: Prime Time," *Vogue*, December 1, 2008, available at https://www.vogue.com/article/jennifer-aniston-prime-time.

5. Stephen Galloway, "Jennifer Aniston Reveals Struggles with Dyslexia, Anger; Shrugs Off Oscar Snub," *The Hollywood Reporter,* January 21, 2015, available at http://www.hollywood-reporter.com/news/jennifer-aniston-reveals-struggles-dyslexia-764854.

6. J. Randy Taraborrelli, "Joe DiMaggio Wanted Marilyn Monroe to Be His Demure House-wife, So When She Posed for This Picture He Beat Her Up," *The Daily Mail*, September 1, 2009, available at http://www.dailymail.co/uk/femail/article-1210384/Joe-DiMaggio-wanted-Marilyn-Monroe-demure-housewife-posed-picture-beat-up.html.

7. Sandra McKee, "Gretzky's Goal: Overcoming Fear," *The Baltimore Sun*, March 9, 1994, available at http://articles.baltimoresun.com/1994-03-09/sports/1994068073_1_fear-star-wayne-gretzky-gretzky-scored.

8. Wayne Drehs, "Michael Phelps' Final Turn," *ESPN*, July 18, 2016, available at http://www.espn.com/espn/feature/story/_/id/16425548/michael-phelps-prepares-life-2016-rio-olympics.

9. Few celebrities have publicly admitted to self-doubt more than Portman. Among the sources to consider: Chris Heath, "The Private Life of Natalie Portman," *Rolling Stone,* June 20, 2002, available at http://www.rollingstone.com/culture/news/the-private-life-of-natalie-portman-rolling-stones-2002-cover-story-20110120; Gill Pringle, "Natalie Portman – More

Than a Woman," *The Independent*, February 28, 2008, available at http://www.independent. co.uk/arts-entertainment/films/features/natalie-portman-more-than-a-woman-789103.html; and Christina Pazzanese, "Portman: I, Too, Battled Self-Doubt," *The Harvard Gazette*, May 27, 2015, available at https://news.harvard.edu/gazette/story/2015/05/portman-i-too-battled-self-doubt/.

10. Arthur Miller, *Timebends: A Life* (New York: Grove, 2013).

11. Sara Boboltz, "Here's What You Might Not Remember About O. J. Simpson's Police Chase," *The Huffington Post*, February 9, 2016, available at http://www. huffingtonpost.com/entry/american-crime-story-oj-simpson-bronco-chase_ us_56b8f737e4b01d80b2475fc7.

12. Chris Spargo, "OJ Simpson's Agent Claims He Admitted to Stabbing Nicole Brown to Death," *The Daily Mail*, June 18, 2016, available at http://www.dailymail.co.uk/news/ article-3648762/OJ-Simpson-s-agent-claims-football-star-chilling-murder-confession-admitted-stabbing-Nicole-Brown-death.html.

13. Twin sources here consist of: Julie Miller, "Jean Fonda Is 'So Jealous' of Jennifer Lawrence and Amy Schumer's Friendship," *Vanity Fair*, February 2, 2016, available at http://www. vanityfair.com/hollywood/2016/02/jane-fonda-jennifer-lawrence; and Maureen Dowd, "'My Life So Far': The Roles of a Lifetime," *Op. Cit.*

14. Jon Meachem, "Nostalgia for the Grace of George H. W. Bush," *The New York Times*, October 15, 2016, available at https://www.nytimes.com/2016/10/16/opinion/nostalgia-for-the-grace-of-george-hw-bush.html.

15. Matt Weinberger, "The Rise of Larry Ellison, the Jet-Setting Billionaire Founder of Oracle," *Business Insider*, January 16, 2017, available at http://www.businessinsider.com/rise-of-oracle-founder-larry-ellison-2017-1.

16. Peter King, "Tom Brady Tells the Story of the Super Bowl 51 Comeback," *Sports Illustrate*d, February 13, 2017, available at https://www.si.com/mmqb/2017/02/13/tom-brady-montana-super-bowl-51-nfl-patriots-peter-king.

17. Brooks Barnes, "Following Her Fears to Greater Heights," *The New York Times*, September 6, 2013, available at http://ww.nytimes.com/2013/09/08/movies/sandra-bullock-may-be-hollywoods-gutsiest-a-list-actress.html?pagewanted+all&_r=0.

18. Peggy Noonan, "Ronald Reagan," *PBS*, available at https://www.pbs.org/newshour/spc/ character/essays/reagan.html.

19. Mikal Gilmore. *Op. Cit.*

Epilogue

1. Yudhijit Bhattacharjee, "Why We Lie," *National Geographic,* June 2017.

2. Timothy Wilson, *Strangers to Ourselves: Discovering the Adaptive Unconscious* (Cambridge, MA: Belknap Press, 2002).

3. David Livingstone Smith, *Why We Lie: The Evolutionary Roots of Deception and the Unconscious Mind* (New York: St. Martin's Griffin, 2004).

4. Yudhijit Bhattacharjee, *Op. Cit.*

5. The video clip, "President Dwight Eisenhower speaks about the U-2 Spy Trials at Moscow Trade Union," is available at https://www.youtube.com/watch?v=ZIddDfbBuBc. Not only did Eisenhower tell his secretary, "I would like to resign" in response to the scandal, he also felt that his U-2 "lie was one of the deepest regrets of his presidency." The incident appears in Sheryl Gay Stolberg's article, "Many Politicians Lie, but Trump Has Elevated the Art of Fabrication," *The New York Times*, August 7, 2017.

6. Lying is discussed in depth in Paul Ekman's book,*Telling Lies: Clues to Deceit in the Marketplace, Politics, and Marriage*, New York: Norton, 1992.

7. Zara Ambadar, Jeffrey Cohn, and Lawrence Ian Read, "All Smiles are Not Created Equal: Morphology and Timing of Smiles Perceived as Amused, Polite, and Embarrassed/Nervous," *Journal of Nonverbal Behavior,* 2008.

8. Regarding 2012, look to stories like the one published in *USA Today* on October 11th, "Biden's Frequent Smiles During Debate Ignite Twitter." In 2016, you can view Biden's remarks at https://www.youtube.com/watch?v=Ueq-hvKLUDM.

9. See "Rachel Dolezal Breaks Her Silence: 'I Identify As Black' / Today" at https://www.today.com/news/rachel-dolezal-speaks-today-show-matt-lauer-after-naacp-resignation-t26371.

10. See "President Reagan's Television Address on the Iran-Contra Affair – 1987" at https://www.youtube.com/watch?v=iOlVfoBouus. Despite Oliver North saying "President Reagan didn't always know what he knew," surely Reagan knew that he had explicitly directed White House officials not to tell the U.S. Congress about the Israelis serving as middlemen in the selling of arms to Iran. Among the coverage, check out "North Says Reagan Knew of Iran Ideal" at http:www.nytimes.com/1991/10/20/us/north-says-reagan-knew-of-iran-deal.html?pagewanted=all and "How the Reagan White House Bungled Its Response to Iran-Contra Revelations" at https://www.thedailybeast.com/how-the-reagan-white-house-bungled-its-response-to-iran-contra-revelations.

11. Paul Ekman, *Telling Lies, Op. Cit.*

12. Despite the erroneous assumption that moments of extreme emoting should be readily associated with a single emotion, Alexander Todorov, *Op. Cit.*, offers many valid examples of mistakes made based on first impressions of others. Physiognomy means "a person's facial features or expression, especially when regarded as indicative of character or ethnic origin." It's similar in intent to phrenology ("the detailed study of the shape and size of the cranium as a supposed indication of character and mental ability") in that both pseudo-scientific approaches invite dubious judgments about an individual's mental and moral qualities. In reality, no physical attribute involving one's head or face makes it possible to, for instance, assess an individual's trustworthiness reliably. (Otherwise, definitive clues to lying would exist.) To take but one example, suddenly lowered eyebrows signify the expression of anger, fear and sadness, but which of these three emotions might be most pertinent benefits from considering the specific context involved as well as the emotive patterns evident for that person over time.

Celebrity Index

Page numbers pertain to a celebrity in the 173–celebrity sample getting cited. Page numbers in parentheses indicate a photograph.

Acknowledgments

"Books are never finished, they are merely abandoned" quipped Oscar Wilde. I've been lucky to have many people who kept me from wrapping up *Famous Faces Decoded* prematurely. First and foremost, gratitude is due to my wife, Karen Bernthal, for bringing her artistic talents to bear on all of the book's many graphic elements. Next up is Joe Bockman, to whom I'm grateful for sourcing and keeping track of photographs and video files, and for compiling the statistics that helped to shape this book.

Holly Buchanan and Anne Jones both read the manuscript in full and offered good, deft suggestions for improvement. Besides my father and in-laws, others who tackled one or more chapters include: Tim Dennis, Paul Feroe, Steve Goodyear, Gary Jader, Dave Kenney, Kristin Kladstrup, Jerry Lee, Kathryn and Scott Mathews, Christie and Mark McLean, Peter Narum, Shirley Ochi-Watson, Anita and David Perry, Emmanuel Probst, Nelson and Patty Rhodus, Margaret Radke, Kathy Seamon, Becky Seavey, Joel Stern, Natalie Sudman, Dan Wallace and John Weddle. Taylor Atkinson and Ron Standord kindly proofread the book's penultimate draft.

Earlier in the process, many people, far too numerous to name here, helped to provide suggestions on which celebrities to facially code. Hundreds of other people then participated in voting on the celebrities' most distinctive emotions. Lauren DeBueriis and Laura Dragne were particularly helpful in securing the voting input. To one and all, my heartfelt appreciation!

About the Author

Dan Hill, Ph.D., is the founder and president of Sensory Logic, Inc., which originated the use of facial coding in business beginning in 1998. Dan has received ten U.S. patents in all, and his research-based consulting company has worked for over half of the world's top 100 business-to-consumer oriented companies.

Dan's TV appearances have included: ABC's "Good Morning America," Al Jazeera, Bloomberg TV, CNBC, CNN, ESPN, Fox, MSNBC, NBC's "The Today Show," PBS, and The Tennis Channel. Radio appearances have included the BBC and NPR's "Marketplace." Print and digital coverage of Dan's work has included: *Admap, Advertising Age, Adweek, Allure, Cosmopolitan, China Forbes, Entrepreneur, Fast Company, The Financial Times, Inc., Kiplinger's The Los Angeles Times, The New York Times, Politico, Time, USA Today*, and *The Wall Street Journal*, in addition to his having been a columnist for *Reuters* during the 2016 presidential race. His essays were noted with commendation in the 1989, 1991 and 1994 editions of *The Best American Essays*.

Since his education at St. Olaf College, Oxford University, Brown University, and Rutgers University, Dan has given speeches and workshops in over 25 countries, Along with his wife, Karen Bernthal, he lives in St. Paul, Minnesota and Palm Desert, California. To sign up for Dan's *Faces of the Week* blog series or to learn about his other offerings, please visit www.sensorylogic.com.

Other Books by Dan Hill

Emotionomics (2007, 2008, 2010 editions)

There are two currencies in business: money and emotions. The book that first brought behavior economics into business on an actionable basis reveals how breakthroughs in brain science have revelatory implications for how companies should be conducting business in the 21st century. Gone is the old consumer and worker model in which appeals to utilitarian benefits alone will carry the day. Instead, step ahead of competitors by stepping closer to customers and employees, the two groups of people on whom profitability depends. *Emotionomics* covers the role of emotions in both the marketplace and workplace, from branding, to offer design, packaging, usability, advertising, sales, and the customer shopping experience, as well as leadership and employee management. Chosen by *Advertising Age* as one of the top ten must-read books of 2009, *Emotionomics* includes a foreword by Sam Simon, co-creator of *The Simpsons*, and is endorsed by business luminaries like Seth Godin, Philip Kotler, Martin Lindstrom, Jeffrey Gitomer, Paco Underhill, and Faith Popcorn.

Two Cheers for Democracy (2019)

Not only in America, but around the globe democracy is under siege. In an era personified by Donald Trump, illiberal—increasingly hollow—democracies, and "strongman" dictatorships, it's time to take a closer look at the nature of the leaders who shape our world. The policies or positions that leaders adopt may change, but rarely their personalities. All of us have signature facial expressions that reveal the emotions we gravitate to most often over time. The difference is that in leading a country, the head of state's feelings can hold sway over events likely to impact every citizen's life and well-being.

In *Two Cheers for Democracy*, the focus is on identifying emotional patterns that help to predict three key things about leaders: will they prove to be competent, compelling, and compassionate in executing their official duties? This book analyzes all 44 U.S. presidents to date and every U.S. presidential debate ever held, from 1960 to 2016, in addition to 79 foreign leaders. With results from the American Political Science Association's presidential greatness rankings, Gallup polls, and Freedom House's annual survey of countries' commitment to democracy as benchmarks, *Two Cheers for Democracy* takes seriously—in a unique way—the central question of today: what's the personality of the people leading us, and can we trust them to look out for the public good?

Two Cheers for Democracy comes richly illustrated with photographs and charts, and includes an epilogue with a look at the likely 2020 Democratic front-runners for The White House.

First Blush (2019)

What we choose to focus on, and how we feel about what we're seeing, defines us. In today's hyper-visual world that stretches from TV shows and advertising to online videos (and more), how good are we at truly understanding what does and doesn't grab our attention and make us care? This groundbreaking book tackles that question by using two unique scientific tools to provide objective, quantifiable see/feel answers. *First Blush* is twice as large in scope as any study ever conducted before that links eye-tracking and world-class art works. This book simultaneously draws on facial coding to capture and identify people's quick, real-time emotional responses to 88 notable art works, spanning the eras from masters like da Vinci and Rembrandt to contemporary painters, photographers, and sculptors like Basquiat, Liebovitz, and Koons. "Art is either plagiarism or revolution," wrote Paul Gauguin. Welcome to revolution. You won't find another richly-illustrated, full-color art book like *First Blush* anywhere else.